海上貨物保險基礎理論與實務 --ICC,2009 逐條釋義

第二版

曾文瑞　著

■ 國家圖書館出版品預行編目資料

海上貨物保險基礎理論與實務：ICC,2009 逐條釋義 /
曾文瑞著. – 第二版. -- 高雄市：麗文文化,
2017.03
　　面；　公分
　　ISBN 978-957-748-923-4（平裝）

1.海上保險　2.貨物保險

563.76　　　　　　　　　　　　　106002787

海上貨物保險基礎理論與實務：ICC,2009 逐條釋義

二版一刷・2017 年 3 月　　二版二刷・2022 年 9 月

著者	曾文瑞
封面設計	黃士豪
發行人	楊曉祺
總編輯	蔡國彬
出版者	麗文文化事業股份有限公司
地址	80252高雄市苓雅區五福一路57號2樓之2
電話	07-2265267
傳真	07-2233073
網址	www.liwen.com.tw
電子信箱	liwen@liwen.com.tw
劃撥帳號	41423894
購書專線	07-2265267轉236
臺北分公司	23445新北市永和區秀朗路一段41號
電話	02-29229075
傳真	02-29220464
法律顧問	林廷隆律師
電話	02-29658212

行政院新聞局出版事業登記證局版台業字第5692號

ISBN 978-957-748-923-4（平裝）

麗文文化事業

定價：430 元

曾序

　　英國海上貨物保險條款自早期的 S. G. Form，直至最新之 2009 年版，其中歷經了多次的修正，以配合航運環境變遷以及國際貿易的需求。臺灣保險市場目前普遍使用之條款為 1982 年版的協會貨物保險條款，然近 30 年來國際貿易型態及貨物運輸型態都已有極大的轉變，傳統的運輸概念已然轉變成全方位的國際物流模式，故因應運輸風險的貨物保險條也勢將重新修改。在國內，不論就理論或實務而言，對新條款的內容了解以及對雙方當事人間之影響為何，均為重要的課題。

　　曾文瑞先生為海洋大學航運管理博士，目前任教於國立高雄海洋科技大學航運管理系，其在海洋大學航運管理研究所取得碩士學位後，隨即在富邦產物保險公司海上保險理賠部服務 5 年時間，並先後在中國海專（現為台北海洋技術學院）航運管理科、長榮大學航運管理學系講授海上保險課程，治學嚴謹，教學經驗豐富，並常於業界分享其理論及實務研討之成果，經多年淬煉後，乃就其實務經驗及教學心得，著手撰寫本書以饗讀者，並為思源航運叢書系列之第 5 本專書。

　　本書先論述海上保險理論，諸如航程保險單、保險利益、定值保險單、保險代位權以及擔保等有關海上貨物保險之基礎，都有詳細深入的探討，再以最新之 2009 年英國協會貨物保險(A)、B) 及 (C) 條款為論述主軸，對保險條款逐條釋義，其中更輔以實務觀點探討條款之應用與問題之因應，誠屬難得，堪稱為一可供理論與實務參考之專業書籍。

　　茲值本書付梓之際，僅以數語為序，期盼本書之問世對理論與實務有所貢獻與助益。

國立臺灣海洋大學名譽教授
長榮大學航運管理學系講座教授 *曾國雄* 謹誌

2011 年 1 月

1

黃序

　　1977 年第一次赴倫敦於英國最好的海事法律事務所 Ince & Co 及 Clyde & Co.實習。Ince & Co 常代表 shipowner's interests, Clyde & Co. 常代表 cargo interests。分別學習得不同的 practice 及英國的人情事故，這是一段充滿夢與飛雪的日子，曾為英國海事法的浩瀚震憾，曾為英國法院如廟堂的莊嚴肅穆感動流淚，也為刻骨的思家之情痛苦，終決定來日再赴倫敦進入大學以系統地學習英國海事法。其後得知 Ince & Co 曾為共同海損理算的 York-Antwerp Rules 出力甚多，而 Clyde & Co.正是此次 2009 年協會貨物保險條款修正工作主要的指引者。

　　1982 年再赴倫敦進入倫敦大學修習法學碩士及法學博士，追隨英國海事法泰斗 Professor E. R. Hardy Ivamy，六年後以 "A Programme of International Shipping and Insurance Law for Our Future World"（未來世界的國際海事與保險法規畫）博士論文完成學業，成為 Professor Ivamy 最後的關門弟子，如此算來文瑞也可稱為英國海事法泰斗 Professor Ivamy 的嫡傳子弟，係屬師出名門了。

　　因於政治大學商學院風管系被馬市長借調臺北市政府工作，學術空白六年，近年重返學術界，適逢聯合國國際貿易法委員會為因應國際社會貨櫃運輸「門至門」（door to door）服務之需求，推動建立「United Nations Convention on Contracts for the International Carriage of Goods Wholly or Partly by Sea，2008」（聯合國官方之中文公約名稱為：「聯合國全程或部分海上國際貨物運輸合同公約」（原文字為以大陸使用之中文表達），依我海商法之法律用語譯為：「聯合國全程或部分海上國際貨物運送契約公約」）。整個心緒都在注意公約的發展，關注公約可能對我國海商法帶來的影響，並著手撰寫約 20 萬字的論文「聯合國全程或部分海上國際貨物運送契約公約之研究」發表於 2009 數位科技與公共事務學術研討會，於 Yahoo 或 Google 輸入相關關鍵字均搜尋得到此論文，顯示其獲得社會的關注。2009 新協會海上貨物保險條款問世，尚來不及深入關注，文瑞業已完成出書，可喜可賀，以文瑞 Professor Ivamy 再傳弟子的功力，此書當有許多可以參考與引注的地方。

1982 年入倫敦大學修習英國海事法時，倫敦海上保險市場，正因聯合國貿易與發展會議（United Nations Conference on Trade and Development）發布 Legal and Documentary Aspects of the Marine Insurance Contract（TD/B/C.4/ISL/27/Rev.1）一文，對傳統的海上貨物與船舶保險條款產生幾近革命性的改革。倫敦海上保險市場拋棄了傳統長久使用的 Lloyd's S.G. Form of marine insurance policy,當時只能以「震撼」形容倫敦海上保險市場的心情。1982 年的協會海上貨物保險條款使用了 26 年，2009 年新協會海上貨物保險條款與 1982 年當時的「震撼」相較，顯得平靜許多，僅在呼應當前環境更進一步的需求(an update)。文瑞這本書當能給我們許多我們亟需的澄清。

1982 年與 2009 年的協會海上貨物保險條款均明示適用英格蘭法（English law），English law 是指 law of England。但事件由中華民國管轄時，即使事件是有涉外因素，違反中華民國公共秩序善良風俗之行為仍然是無效的。保險最重要的「公共政策」是「保險利益」，1982 年與 2009 年的協會海上貨物保險條款均明示要求：被保險人於損失發生時於保險標的上要有保險利益始得有保險給付請求權（11.1 In order to recover under this insurance the Assured must have an insurable interest in the subject−matter insured at the time of the loss.）。這是英美法的定位。但我國保險法第三條規定「要保人是有保險利益之人」，同法第十七條復規定「要保人或被保險人對於保險標的物無保險利益者，保險契約失其效力」，這個邏輯必須需依德國保險契約法始有可能詮釋：要保人是以其自己的被保險利益為保險標的向保險人投保，故被保險利益消失時意謂保險標的消失，保險契約無保險標的自然失其效力；要保人以他人的被保險利益為保險標的向保險人投保時，該他人為被保險人，故保險標的為被保險人的被保險利益。但我國保險法第四條規定：被保險人為保險事故發生時遭受損害，享有賠償請求權之人。這如協會海上貨物保險條款是英美法的邏輯，被保險人於損害保險（indemnity insurance），應於損失發生時於保險標的上要有保險利益，始會發生損失而對保險人有損失補償性質的保險給付請求權，除保險契約是賭博契約，被保險人永遠無法於保險標的有保險利益，否則不致影響保險契約之效力。我國保險法前後的邏輯是矛盾的。這矛盾的邏輯也造成以我國法解讀協會海上貨物保險條款的困難。

學海事法，海上保險是最深邃的地方，因他主要承保各種海上的風險，觸及海事法每一個地方，我國海商法海上保險章幾十年來仍是一個荒蕪尚未開發的地方，海商法海上保險章對共同海損（general average loss）及單獨海損（particular average loss）的承保理賠、救助費用（salvage charges）、特別費用（particular charges）等核心觀念均未規範，致使我國海商法海上保險章幾僅係備而無法實際運作使用，文瑞這本書相信對我國海商法海上保險章未來的修正會有所助益。

黃正宗 博士

二〇一一年元月二十一日
於稻江學院財經法律學系

廖序

　　論及保險發展歷史，無疑地當屬海上保險發展最早。十四世紀末期，最早海上保險單在義大利被製作完成。其後，隨著國際貿易日益頻繁，海上保險經營重鎮更迭遷移，遊走葡萄牙、西班牙等各大城市，最後傳入英國並發揚光大之。由上述歷史可知，海上保險發展時間遠較其他保險為早，且其更具有濃厚國際性質，故謂保險因海上保險而起實不為過，而藉由海上保險促成保險國際化已有600年以上之歷史。

　　海上保險涉及範圍廣泛，且又深具高度專業性，尤其是英國海上貨物保險條款，每一條款所使用之字義，在其背後均隱含海上貨物運送過程發生歷史典故，此非深具有海上保險理論與實務者，實難能詮釋其真諦。本書作者大學就讀淡江大學保險學系，接受良好正統保險基礎教育；隨後，在海洋大學航運管理研究所專攻海上保險取得博士學位，奠定紮實嚴謹海上保險學術基礎。完成學業後，亦曾在國內著名產險公司海上保險部門工作多年，累積豐富保險實務工作經驗，此對日後轉任教職，講授海上保險相關課程助益良多。

　　本書主要架構包括三大構面：緒論（一至三章）、海上貨物保險之基礎理論（四至八章）、2009年英國協會貨物保險條款逐條釋義（九至十六章），顯見本書結構與內容堪稱十分完備。基於海上貨物保險條款文義艱深難懂，作者撰寫方式著重於保險單條款逐條釋義，俾能讓讀者能確實掌握海上貨物保險之核心議題，進而建構海上貨物保險經營完整基本理念。基此，本書除可做為大學教科書外，亦可做為業界人士實際經營參酌之用；此外，對於準備參加相關保險證照資格考試者，本書亦可供為自修研讀重要參考書籍。

此值本書付梓之際，由衷感佩作者治學嚴謹，在教學之餘辛勤撰寫，其努力不懈堪稱楷模，爰樂為推薦之。

廖述源 謹識

2011 年 1 月 15 日

自序

書本完成之際，心中除了圓滿的喜樂外，更多的是滿滿的感謝！

撰寫本書之過程，思緒常常不斷回到 1988 年與「保險」結緣的淡江大學保險學系，種種理論根基是保險系上老師一字一句引導講解而來，方得以奠下今天撰寫本書的基礎，感銘至今。尤其，擔任班上導師的廖述源教授，對我影響至深。溫文儒雅的廖老師不僅學識淵博，除了對保險課程的教導外，對待我們這群少不經事的大學生，總是循循善誘的要我們將來進保險界服務後，要竭力為客戶付出專業，才不負學保險科班的畢業生。至今，言猶在耳，雖已不在實務界服務，但仍銘記老師的教誨。

大學畢業後，進入海洋大學航運管理研究所就讀，碩士論文指導教授黃正宗教授，是我海上保險的啓蒙恩師。黃老師是極為專業的海上保險法教授，感謝黃老師在研究所課程中逐條解釋英國海上保險法精義，詳細討論國內保險市場使用英國條款的法律與實務問題，點點滴滴的學識累積，匯流為專業的學術基礎，致使在過去業界工作時，能遊刃於海上保險理賠，而今的課堂教學上，也能集結理論與實務，與學生們侃侃而談。

研究所中除了確定未來工作的發展，與現在的學術研究方向外，更可貴的是遇到了海商法的啓蒙恩師 —— 曾國雄教授，曾老師也是我在博士班中，一路教導、提攜及扶持我的博士論文指導教授，他是國內海商法研究的權威泰斗，不論在碩士班或博士班求學過程中，曾老師都毫不露倦的傾囊相授，引導我從保險及法學基礎理論開始，將海商與海上保險進行整合與分析，培養我在學術研究的基本能力。老師常說做學問的結果，是要能夠「用」之於社會，不能夠「用」的學問並不是真的學問！曾老師一語道盡學術研究的核心價值，這樣的教誨更深深影響我後來的學術研究方向，希望都盡力的與實務問題結合，也直接促使本書撰寫以理論為基，實務討論為主的思惟架構。

曾老師宏儒碩學、識量弘恢，待人謙和有容，與學生間之相處更如父子，教導學生也關愛學生，心中對老師的欽服難以筆墨形容。常常想，雖然專業學識不及老師之萬一，但也應盡力努力學習老師對學生無私付出的良師典範。

距離上一本和徐當仁老師合著《海上保險基礎理論與實務》算起，不知不覺已經快 12 年了，這個不算長也不能說短的時間裡，不論是海運界或者海上保險界都有了許許多多的變化，如 2003 年的國際船舶保險條款、2004 年的約克安特衛普規則、2009 年的鹿特丹規則、以及 2009 年的協會貨物保險條款等，都反應了航運與保險不斷改變的趨勢。因此，海上保險雖為海商法之其中一章，但在理論與實務上與海商法是既獨立又連結，密不可分，所以在學校課程中雖獨立開課，但絕不是跳脫海商法以及航運實務而獨立研究學習，反而必須與海商與航運結合方可大成。

國內海上保險相關之專門書籍並不多見，可能是在大學院校中開「海上保險」這門課的系所不多，而實務上，海上保險也不是公司營運的主流險種之故。然筆者認為海上保險雖非明日之星，但卻也絕不是末日黃花，因為航運產業、國際貿易都與海上保險習習相關，臺灣的航運發展不論是港口或航商在國際上已有一席之地，國際貿易業者更是一改傳統之單點運送的貿易方式，而是轉而以三角貿易甚或國際運籌的模式，將全世界的貨物配銷全世界，而成為網狀運送模式，自然國際物流的風險也比過去傳統運輸風險複雜許多。海上保險是國際運輸的衍生需求，也是轉嫁國際物流風險的風險管理工具，實為國際貿易實務中極為重要之一環。

筆者從過去實務工作經驗，及透過學術研究及在實務授課之互動討論中，更深刻體會海上保險理論與實務的同與異。然法律或理論是不是真的跟不上實務，或實務作法只是人云亦云的累積，我想不論是法律規定、條款內容或實務概念，或多或少都存有匪解的盲點亟待澄清，可能是航運或國貿環境變遷，造成法律規定過時，也可能是因實務操作時，夾雜在「業績」、「核保」與「理賠」間的不同立場因素，幾經協商酌量後，所不得不為的權宜行便方式，以致造成學術界與實務界的對話常存歧異。

有感與此，時值 2009 年英國海上貨物保險條款問世，筆者嘗試藉由此書，做為學術與實務之溝通橋樑與對話管道，故全書除於第一篇比較 1982 年版條款與 2009 年版條款之異同外，於第二篇乃開始著手討論與海上貨物保險有關的英國海上保險法規定及其理論義涵，以及在實務上這些基礎理論如何與實務配合；接著，第三篇則是對 2009 年協會貨物保險(A)、(B)及(C)條款進行逐條的釋義，全篇分成承保範圍、除外條款、保險期間、理賠事項及其他事項等五大區塊進行討論，透過基礎理論之探討為基，再逐句逐條解釋條款之義，以及在實務上之應用，希望藉由本書之出版可澄清學術界與實務界間的疑問，更希望在校學生研讀本書後，能有更清楚的海上保險輪廓與概念。

本書內容是多年來之實務與教學心得撰寫而成，也有些是過去曾指導過的研究生或專題所共同發表的期刊論文片段再編撰而融入書本中，如長榮大學的芊妤、紀薇、桂華、雲雁，以及高雄海洋科技大學的于瑄、芊蓁、芳伶、慧珊等，尤其本書第一篇多處表格內容乃是引用慧珊碩士論文內所整理的詳細資料，謝謝這些研究生過去對海上保險研究的貢獻，讓我體會到教學相長的真義，在此一併致謝。

學海無涯，本書僅為個人見解，謹希望藉由本書之出版，收拋磚引玉之效，引起航運、國貿、金融與保險各界對 2009 年新條款之共鳴與討論。筆者才疏學淺，書本內容若有遺誤，或存有不成熟之見解、謬誤而未察，更祈盼諸方賢達不吝指較是幸。

100 年 1 月誌於高雄海洋科技大學航運管理系研究室

CONTENTS

曾序 **1**

黃序 **2**

廖序 **5**

（依姓氏筆劃排列）

自序 **7**

第一篇　緒論

第一章　英國協會貨物保險條款之沿革　**003**

第二章　2009 年英國協會貨物保險條款之產生背景　**007**

第三章　2009 年條款之主要增修內容　**009**

第二篇、海上貨物保險之基礎理論

第四章　航程保險單　**021**

第五章　海上貨物保險之保險利益　**031**

第六章　定值保險單　**043**

第七章　保險代位求償權　**053**

第八章　擔保　**069**

第三篇、2009年英國協會貨物保險條款逐條釋義

第九章　ICC,2009 之承保範圍　*083*

第十章　ICC,2009 之除外條款　*119*

第十一章　ICC,2009 之保險期間　*145*

第十二章　ICC,2009 之理賠事項　*165*

第十三章　保險權益　*187*

第十四章　被保險人之減少損失義務　*191*

第十五章　避免遲延　*211*

第十六章　法律與慣例　*215*

附錄一　Institute Cargo Clauses, 2009 (A)　*219*

附錄二　Institute Cargo Clauses, 2009 (B)　*229*

附錄三　Institute Cargo Clauses, 2009 (C)　*239*

附錄四　Marine Insurance Act 1906　*249*

附錄五　保險法（摘錄）　*289*

附錄六　海商法　*305*

參考文獻　*329*

CONTENTS

第**1**篇

緒 論

第一章　英國協會貨物保險條款之沿革

第二章　2009 年英國協會貨物保險條款之產
　　　　生背景

第三章　2009 年條款之主要增修內容

第 一 章 ‧‧‧‧‧‧‧‧

英國協會貨物
保險條款之沿革

　　臺灣為海島型經濟國家，國際貿易對臺灣經濟發展之重要性不言可喻，加上臺灣有其航運地理上之優勢，更維繫著海島經濟之不斷成長。而依據交通部之統計資料顯示，我國進出口貨物約有 99% 以上是以海上運輸之方式來運送，足見海上運輸在我國貨物運送中扮演著舉足輕重的角色。早期國際貿易的生產純係以「生產地」具比較利益做為考量，直接於該地生產完成之後，就直接運送到出口地，就國際貿易業者之風險而言，不論貿易條件為何，均可謂僅於「運輸」風險而已。

　　國際間隨著區域經濟的整合及全球產業分工模式，國際貿易業者在微利競爭的壓力下不斷調整其產銷策略與整合供應鏈管理，「全球物流管理（Global Logistics Management, GLM）」新興概念逐而成型。臺灣於 2002 年加入 WTO 之後，從事國際貿易的企業，面臨全球競爭劇烈與資訊數位快速發展的環境下，企業產銷及配送體制自也需要創新改革來維持強化企業的優勢與競爭力；換言之，傳統倉儲與運輸模式隨著企業貿易全球化的同時，其作業型態也轉向於專業分工及功能整合。國貿企業為獲取最大利潤，皆選擇在勞工成本、土地成本低廉的國家進行生產組裝，再透過「物流系統」將商品行銷到全世界；在此整體物流過程中，貨主所需面對的風險也自然提高及多樣化。面對著現今多樣且複雜之運輸、倉儲、生產、流通加工等多變的運輸風險，國際貿易業者大多透過投保海上保險方式轉嫁其所承擔之風險，以便於物流過程中發生損失時可獲得及時的補償，降低財務衝擊。

然海上貨物保險雖從名稱上使人容易認知是承保「海上」運輸風險，但為配合前述之多樣且複雜的運輸與物流風險，海上貨物保險也不斷修改承保範圍或限制責任範圍，以因應航運實務的變化。我國海上貨物運輸保險實務，幾乎都是使用由英國倫敦保險人協會（The Institute of London Underwriters）中的技術及條款小組（Technical and Clauses Committee）所制定的協會條款（Institute Clauses）。在貨物方面為協會貨物運輸條款（Institute Cargo Clauses，簡稱ICC），最早的版本為1912年版，經過保險及航貿市場變遷後，保險條款亦隨著更替，陸續乃有1930年、1963年及1982年等三個版本，目前國內實務大都採用1982年版，習慣上將其稱之為ICC,1982。直至2009年，最新的ICC,2009亦由英國倫敦保險人協會公布推薦給全世界使用。

英國協會貨物保險條款版本最早可以追溯到1912年的8個條款版本，全名為Institute Cargo Clauses–With Average, Free Particular Average，其中1至7條為基本條款，第8條為特約條款；ICC,1912為一合併保單，所謂With Average（簡稱W.A.），正確譯文應為海損賠償，國內通常翻譯為水漬險；第8條則為Free From Particular Average條款（簡稱F.P.A.），正確譯文應為單獨海損不賠條款，國內則翻譯為平安險。若保險單中並未刪除第8條，則保險人除因擱淺（stranded）、沉沒（sunk）及焚毀（burnt）外，對單獨海損不負賠償責任。此套條款在當時是與Lloyd's S.G. Policy––Cargo以附註補充方式使用於貨物保險市場。至1930年代初期，英國倫敦保險人協會所屬之技術與條款小組對ICC,1912年版進行修訂，就是ICC,1930，共計 10 條條文，並由第四條區分為 With Average Clause 以及 F.P.A. Clause 兩種承保範圍。1951 年則首度出現全險條件（All Risk），並與 W.A.及 F.P.A.三種條件並列，亦為 10 個條文[1]。惟這三個條款年代久遠，實務上也早已不再使用。

隨著時代更迭以及運輸方式的演進與革命，Lloyd's S.G. Policy 已無法因應當時的海運市場與海上危險，但考慮這個保單已經在國際保險市場中使用近兩百年，雖然保單用語艱澀難懂，但其內容的解釋與精確意義仍須參酌過去兩百年來之無數判決方能確定，因此倫敦保險人協會持續沿用 Lloyd's S.G. Policy 並將內容訂為貨物保險契約之基本條款（General Clause），而再研擬特別條款以配合實務需要，1963 年協會貨物保險條款便因應而生。ICC,1963 為一綜合保險單，由 14 條條款所組成，且係配合 Lloyd's S.G. Policy 使用，以做為補充或限制原保險單之用。條款除第 5 條外，其餘條款內容都一樣，也就是第 5 條分別為平安險條款（Institute cargo clauses, F.P.A.）、水漬險條款（W.A., Average Clause）以及全險條款（All Risks, All risks Clause）。

再隨著貨櫃運輸之興起，全球航運環境產生極大之質變，國際間也相繼出現國際公約，如 1968 年海牙威士比規則，以及 1978 年漢堡規則、1980 年國際複合運送公約、1989 年海難救助公約等，均為國際航運法律帶領進入另一個新的時代，如以特別提款權為計算的單位責任限制、運送人之強制責任期間、運送人之法定免責事由及短期時效利益、複合運送責任規定等，更直接使運送人與貨主間或保險人與被保險人間，以及保險人與運送人間之風險承擔與轉嫁，產生了跳躍式的轉變。

因此，聯合國貿易暨發展委員會（UNCTAD）提出改革報告，並

---

[1] 鄭鎮樑、范姜肱、謝宗興，〈英國 2009 協會貨物條款修正之探討〉，《核保學報》第十八卷，頁 287。

要求技術與條款委員會起草修訂條款之工作，期望設計出一套用字清楚且明白顯示承保範圍之新條款，ICC,1982 乃因應而生。新條款大幅修改 ICC,1963 條款，可謂協會條款歷年來之最大幅度修改；除修改傳統古老用字的條款外，也配合複合運送設計內陸運輸風險，並分別清楚規範三套不同條款保險人的責任範圍。1982 年版的協會貨物保險條款名稱係由 1963 年之條款名稱簡化而來，條款數目亦由原先的 14 條增加至 19 條；三套條款分別為 ICC（A）、ICC（B）以及 ICC（C）條款。

由於 ICC,1982 條款用字清楚易懂，使保險契約雙方對於承保範圍等規定更能明瞭，減少當事人的紛爭；另新式海上保險單跳脫舊有保單之紊亂內容，改以條列式方式規範相關事項，條款文字清晰易懂與保單格式內容分明等因素皆讓 1982 年版之 ICC 條款受到國際海上貨物保險市場之廣泛採用，ICC,1982 至今仍是國際海上貨物保險市場最普遍使用之保險條款。

第二章••••••••••

2009年英國協會貨物保險條款之產生背景

　　ICC,1982 廣為被國際社會採用 20 多年後，全球國際貿易型態由文件訂單轉變成電子 e 化的無紙化訂單，運輸型態也從港到港轉變成戶到戶；整合型全球物流活動的趨勢亦帶領貨櫃集散站經營業者與物流配銷中心經營貨物（櫃）拆併裝、進出口與轉口物流、配銷運送以及倉儲等物流業務活動，貨主於國際貿易商業活動中提供商品服務時，貨物的安全送達目的地已成為最低門檻的要求，貨主更希望運送人能提供整合性（integrated）的運送方式，有效的整合運輸、倉儲、裝卸、包裝、流通加工等相關動作以節省物流成本。

　　特別是當貿易雙方採用 2000 年貿易條件的 D 類條件（到達指定地／港交貨）時，如 DAF（Delivered at Frontier，邊境交貨條件）、DES（Delivered Ex Ship，目的港船上交貨條件）、DEQ（Delivered Ex Quay，目的港碼頭交貨條件）、DDU（Delivered Duty Unpaid，輸入國稅前交貨條件）以及 DDP（Delivered Duty paid，輸入國稅迄交貨條件）等五種貿易條件下，除買賣雙方另有約定之外，賣方在規定的日期或期限之內，必須要先自行負擔一切風險與費用，如倉儲、配送甚至流通加工過程等，直到將貨物安全運抵指定目的港或目的地點交至買方處置之後，一切風險及費用才由買方負擔。因此，對於國際貿易 D 條件之出口託運人而言，如何管理國際物流過程中所造成的風險或是否可以透過現行海上運輸保險轉嫁風險，是非常重要的風險管理議題。

　　總言之，就運輸風險而言，此全球運籌模式無疑係自複合運輸以來，又是另一對國際貨物運輸風險的重大變革，其影響將改變過去保險人與被保險人的運輸風險評估，也考驗著現行 ICC,1982 條款的實用價值。除了上述全球貨物運籌模式考量，實務上對於 ICC,1982 的部分保單條款文字解釋仍存有爭議，如第 4.3 款、第 12 條及第 16 條的「servants」之義，第 8 條有關保險期間之「delivery to」之實務認定問題，如第 10 條變更航程之「Held Covered」的解釋等。又 2001 年 9 月 11 日美國遭恐怖分子攻擊後，防恐議題逐成為美國及國際社會之焦點，反應於保險契約，亦成為保險人是否將恐怖攻擊造成之損失明列為除外事項的理賠問題。基於上述原因英國協會貨物保險條款再度面臨被修訂的挑戰。

　　由國際保險協會（International Underwriter Association）以及勞依茲市場協會（Lloyds Market Association）所組成之聯合貨物保險委員會（The Joint Cargo Committee，簡稱 JCC）為統一保單用語並調整保險契約雙方當事人的風險承擔與權利平衡，以及修改易混淆及簡化條款文字等考量，於 2006 年 2 月開始著手修改工作，以問卷方式廣徵意見，於 2008 年 5 月 JCC 將回收的問卷分析後，同年 10 月提出修改版草案供國際海上保險市場參考，最後於 2009 年 1 月 1 日正式公布新保險條款，即為 ICC,2009。ICC,2009 的問世從保單用語之修改，恐怖攻擊列入除外不保以及修正最多的保險期間條款可知，新條款的公布已使國際海上貨物保險市場之雙方當事人風險承擔天平，再度發生實質改變。

第三章 •••••••••

2009年條款之主要增修內容

　　ICC,1982 與 ICC,2009 年貨物保險比較後發現條款數目並無增刪，仍維持 19 個條款並區分為 Risk Covered、Exclusions、Duration、Claims 等四大部分及 Benefit of Insurance、Minimising Losses、Avoidance of Delay、 Law and Practice 等項目。其主要修改部分為刪除部分原於 ICC,1982 保險單右側的條款名稱，如 Exclusions 中的第 4 至第 7 條，以及保險權益規定的第 15 條，以及第 18 條與 19 條，其中第 15 條已改名為 Benefit of Insurance。另，為使被保險人於閱讀條款時能夠清楚了解其條款分類與內容，ICC,2009 保險單中，將部分條款名稱增列於條款上方形成次標題，如第 12 條轉運費用條款（Forwarding Charges Clause）以及減輕損失（Minimising Losses）規定的第 16 條被保險人義務條款（Duty of Assured Clause），及第 17 條的棄權條款（Waiver）等。

　　至於修改的部分則可區分為條款內文句刪除，如第 4 條、第 5 條、第 12 條，刪除部分詳如表 3–1 所示：

表 3-1 ICC, 2009 條款內文句刪除表

條次	ICC, 1982	ICC, 2009	說明
第 4 條	4.3 loss damage or expense caused by insufficiency or unsuitability of packing or preparation of the subject-matter insured (for the purpose of this Clause 4.3 "packing" shall be deem to included stowage in a container or **liftvan** but only when such stowage is carried out prior attachment of this insurance or by the Assured or their servants)	4.3 loss damage or expense caused by insufficiency or unsuitability of packing or preparation of the subject-matter insured to withstand the ordinary incidents of the insured transit where such packing or preparation is carried out by the Assured or their employees or prior to the attachment of this insurance (for the purpose of these Clauses "packing" shall be deem to included stowage in a container and "employees" shall not include independent contractors)	刪除 ICC,1982 中 "liftvan" 一字。
第 5 條	5.2 The Underwriters waive any breach of the implied warranties of seaworthiness of the ship and fitness of the ship to carry the subject-matter insured to destination, **unless the Assured or their servants are privy to such unseaworthiness or unfitness**.	5.3 The Insurers waive any breach of the implied warranties of seaworthiness of the ship and fitness of the ship to carry the subject-matter insured to destination.	除 5.2 條次變稱為 5.3 外，並將 ICC,1982 原 5.2 條款後段之但書 "unless the Assured or their servants are privy to such unseaworthiness or unfitness." 刪除。
第 12 條	12. Where, as a result of the operation of a risk covered by this insurance, the insured transit is terminated at a port or place other than that to which the subject-matter is covered under this insurance, the Underwriters will reimburse the Assured for any extra charges properly and reasonably incurred in unloading storing and forwarding the subject-matter insured to the destination to which it is insured **hereunder**.	12. Where, as a result of the operation of a risk covered by this insurance, the insured transit is terminated at a port or place other than that to which the subject-matter insured is covered under this insurance, the Insurers will reimburse the Assured for any extra charges properly and reasonably incurred in unloading storing and forwarding the subject-matter insured to the destination to which it is insured.	刪除 ICC,1982 中 "hereunder" 一字。

資料來源：作者整理自林慧珊，《2009年協會貨物保險條款增修內容之研究》，頁48。

條款內文字改變則如第 1 條、第 2 條、第 3 條、第 5 條、第 8
條、第 9 條、第 11 條、第 12 條、第 13 條、第 14 條、第 15 條、第
16 條、第 17 條等，詳如表 3-2 所示。

表 3-2　ICC, 2009 與 ICC, 1982 條款文字改變比較彙整表

ICC, 2009 條款	ICC, 1982 條款用字	變更後用字
Clause 3、Clause 5.3、Clause 9、Clause 11.2、Clause 12、Clause 14.1、Clause 14.2、Clause 16.2、Clause 17、NOTE	underwriter	insurer
Clause 2、Clause 3、Clause 8.3	contract of affreightment	contract of carriage
Clause 4.3、Clause 12、Clause 16	servants	employees
Clause 3、Clause 8.3	shipowners	carriers
Clause 4.6、Clause 4.7	arising from	caused by
Clause 4.7	war employing atomic	device employing atomic
Clause 8.1.4、Clause 8.2、Clause 9.1、Clause 9.2	goods	subject-matter insured
Clause 12、Clause 13	subject-matter	
Clause 14.1	cargo	
Clause 14.1	herein	under this insurance
Clause 8.1.1、Clause 8.1.2、Clause 9.2		in the contract of insurance
Clause 15.2	inure to	extend to
Clause 1	provided in	excluded by the provisions of
Clause 2	elsewhere in this insurance	below
Clause 8.3	for above	in Clauses 8.1.1 to 8.1.4

資料來源：林慧珊，《2009年協會貨物保險條款增修內容之研究》，頁55。

ICC,2009 最重要者乃在於條款內容實質修改，分別爲第 3 條、第 4 條、第 5 條、第 7 條、第 8 條、第 9 條、第 10 條、第 15 條以及附註等，詳如表 3-3 所示。

表 3-3　ICC, 2009 條款實質修改內容表

條次	ICC, 1982	ICC, 2009	說明
第 3 條	3. This insurance is extended to indemnify the Assured against such proportion of liability under the contract of affreightment "Both to Blame Collision" Clause as is in respect of a loss recoverable hereunder. In the event of any claim by shipowners under the said Clause the Assured agree to notify the Underwriters who shall have the right, at their own cost and expense, to defend the Assured against such claim.	3. This insurance **indemnifies the Assured, in respect of any risk insured herein, against liability incurred under any Both to Blame Collision Clause in the contract of carriage**. In the event of any claim by carriers under the said Clause, the Assured agree to notify the Insurers who shall have the right, at their own cost and expense, to defend the Assured against such claim.	除 將 ICC,1982 之 " is extended to" 刪除外，並修改條文文句如粗黑體部分。
第 4 條	4.3 loss damage or expense caused by insufficiency or unsuitability of packing or preparation of the subject–matter insured（for the purpose of this Clause 4.3 "packing" shall be deem to included stowage in a container or liftvan but only when such stowage is carried out prior attachment of this insurance or by the Assured or their servants）	4.3 loss damage or expense caused by insufficiency or unsuitability of packing or preparation of the subject–matter insured **to withstand the ordinary incidents of the insured transit where such packing or preparation is carried out by the Assured or their employees or prior to the attachment of this insurance**（for the purpose of **these Clauses** "packing" shall be deem to included stowage in a container and "employees" shall not include independent contractors）	1.增訂條款文字如粗黑體部分。 2. 將 ICC,1982 之 "this Clause 4.3" 改為 "these Clauses"

第 5 條	5.1 In no case shall this insurance cover loss damage or expense arising from unseawothiness of vessel or craft, unfitness of vessel craft conveyance container or liftvan for the safe carriage of the subject–matter insured, where the Assured or their servants are privy to such unseawothiness or unfitness, at the time the subject–matter insured is loaded therein. 5.2 The Underwriters waive any breach of the implied warranties of seaworthiness of the ship and fitness of the ship to carry the subject–matter insured to destonation, unless the Assured or their servants are privy to such unseaworthiness or unfitness.	5.1 In no case shall this insurance cover loss damage or expense arising from 5.1.1 unseaworthiness of vessel or craft or unfitness of vessel or craft for the safe carriage of the subject–matter insured, where the Assured are privy to such unseaworthiness or unfitness, at the time the subject–matter insured is loaded therein **5.1.2 unfitness of container or conveyance for the safe carriage of the subject–matter insured, where loading therein is carried out prior to attachment of this insurance or by the Assured or their employees and they are privy to such unfitness at the time of loading. 5.2 Exclusion 5.1.1 above shall not apply where the contract of insurance has been assigned to the party claiming hereunder who has bought or agreed to buy the subject–matter insured in good faith under a binding contract.** 5.3 The Insurers waive any breach of the implied warranties of seaworthiness of the ship and fitness of the ship to carry the subject–matter insured to destination.	1.將原 5.1 款之規定分為 5.1.1 船舶、駁船之不適航規定與 5.1.2 貨櫃、運輸工具之不適運規定。 2.新增第 5.2 款之規定如粗黑體部分。排除善意受讓第三人之適用。
第 7 條	7.3 caused by terrorist or any person acting <u>from a political motive.</u>	7.3 caused by any act of terrorism being an act of any person acting **on behalf of , or in connection with, any organization which carriers out activities directed toward the overthrowing or influencing, by force or violence, of any government whether or not legally constituted 7.4 caused by any person acting from a political, ideological, or religious motive.**	1.修改並擴大 ICC,1982 有關恐怖行為除外之規定。 2.增列 7.4 款如粗黑體部分,加入因政治、意識型態或宗教動機除外之規定。

| 第 8 條 | 8.1 This insurance attaches from the time the goods leave the warehouse or place of storage at the place named herein for the commencement of the transit, continues during the ordinary course of transit and terminates either
8.1.1 on delivery to the Cosignees' or other final warehouse of place of storage at the destination named herein.
8.1.2 on delivery to any other warehouse or place of storage, whether prior to or at the destination name herein, which the Assured elect to use either
8.1.2.1 for storage other than in the ordinary course of transit or
8.1.2.2 for allocation or distribution, or
8.1.3 on the expiry of 60 days after completion of discharge overside of the goods hereby insured from the oversea vessel at the final port of discharge, whichever shall first occur.
8.2 If, after discharge overside from the final port of discharge, but prior to termination of this insurance, the goods are to be forwarded to a destination other than that to which they are insured hereunder, this insurance, whist remaining subject to termination as provided for above, shall not extend beyond the commencement of transit to such other destination. | **8.1 Subject to Clause 11 below, this insurance attaches from the time the subject−matter insured is first moved in the warehouse or at the place of storage（name in the contract of insurance）for the purpose of the immediate loading into or onto the carrying vehicle or other conveyance for the commencement of transit,** continues during the ordinary course of transit and terminates either
8.1.1 on completion of unloading from carrying vehicle or other conveyance in or at the final warehouse or place of storage at the destination named in the contract of insurance,
8.1.2 on completion of unloading from the carrying vehicle or other conveyance in or at any other warehouse or place of storage, whether prior to or at the destination named in the contract of insurance, which the Assured or their employees elect to use either for storage other than in the ordinary course of transit or for allocation or distribution, or
8.1.3 when the Assured or their employees elect to use any carrying vehicle or other conveyance or any container for storage other than in the ordinary course of transit or
8.1.4 on the expiry of 60 days after completion of discharge overside of the subject−matter insured from the oversea vessel at the final port of discharge, whichever shall first occur.
8.2 If, after discharge overside from the oversea vessel at the final port of discharge, but prior to termination of this insurance, the subject−matter insured is to be forwarded to a destination other than that to which it is insured, this insurance, whist remaining subject to termination as provided **in Clauses 8.1.1 to 8.1.4,** shall not extend beyond **the time the subject−matter insured is first moved for the purpose of** the commencement of transit to such other destination. | 1. 修訂 8.1 款 將保險生效 點提前到為 了運送目的 裝上運送工 具之第一次 動作。
2. 修訂原 8.1.1 與 8.1.2 條 款規定，將 ICC1982 中 "on delivery to"修改為 "on completion of unloading"。
3. ICC,1982 的 8.1.2.1 及 8.1.1.2 之內 容合併修訂 成 ICC,2009 的 8.1.2。
4. 新增訂 8.1.3 如粗黑體部 分，規範以 運輸車輛為 通常運輸過 程以外之儲 存的終止規 定。
5. 將 ICC,1982 的 8.1.3 改 成 ICC,2009 之 8.1.4。
6. 於 8.2 中修 改成為了運 往其他目的 地而裝上運 送工具之第 一次動作時 保險終止。 |

第 9 條	9.If owing to circumstances beyond the control of the Assured either the contract of carriage is terminated at a port or place other than the destination named therein or the transit is otherwise terminated before delivery of the goods as provided for in Clause 8 above, then this insurance shall also terminate unless prompt notice is given to the Underwriters and continuation of cover is requested when the insurance shall in force, subject to an additional premium if required by the Underwriters, either	9.If owing to circumstances beyond the control of the Assured either the contract of carriage is terminated at a port or place other than the destination named therein or the transit is otherwise terminated before **unloading of the subject−matter insured** as provided for in Clause 8 above, then this insurance shall also terminate unless prompt notice is given to the Insurers and continuation of cover is requested when the this insurance shall in force, subject to an additional premium if required by the Insurers, either	1.將 ICC,1982 之"delivery of the goods"改為 "unloading of the subject−matter insured"。
第 10 條	10. Where, after attachment of this insurance, the destination is changed by the Assured, held covered at a premium and on condition to be arranged subject to prompt notice being given to the Underwriters.	10.1 Where, after attachment of this insurance, **the destination is changed by the Assured, this must be notified promptly to Insurer for rates and terms to be agreed. Should a loss occur prior to such agreement being obtained cover may be provided but only of cover would have been available at a reasonable commercial market rate on reasonable market terms.** 10.2 Where the subject−matter insured comments the transit contemplated by this insurance（in accordance with Clause 8.1）, but, without the knowledge of the Assured or their employees the ship sails for another destination, this insurance will nevertheless be deemed to have attached at commencement of such transit.	1. 將 ICC,1982 分成 10.1 及 10.2 兩款規定。 2. 刪除 ICC, 1982 中 "held cover" 之規定並改以條款詳細規定。 3. 新增於新費率條件談妥前發生事故，保險之責任規定。 4. 新增 10.2 款規定如粗黑體部分，被保險人不知情船舶將變更航程時，保險之效力仍自開始運送該保險標的物時生效。

| 第 15 條 | 15. This insurance shall not inure to the benefit of the carrier or other bailee. | **15. This insurance**
15.1 covers the Assured which included the person claiming indemnity either as the person by or on whose behalf the contract of insurance was effected or as an assignee,
15.2 shall not extend to or otherwise benefit the carrier or their bailee. | 1. 將 ICC,1982 第 15 條全部改寫，並分成為 15.1 及 15.2 兩款，如粗黑體部分。
2. 清楚定義被保險人，及聲明保險權益不擴及運送人及其他受託人。 |

資料來源：作者整理自林慧珊，《2009年協會貨物保險條款增修內容之研究》，頁19-46。

　　ICC,2009 完全沒有修改 1982 版的條款為第 6 條、第 18 條、第 19 條等三個條款。整體而言，ICC,2009 之修改以條款內文字改變為最多，共有 14 個條款有改變，而第 5 條則是整體修改最多的條款。至於條款內容實質修改部分則是 Duration 內的 3 個條款均有變動，應可以說是 ICC,2009 最重要且影響較大的修改條款。茲將 ICC,2009 之條款相較於 ICC,1982 的增修情況列於表 3-4。

表 3-4　ICC, 2009 增修整理表

項目		文句刪除	文字改變	實質修改	合計
Risk Covered	Clause 1. Risks		√		1
	Clause 2. General Average		√		1
	Clause 3. Both to blame Collision Clause		√	√	2
Exclusions	Clause 4	√		√	2
	Clause 5	√	√	√	3
	Clause 6				0
	Clause 7			√	1
Duration	Clause 8. Transit Clause		√	√	2
	Clause 9. Termination of Contract of Carriage		√	√	2
	Clause 10.Change of Voyage			√	1
Claims	Clause 11.Insurable Interest		√		1
	Clause 12.Forwarder Charges	√	√		2
	Clause 13.Constructive Total Loss		√		1
	Clause 14. Increased Value		√		1
Benefit of Insurance	Clause 15.		√	√	2
Minimising Losses	Clause 16. Duty of Assured		√		1
	Clause 17. Waiver		√		1
Avoidance of Delay	Clause 18.				0
Law and Practice	Clause 19.				0
NOTE			√		1
合計		**3**	**14**	**8**	**25**

資料來源：作者整理自林慧珊，《2009年協會貨物保險條款增修內容之研究》，頁19。

第2篇

海上貨物保險之基礎概念

第四章　航程保險單

第五章　海上貨物保險之保險利益

第六章　定值保險單

第七章　保險代位求償權

第八章　擔保

第 四 章 ● ● ● ● ● ● ● ●

航程保險單

　　海上貨物保險為一動態保險單，保險標的（貨物或其他動產）並不是僅固定停留在某一特定地點，由保險人承保，而是從一地點運送到另一地點，倘若尚未自該約定地點開始運送移動，則保險契約還沒有生效；而若已到達約定地點，則保險契約的效力即為終止。這樣的概念與靜態保險單為原則的保險契約概念恰好相反；所謂靜態保險單如以火災保險為例，其保險標的（建築物）是靜止不動，建築物內動產原則上也是應該在約定的建築物範圍內，若離開該處所將被認為是危險變更，將影響保險契約的效力，此即為動態保險與靜態保險的最大差別。

　　所謂保險期間為保險人對於保險事故發生時之應負責任期間，或者稱為保險人承保責任之開始至結束期間。保險期間依不同性質可分為兩類：一為以時間為界定的保險期間（time policy），另一為以航程為界定的保險期間（voyage policy）。非海上保險的財產保險通常為一年期，如汽車保險、火災保險等。此外，人壽保險的保險期間則以最短一天為限，如旅行平安保險；反之，最長期限則至被保險人身故為止，如終身壽險。而以航程為界定的航程保單，其保險期間的約定並不以「時間」的開始與結束為概念，而是以「距離」的空間概念為約定，即以一起航點保到另一個航程終止點的運送航程為「保險期間」，如海上與航空貨物保險均屬之。

第一節　英國海上保險法保險期間之規定

英國海上保險法（Marine Insurance Act, 1906，以下簡稱 MIA, 1906）中有關保險期間之規定詳見第 25 條規定：

Where the contract is to insure the subject–matter "at and from", or from one place to another or others, the policy is called a "voyage policy" and where the contract is to insure the subject matter for a definite period of time the policy is called a "time policy." A contract for both voyage and time may be included in the same policy.

由條文可知，海上保險期間的約定可分為兩類：一類為以約定航程的保險期間；另一類為以約定固定時間的保險期間。在固定時間之保單中，關於時間的記載，應指明確切之期間（definite period of time），除了保險單上另有特別規定外，否則實務上認定保險期間開始於某日凌晨零時，終止於某日午夜 12 時。其概念圖 4-1。

| xx 年xx月xx日零時 | | yy 年xx月xx日零時 |

圖 4-1　時間保險單概念圖
資料來源：作者自繪

另外，若保險單約定某日到某日為保險期間，則所約定的第一天與最後一天應解釋包含於保險期間之內，於實務上為避免爭議，可於保險單開始日與最後一日加上 "b.d.i"（both days inclusive）的字

4

句，則更可確定第一天與最後一天均爲保險期間。若是國際性的保險，則因保險標的物可能於保險期間內在世界不同地點遊走，實務上將出現地域時差的問題，故保險期間所指某日某時開始，應依保險契約簽訂地的時間爲準，較能反應締約時雙方當事人的眞意。

於定期航運實務上，船公司通常都將船期刊登於船報上，讓託運人參考，因此會有預定啓航日（Estimated Time of Departure, ETD）以及／預定到港日（Estimated Time of Arrival, ETA）出現在船期表上，在解釋上依最高法院 17 年上字第 1118 號判例指出：「契約文字業已表示當事人之眞意無須別事探求者，即不能反捨契約文字而爲曲解。」所以，當船期中明示裝船通知中所載的日期係「預定到期日」就不應認爲雙方曾就運送物有約定交付的特定期限。因此，「預定」的日期僅爲日期之初估，並不能認爲即爲運送期間的約定，也更不能據以爲保險期間的約定。

所謂航程保單則是以一特定地點保到另一個特定地點爲保險期間之保險契約。依 MIA,1906 的規定爲當保險標的物是以「在及從（at and from）」，或者「從一個地點到另外一個地點（from one place to another or others）」爲約定保險期間之保險單，就稱爲航程保險單。其概念如圖 4-2。

圖 4-2　航程保險單概念圖
資料來源：作者自繪

在英國海上保險法附則之保險單解釋規則（Rules for Construction of Policy）中進一步解釋 "from" 之義，"Where the subject-matter is insured 'from' a particular place, the risk does not attach until the ship starts on the voyage insured." 即當保險標的是From（從）一特定地點開始，船舶若尚未開始被保險航程，該保險並不生效。此概念就時間上而言，保險契約的成立時間點，並不等同於就是保險期間的開始。保險期間可能於訂約當時即開始，亦可能經過一段時間後才開始，需以船舶為進行航程而「發航」動作開始之時，保險期間才開始。

除此，船舶雖開始航程，但還要看是否是從保險單所約定的「特定地點」發航，保險期間才可說是由此開始。綜上所述，決定航程保險單開始生效須考量三項要件，即：1.運輸工具必須開始「航程」；2.必須於「特定地點」開始航程；3.該航程必須是「保險航程」。故就保險契約的訂立與保險期間開始的時間而言，將可能會產生兩種情況：其一為先訂立保險契約，但訂約後經一段時間，貨物才開始自保險航程運送，在此情況下，訂約後至裝載前保險並未生效。另一種情形則是保險契約訂立之前，貨物就已經在運送途中，所以若在還沒有發生損失情況下，契約訂立的同時，保險期間也即刻開始，保險契約也開始生效。

實務上，貨物的出口流程為工廠完成包裝之後，出口商需將貨物送至指定的貨櫃場或倉庫存放，由報關行向海關申請完成出口報關後，再將出口貨物裝櫃及裝船，最後才發航開始航程。故就海上貨物保險而言，若保險單上所記載的航程為「從高雄至安特衛普」（from Kaohsiung to Antwerp），其中高雄港即為「特定地點」，From（從）則指運輸工具從高雄港特定地點開始航程之時，保險人才開始承擔危險，負擔保險人責任，此時再搭配 ICC,1982 或 ICC,2009 第 8 條的解釋，決定保險期間之開始。另一與航程保險相關之保單用語為 "at and from"，依 MIA,1906 保險單解釋規則說明 "Where a ship is insured 'at and from' a particular place, and she is at that place in good safety, and, unless the policy otherwise provides, it is immaterial that she is covered by another policy for a specified time after arrival." 。即貨物之保單若記載 "at and from" （在及從）並載明裝船港時，則貨物於裝船港裝載至約定的船舶，保險人應負之保險責任即開始。

　　當貨物或其他動產是以 "From the loading thereof" （從裝載之時起）的條件投保，MIA,1906 保險單解釋規則說明 "Where goods or other moveables are insured 'from the loading thereof', the risk does not attach until such goods or moveables are actually on board, and the insurer is not liable for them while in transit from the shore to ship." 指在該貨物或動產實際裝載於船舶之前，保險不生效，保險人也不負擔裝船期間的風險，亦即貨物的航程保險，係以貨物裝載於船舶之時，保險人開始承擔保險責任。此處所謂「裝載」，當亦為一事實認定之問題，但依此規則之義，當貨物準備裝載於大船之上，起重機起吊貨物之時，非為「裝載」，保險人責任尚未開始，而是當貨物已卸置於大船上，無論其卸於甲板上或貨艙內，保險期間方可稱為開始。

　　依此解釋在實務上對貨主較為不利，後來經過航運習慣之轉變及條款的特別約定，MIA,1906 保單解釋規則僅於傳統船邊交、提貨之實務可以適用，如散裝雜貨以抓斗或起重機裝貨的裝船模式。然以現今貨櫃運送為主流的運輸模式，輔以協會保險條款的解釋，ICC,1982 之保險期間為貨物自離開海關倉庫時保險期間開始，也就是以開始運送（for the commencement of the transit）而「離開」（leave）倉庫或儲存處所之事實，為貨物保險開始生效的決定關鍵，所以船邊橋式起重機吊裝貨櫃過程，已經是保險期間之內，不應再如 MIA,1906 保單解釋規則之以貨物已卸置於船舶上保險期間才開始。但是 ICC,1982 並不包括在倉庫內之裝併櫃危險，若被保險人為求裝貨期間也可獲得保險保障，則與保險人再約定以批單（endorsement）方式加保 loading clause，使保險人承保裝併櫃時的意外危險事故。惟 ICC,2009 已將保險期間之生效提前至為了立即裝上或裝進運送車輛或其他運輸工具,並開始以運送為目的的第一次移動時開始生效,則依此條款文義可知,保險期間已然包括倉庫內之裝貨期間。

另於 MIA,1906 保單解釋規則中之 "Safely Landed" 規定為 "Where the risk on goods or other movables continues until they are 'safely landed' they must be landed in the customary manner and within a reasonable time after arrival at the port of discharge, and if they are not so landed the risk ceases." 依此規則可知,所謂安全卸載(safely landed)之意義,係貨物於港口以習慣性方式卸下,並予以保護至陸上。規則中的「習慣方式」(customary manner),係指安全的卸於卸貨港範圍內的正常碼頭或習慣地點而言,如香港著名的中流作業模式,此作業模式為遠洋船舶進港後並不靠泊船席,而是直接繫泊在港內浮筒或碇泊位,由駁船往返靠泊於貨船與公共裝卸區碼頭間,利用裝有吊臂的駁船把碇泊船隻上的貨物運載上岸進行貨物裝卸。因此,若所謂習慣方式當由各不同港口、不同貨種之不同卸貨方式而定,例如:實務上若某港的某種貨物,習慣上用小艇駁轉運至岸邊者,保險人仍須自負卸岸前之小艇運送危險責任。

解釋規則中所稱之「合理期間」(reasonable time)乃屬事實認定之問題,應參閱 MIA,1906 第 88 條的規定:"Where by this Act any reference is made to reasonable time, reasonable premium, or reasonable diligence, the question what is reasonable is a question of fact." 故所謂事實認定問題,即被認定為合理期間的標準,應以客觀、理性之判斷,考量同樣情況於其他場合是否合理而論,如航運習慣、港口特性、貨載之種類等情況而決定。

第二節　我國法中有關貨物保險期間之規定

保險法第 86 條規定:「貨物之保險,除契約另有訂定外,自交運之時以迄於其目的地收貨之時為其期間。」按其文義，可知除於保險契約有不同於保險法的之約定，貨物保險期間應該為「貨物交付運送之時」至「到達貨物目的地之時」為保險期間，由條文可知乃採航程的概念而立法，保險期間始於「貨物交付運送」之行為開始，而終止於貨物「到達目的地」之動作完成。

海上貨物保險期間則依海商法第 128 條的規定，即「保險期間除契約另有訂定外，關於船舶及其設備屬具，自船舶起錨或解纜之時，以迄目的港投錨或繫纜之時，為其期間；關於貨物，自貨物離岸之時，以迄目的港起岸之時，為其期間。」依此條文之義可知，海上貨物保險的保險期間乃始於裝貨港「貨物離岸」之動作開始，而終止於目的港「貨物起岸」之動作完成。換言之，海商法下的貨物保險期間如同保險法一樣，並非以確定的「時間」如某年某月某一天開始，至某年某月某一天中止為保險期間之約定，而是以貨物於出口港「離岸」，直到目的港「起岸」，兩個動作之開始與完成為保險期間之規定。

海商法此原則性的規定應僅船邊交提貨之傳統貨物運送情況，此船邊交提貨的方式，雖仍見於散雜貨物，惟隨著貨櫃化運輸的興起，貨櫃貨不論是整櫃運送或併櫃運送，就出口情形而言，大都先送至貨櫃集散站儲存或併櫃，待報關放行後再由貨櫃卡車載運至船邊裝船。故貨主投保貨物保險不宜如海商法之規定僅由船邊交貨甚至貨物離岸時才開始保險期間，即除了應考量海上運送過程之外，仍應再將內陸運輸之風險，視國際貿易條件的不同而於投保時加以約定。於解釋海商法的貨物保險期間規定時，當應配合實務現況，決定保險期間的起迄點，即除以原則性之概念規定保險期間外，不同貿易條件有不同的危險負擔轉移時點，由誰投保或如何安排保險航程，則應視國際貿易條件而論，若有必要仍應於保險契約中另外約定港到港以外的保險航程。

如以 CIF 做為貿易條件進口的情況，依條件之約定，賣方應自行負擔保險費，以使買方或其他任何擁有保險利益者，可直接向保險人索賠，同時提供買方保險單或其他保險單據。就 2000 年國貿條規CIF的條件特性而言，它是由三個契約所組成，即買賣契約、運送契約及保險契約等三種契約構成。賣方安排裝貨手續，並購買保險，取得提單及保險單，再將這些單證背書轉讓給買方，表示貨物所有權及保險請求權均移轉予買方。若貨物在運送途中發生損失，只要貨物已越過出口船舶之船舷，則原則上由買方取得保險利益向保險人索賠[1]。CIF 的貿易條件雖由出口商（託運人）投保，而就危險負擔之概念，出口商（託運人）之危險負擔為出口地內陸運送至裝船前，危險負擔於貨物越過船舷時即轉由買方，然因貿易條件中約定是應由賣方辦理保險，故若僅依海運提單上之航程記載而投保貨物保險，賣方安排的保險航程可能會由賣方倉庫起保或港口起保至目地港為止，依英國協會貨物保險條款的規定，貨物於到達目的港海關倉庫時，保險效力即終止；即進口商於進口港卸貨後，依 ICC,1982 的規定，貨物於到達目的港海關倉庫時，保險效力即終止，縱使是投保 ICC,2009 也是於海關倉庫完成卸貨後終止；若保險單未特別載明貨主的內陸倉庫，則保險公司的承保責任僅及於貨物到達卸貨港的海關倉庫時，並不包括將貨物進一步運往內陸的貨主倉庫之風險。因此，進口商必須自行安排保險承保該段內陸風險，或要求出口商購買保險時即涵蓋此風險。例如可將承保航程載明為 up to buyer's warehouse，則該風險即可移轉由保險公司承擔。

保險實務上以 CIF 的貿易條件投保，出口商除投保港到港之航程外，也常附加以 from seller's warehouse to buyer's warehouse 為保險航程的約定，故若事故發生於裝船前則由託運人索賠，但若發生裝船後則因危險負擔移轉，則於保險單背書轉讓後由受貨人向保險人索賠。惟此保險實務在國貿條件危險負擔的概念下，乃是將託運人應投

---

[1] 莊雲雁，《海上貨物保險之航程之研究》，頁 86。

保的保險及保險費，以約定 Door to Door 為保險航程的方式，「夾帶」至受貨人（進口商）付費之保險單內，似有違 CIF 的危險負擔條件與代為投保之精神，但在臺灣此實務投保方式可謂根深蒂固，只要受貨人並無意見，則似也並無大礙，雙方均相安無事。惟若是賣方倉庫離出口港有一相當距離時，如中國內地到沿海港口或歐洲內陸到港口時，因內陸運送距離長，風險變化及程度都大，尤其三角貿易情況由第三地出貨時，保險人於核保時應加以考量評估此段運輸風險，而不宜完全比照臺灣出口保單，一律附加 from seller's warehouse to buyer's warehouse 的航程。

反之，若貿易條件為 FOB，當貨物於指定裝船港越過船舷時，賣方即已履行其交貨義務，買方必須負擔自那時起貨物毀損或滅失的一切費用及危險，並投保海上運輸保險。賣方對貨物的危險責任直至貨物吊上船舶確實越過船舷為止，故貨物自工廠運至上船前的運輸或操作意外危險，都需由賣方投保。買方之危險負擔則自貨物上船後開始，故航程保單的約定除涵蓋海上運送期間外，也應包括自港口卸貨後的內陸運送期間，才能保障進口商所有危險負擔的期間。

前已述及，於 FOB 之條件下，裝船港越過船舷前的風險仍屬賣方，縱使買方自行購買此段之保險，然由於其未獲保險利益，因此仍無權向保險公司求償，所以賣方在 FOB 的貿易條件下，僅是不用投保海上運輸保險，但對於從倉庫到裝船前之風險仍應自行投保。（如圖 4-3）

出口商倉庫　　內陸運送

risk　　　　　　　　　　　出口港過船舷前

圖 4-3　FOB 出口商之危險負擔示意

資料來源：作者自繪

實務上，賣方可藉由投保「託運人利益保險」的方式來轉嫁其風險，託運人利益保險所承保的航程其條款規定大致爲：「本保險之效力自貨物離開被保險人之倉庫或儲存處所開始，並繼續有效至下列兩種情況下終止，其中並包括貨物於港口倉庫等待裝船期間之風險（惟以7天爲限）。(A)若貿易條件爲 CIF 或 C&I 時，直到貨物離開任何臺灣港口之海關倉庫或最後儲存處所，或(B)若貿易條件爲 FOB 或 C&F 時，直到貨物裝載於任何臺灣港口之指定船舶上爲止。」故賣方可依其需求投保其內陸運輸段的風險，或投保此「託運人利益保險」以轉嫁以 FOB 爲貿易條件時，於貨物裝船前的風險。

第五章

海上貨物保險之保險利益

第一節　海上貨物保險利益之意義

　　MIA,1906 第 5 條對海上保險利益之定義甚為完整，其條文定義如下：

Insurable interest defined

5–(1) Subject to the provisions of this Act, every person has an insurable interest who is interested in a marine adventure.

5–(2) In particular a person is interested in a marine adventure where he stands in any legal or equitable relation to the adventure, or to any insurable property at risk therein, in consequence of which he may benefit by the safety or due arrival of insurable property, or may be prejudiced by its loss, or by damage thereto, or by the detention thereof, or may incur liability in respect thereof.

　　由條文可知，凡與海上航行有利害關係之人，都依海上保險法規定有保險利益。而第 2 項進一步說明凡對海上航行為或危險中的任何可保財產具有法律上關係，即對該財產之安全或如期抵達即可獲得利益，或對該財產發生滅失、毀損、扣押或有責任產生時，即遭受損害時，則具有保險利益。因此，由 MIA,1906 的海上保險利益為被保險人對保險標的一種「利害關係」，此利害關係之發生則來自於合法海上航行，舉凡海上航程中與海上交易有關的船舶、貨物、其他動產、運費、佣金、交易利益、金錢利潤、貸款、責任等均是，對保險利益的定義及範圍乃採概括式的認定。

就貨物保險而言，保險利益主要是指與積極性財產有關的「所有權利益」，即該利益關係將因被保險人的現有財產因海上危險的發生而喪失。如 MIA,1906 第 3 條第 2 項(a)款所規定之任何船舶、貨物其他動產有可能遭受海上危險事故時，該財產即稱為「可保財產」（any ship goods or other moveables are exposed to maritime perils such property is in this Act referred to as "insurable property"），貨主基於這個可保財產之所有權關係即產生保險利益。

另於國際貿易之貨物而言，因所有權可能轉讓，託運人可能行使中止運送權，或者受貨人拒絕收受貨物等，都可能產生保險利益歸屬有不同考量。因此，在英國海上保險法即規定了或有性保險利益及消滅性保險利益之規定。如 MIA,1906 第 7 條第 1 項規定 "A defeasible interest is insurable, as also is a contingent interest." 即不論是或有性利益或者是消滅性利益都可以是保險利益。條文所指的或有性利益（contingent interest）及可消滅性利益（defeasible interest），乃為國際貿易貨物買賣下特有的保險利益種類。同條第 2 項再進一步規定 "In particular, where the buyer of goods has insured them he has an insurable interest, notwithstanding that he might, at his election, have rejected the goods, or have treated them as at the seller's risk by reason of the latter's delay in making delivery or otherwise."

按條文文義，所謂「contingent interest（或有性保險利益）」指若買方於貨物到達約定地點後，發現貨物有不符合買賣契約規定情形時，買方可拒絕受領貨物，此時貨物之危險負擔將再度從買方復歸於賣方，並且恢復其對貨物所有權，是故賣方又重新取得保險利益。對買賣雙方而言，由於此利益之取得與否繫於某一未來偶發或意外事件的發生，故為「或有性保險利益」。而所謂「defeasible interest（可消滅性保險利益）」指賣方本其所有權對貨物有保險利益，在買方收受貨物或喪失其拒絕受貨權前，若賣方持有載貨證券，則對於尚在運送中的貨物，可以請求運送人中止運送、返還貨物或為其他處分的權利（詳見民法第 642 條），或因買方破產，賣方為保障價金債權，請求運送人中止運送，故重新取得貨物之占有；在此情況下，由於此利益的喪失與否繫於不確定的條件賣方是否行使停止運貨權，故稱為可消滅性保險利益。

儘管買賣契約雙方存在可消滅性及或有性的保險利益，然保險實務上較易產生爭議者，並非是否有保險利益的存在，而是係於損失發生時，此保險利益究由何人擁有。蓋賣方是否行使中止運送貨物權，買方是否拒絕接受貨物，再加上實務上貨物所有權人將轉讓所有權，以及運送過程中所約定的危險負擔轉移，更造成認定何人應有保險利益，或損失發生時是否具有保險利益的理賠困難。

第二節　被保險人與海上貨物保險利益

「保險利益原則」在保險理論是補償性保險（indemnity insurance）的基礎，在保險實務上則是保險人決定賠償給何人與衡量補償額度的依據。所謂保險利益乃指被保險人與保險標的之間的利害關係，或稱為合法的經濟利益。此種經濟利益，被保險人因保險事故發生而受損，或因保險事故不發生得繼續享有。故「被保險人與保險標的間的經濟上利害關係」概念，誠為財產保險損害賠償的理論基礎；換言之，保險契約的基本概念即為「無利益關係，則事故發生時無損失；無損失，則無保險契約」。保險利益與保險請求權概念如圖 5–1。

圖 5-1　保險利益與保險請求權概念圖
資料來源：作者自繪

　　就理賠角度而言，當保險標的毀損或滅失，保險人常以「恢復原狀」為保險責任之履行，但就其本質其實應稱之為填補該保險標的物所失去的價值，對被保險人而言，就是補償這個失去的「價值」或「經濟利益」；因此，若本身無須承擔財產上的危險，則其財產價值或經濟利益即無喪失之虞，也就不會有保險理賠的問題，這是最基本的保險損害賠償的實務理賠邏輯。

　　國際貿易貨物隨著國際貿易與銀行押匯程序，以及貨物所有權移轉情況，在一連串的運輸過程及單證轉讓後，實務上保險利益將可能存在於出口商或進口商或者是轉讓後的受讓人，於理賠時是必要的確認事實。

　　我國海上貨物保險實務通常將被保險人與要保人視為同一人，此由實務上絕大多數之要保書格式以及保險單中僅有「被保險人」的欄位，而無「要保人」的欄位可知；但是某些大型企業往往透過保險經紀人向保險公司洽商保險，此時雖由保險經紀人出面要保，但因為宥於保險法第 3 條要保人必須有保險利益之規定，保險經紀人對保險標的沒有保險利益，故要保人（同時也是被保險人）仍是貨物所有權人，雖保險法第 45 條規定要保人得不經委任為他人的利益訂立保險契約，但前提仍須有保險利益才可以為他人利益訂立保險契約，此規定於人壽保險實務中如要保人爲母親，被保險人是子女，滿期保險金受益人是子女，與海上貨物保險實務由保險經紀人洽談的保險契約不同，故保險法第 45 條規定，因保險經紀人對貨物沒有保險利益，自無法成爲要保人，無法適用於保險經紀人的保險實務，此當爲我國保險法規定所造成保險實務的限制。

然 MIA,1906 第 53 條（Policy effected through broker）及第 54 條（Effect of receipt on policy）中對於保險經紀人之代爲被保險人洽商投保則有明確規定。第 53 條條文如下："Unless otherwise agree, where a marine policy is effected on behalf of the assured by a broker, the broker is directly responsible to the insurer for the premium, and the insurer is directly responsible to the assured for the amount which may be payable in respect of losses, or in respect of returnable premium." 第 54 條："Where a marine policy effected on behalf of the assured by a broker acknowledges the receipt of the premium, such acknowledgement is , in the absence of fraud, conclusive as between the insurer and the assured, but not as between the insurer and broker."

綜合兩個條文可知，若海上保險是由保險經紀人代爲簽訂，且保險費已經由保險經紀人代爲繳交後，在沒有詐欺的情況下，保險契約將於保險人及被保險間產生絕對拘束力，亦即保險人直接向被保險人負保險事故發生時的損害賠償責任，保險契約並不及於保險人與保險經紀人間。

第三節　海上貨物保險利益的認定

國際貿易雙方當事人間通常會約定「危險負擔（risk transfer）」的移轉點，做爲意外事故發生時由何人承擔損失的認定。如 2000 年國際貿易條規（International Rules for the interpretation of Trade

Terms，簡稱 INCOTERMS）中規定，無論是 CIF、FOB 或 CFR，買方與賣方危險負擔的移轉，都是以貨物是否越過船舷（rail）為準，也就是當裝載貨物越過船舶船舷時，危險負擔即移轉予買方，必須承擔因貨物毀損滅失所致的任何損失，將此概念移至保險契約觀之，具危險負擔者也就是事故發生時會遭受損害者，故也認定具有保險利益，可享有保險契約的賠償請求權。故在保險理賠實務，凡是具負擔危險者即可「原則性」認為有保險利益。然而在保險理賠實務中，貿易條件危險負擔之認定也不宜直接與保險利益劃上等號，因貿易條件是於買賣契約中約定危險負擔在何時移轉，與保險利益之認定是以何人在事故發生時遭受損害之概念，雖大致相同，但也有例外之情況。如 CIF 貿易條件下，若於海上發生意外事故，買方卻因此貨損而違約拒付貨款，賣方無法順利取得貨款，雖然可消滅性以及或有性保險利益均已不存在，但因為危險負擔已經移轉，但買方拒絕貨款償付，造成危險負擔之規定與實際損害承擔的人發生不一致的情況；亦即，因買方違約拒付貨款，賣方當視為實際遭受損失之人，雖 CIF 條件下保險之前提乃是為買方之利益而代訂，但是因買方拒付貨款，所以可謂沒有任何損失，反倒是賣方因貨物已經毀損卻又無法收回貨款，其為所投保之保險契約上的被保險人，故此保險契約上之請求權仍應為賣方，除非買方償付貨款，則所有權移轉與危險負擔移轉以及價金之給付完全一致，買方才可謂損失發生時具保險利益，而向保險人請求賠償。

換言之，買方因貨損而拒付貨款，雖依國貿條規之規定已承擔危險，但是其因未實際支付價金，故就其實質經濟觀點而言，難謂受有損失，自不應視為具有保險利益。建議買方若已持有載貨證券或待載貨證券收到後，應再退還回予出口商（賣方），並聲明放棄貨物之所有權，且為周延起見，同時出具轉讓書將保險給付請求權讓與出口商，以利出口商向保險公司求償。

其他有關貨物在國際運輸過程中，依 2000 年版國際貿易條規的規定，不同貿易條件的危險負擔歸屬時點詳列如表 5-1。

表 5-1　2000 年版國際貿易條規與歸屬時機

危險負擔之移轉時機	貿易條件
賣方工廠或倉庫交付後危險負擔歸買方	EXW
貨物越過船舷後危險負擔歸買方	FOB、CIF、CFR
指定裝載港船邊移轉危險負擔歸於買方	FAS
貨物交付第一運送人或貨櫃場時危險負擔歸買方	FCA、CPT、CIP
目的港船上交貨後危險負擔歸買方	DES
目的港船邊交貨後危險負擔歸買方	DEQ
目的地指定地點交貨後危險負擔歸買方	DDU、DDP
目的地邊境交貨後危險負擔歸買方	DAF

資料來源：作者整理

　　自表 5-1 可知，不同貿易條件下應分辨不同的危險負擔移轉時間點，保險人處理理賠案時，若是進口案件，通常會委請海事保險公證公司進行查勘確認事故原因及金額；若是出口案件，同樣也會請國外理賠代理（claim agent）委託公證公司進行公證。公證報告內應該有整個案件的人（託運人、受貨人、運送人、被保險人爲何）、事（事故原因）、時（何時裝運、何時卸貨、何時提貨）、地（事故發生或發現損失時於何處、何處公證）、物（保險標的物損失情況）等調查事宜，雖然某些情況下無法確知事故發生的地點，但公證人仍應依相關人的表述及文件表單中研判事故發生於何時何處，從國際貿易角度而言，即是確認事故發生當時危險負擔歸於何方，不僅有助於貿易糾紛的釐清，更可幫助保險人確認保險利益的歸屬，做爲賠償依據。爲便於參考再將不同貿易條件的危險負擔移轉時點如圖 5-2 所示。

貿易條件	seller	carrier	frontier	Port		Port	customs	buyer
EXW	·····━━━━━━━━━━━━━━━━━━━━━━━━━━							
FCA	·········━━━━━━━━━━━━━━━━━━━━							
FAS	·············━━━━━━━━━━━━━━━━							
FOB	················━━━━━━━━━━━━							
CFR	················━━━━━━━━━━━━							
CIF	················━━━━━━━━━━━━							
CPT	·········━━━━━━━━━━━━━━━━━━━━							
CIP	·········━━━━━━━━━━━━━━━━━━━━							
DAF	··························━━━━							
DES	·············━━━━━━━━━━━━							
DEQ	·················━━━━━━━━							
DDU	·····························							
DDP	━━━━━━━━━━━━━━━━━━━━━━━━━━━━━							

Risk 圖示:

········ ：由賣方承擔

━━━━━ ：由買方承擔

圖 5-2 國際貿易條規買賣雙方危險負擔移轉點

資料來源：整理自莊雪雁，《海上貨物保險航程之研究》，頁 77-84。

　　2010 年 9 月國際商會繼 10 年前之 2000 年版條規，再推出 2010 年新版國貿條規，並宣布於 2011 年 1 月份正式實施新版本。新版本中明確定義買賣雙方 "delivery" 的權利及義務，並清楚規範風險移轉的時點；2010 年國貿條規主要改變乃是廢除了以往以 E、F、C、D 字頭的分類，改以適合複合運送的或沒有海上運送的「任何或多種運輸方式（Rules for any mode or modes of Transports）」；以及交貨地點和貨物運載至買方的地方都屬港口的「海運及內陸水路運輸（Rules for Sea and Inland Waterway Transports）」兩大類。2010 年版條規並刪除了目的地碼頭交貨之 DEQ、邊境交貨之 DAF、目的地船邊交貨之 DES，以及稅前交貨之 DDU 等四類條件；而改以新增兩條規為終站交貨（Delivered at Terminal, DAT）與目的地交貨（Delivered at Place, DAP）。將 2010 年國貿條規整理如表 5-2 所示。

表 5-2　2010 年國貿條規類型

2010 年國貿條規之類型	貿易條件
任何或多種運輸方式（Rules for any mode or modes of Transports）	EXW（工廠交貨條件） FCA（貨交運送人條件） CPT（運費付訖條件） CIP（運保費付迄條件） DAT（終站交貨條件） DAP（目的地交貨） DDP（稅訖交貨條件）
海運及內陸水路運輸（Rules for Sea and Inland Waterway Transports）	FAS（船邊交貨條件） FOB（船上交貨條件） CFR（運費在內條件） CIF（運保費在內條件）

資料來源：作者整理

　　2010 國貿條規新增之終站交貨條件（Delivered at Terminal, DAT）中，所謂 "Terminal" 可譯成「貨運終站」，也就是海關管制或申請自主管理的貨櫃集散站，或機場的航空貨運站等，航運實務上因進口地買方無法控制貨物裝卸進站作業，所以本條件要求賣方必須負擔危險到卸貨進入終站，將貨物自到達的運送工具卸貨為止。DAT之 A4 Delivery 原文為："The seller must unload the goods from the arriving means of transport and must then deliver them by placing them at the disposal of the buyer at the named terminal referred to in A3 a at the port or place of destination on the agreed date or within the agreed period." 再依 A5 Transfer of risks（危險移轉）之規定："The seller bears all risks of loss of or damage to the goods until they have been delivered in accordance with A4 with the exception of loss or damage in the circumstances described in B5."[1] 依其規定可知，賣方必須負擔貨物毀損滅失一切危險，直到已依照 A4 之規定交付為止；換言之，貨物到達指定貨物終站卸貨完成前的危險均由賣方負責。而在 DAT 條件下，進口稅及進口報關均由買方負責，惟買方並無辦理進口報關、繳規稅的義務，除非在買賣契約內載明。

DAP 的特點乃是約定 P（Place）為何處，在原文中 A4（交貨）之規定為 "The seller must deliver the goods by placing them at the disposal of the buyer on the arriving means of transport ready for unloading at the agreed point, if any, at the named place of destinationon the agreed date of within the agreed period."[2] 故依此規定可知，"Place" 是經由雙方當事人約定的且最好是註明詳細地址。Incoterms 2010 的 Introduction 第 3 條 "specify your place or port as precisely as possible" 指出如果當事人盡可能精確的註明該交貨地點或港口，則國貿條件效果將更好。"The chosen incoterms rule can work only if the parties name a place or port, and will work best if the parties specify the place or port as precisely as possible."[3] 在 DAP 條件下，依 A4 之規定賣方必須在約定期間及約定的地點，將放置於到達的運送工具上準備卸貨的貨物交由

---

[1] 2010 年版國貿條規編譯委員會，《國貿條規 2010》，頁 98–99。
[2] 2010 年版國貿條規編譯委員會，《國貿條規 2010》，頁 112–113。
[3] 2010 年版國貿條規編譯委員會，《國貿條規 2010》，頁 21。

買方處置；再依 A5 危險移轉之規定，賣方也必須負擔一切貨物毀損滅失之危險，直到依 A4 之規定交付時止。茲將 DAT 及 DAP 有關交付及危險負擔之規定比較如表 5-3。

表 5-3　DAT 及 DAP 條件交付及危險負擔規定

	DAT		DAP	
	賣方	買方	賣方	買方
交貨／收貨 Delivery／Taking delivery	員責於期限內卸貨到指定的終點	如賣方如依規定交付，則買方必須收貨	員責於期限內送達指定的目的地地點（不包括卸貨）	如賣方如依規定交付，則買方必須收貨
風險移轉 Transfer of risks	賣方承擔交貨前風險	買方承擔交貨後風險	賣方承擔交貨前風險	買方承擔交貨後風險

資料來源：作者整理

　　另一項在 2010 年新條件有關危險負擔極大不同的改變，則是將 FOB、CIF、CFR 等三項貿易條件危險負擔時點，從 2000 年版的貨物越過船舷（ship rail）改為貨物放置於船上（on board），此改變不僅可更符合現代商業及航運概念，且可避免過去貨物危險移轉時點，是以虛擬的船舷垂直線的左或右的荒謬判斷方式。2010 年國貿條規更具體建議上述三種船上交貨條件，並不適合於貨物在裝船前就交給運送人之運送模式，如併櫃運送（CFS）實務乃是將先貨物交由運送人指定的貨櫃集散站併櫃後，再進港裝船出口，故若採 FOB、CIF、CFR 為貿易條件時，危險負擔的移轉點將與事實控制危險的情況不同，故若貨物是以貨櫃運送時，不應使用 FOB、CFR 或 CIF 條件，而應改而使用 FCA、CPT 或 CIP 條件。

第 六 章·········

定值保險單

第一節　定值保險的意義

　　財產保險實務中因保險標的物之稀有或單一特性，往往造成投保時確定保險金額鑑價的困難，例如藝術品、古董等特殊標的於實務投保時因為保險標的物之價值估價困難，所以於訂立保險契約時，雙方當事人乃約定保險標的之價值。另一種情形則是依損害補償原則之下，保險人於理賠時必須確認損失並依實際損害金額損害補償，但若是事故發生後的損失很難衡量，可能因為價值波動太大，或是因為該保險標的具稀少性及獨一性，所以實務上面對這類保險標的最理想的方法就是投保當時約定保險標的之價值。綜合上述，如果保險人與被保險人於訂立保險契約當時，便約定保險標的物之價值而成為約定價額（agreed value），這個記載於保險契約上的約定價額於保險期間內就不再變動，當保險事故發生時，則以此約定價額做為理賠計算的標準，此保險契約就稱之為定值保險契約（valued insurance: valued policy）。

　　在 MIA,1906 第 27 條第 2 項規定：“A valued policy is a policy which specifies the agreed value of the subject-matter insured.” 即規定

當保險單上載明保險標的物的價值者，稱之爲定值保險單。海上保險不論是船體保險還是貨物保險，因爲保險標的物並非固定在一地而是經常移動，尤其貨物保險主要是因爲國際貿易下的保險需求產物，生產地或出口地往往與消費地或進口地之價值不一樣，所以要在「損失發生地」及「損失發生時」確定保險標的物之價值是件相當不容易的事，爲了避免理賠時損害賠償原則適用的困擾，因此海上保險實務大多係探定值保險的方式投保。

　　MIA,1906 第 27 條第 3 項再進一步規定："Subject to the provisions of this Act, and in the absence of fraud, the value fixed by the policy is, as between the insurer and assured, conclusive of the insurable value of the subject intended to be insured, whether the loss be total or partial." 依條文之義乃指在無詐欺之情況下，保險單上之約定價額，就是保險人與被保險人雙方所確定的保險標的物價值，且不論以後發生全部損失或部分損失均以此金額爲準。本條文之解釋須搭配 MIA, 1906 第 67 條、第 68 條第 1 項、第 70 條及第 71 條第 1 項的規定，就可以非常清楚，請見列表 6-1。

表 6-1　MIA,1906 中賠償限度之規定

MIA,1906 條次	內容	譯文
第 67 條	**67. Extent of liability of insurer for loss** (1) The sum which the assured can recover in respect of a loss on a policy by which he is insured, in the case of an unvalued policy to the full extent of the insurable value, or, in the case of a valued policy to the full extent of the value fixed by the policy, is called the measure of indemnity (2) Where there is a loss recoverable under the policy, the insurer, or each insurer if there be more than one, is liable for such proportion of the measure of indemnity as the amount of his subscription bears to the value fixed by the policy in the case of a valued policy, or to the insurable value in the case of an unvalued policy.	67.保險人對損失責任之限度 (1)被保險人對保險契約所承保之損失可得而獲償之數額是為補償額度：於不定值保險契約為保險價額的全部，於定值保險契約則為保險契約上約定價額之全部。 (2)保險人或各保險人對得由保險契約獲償之損失，依其保險金額員補償限度比例之責任，於定值保險契約以保險契約定價額為標準，於不定值保險契約則以保險價額為標準。

	68. Total loss	68.全部損失
第 68 條 第 1 項	Subject to the provisions of this Act and to any express provision in the policy, where there is a total loss of the subject-matter insured,— (1)If the policy be a valued policy, the measure of indemnity is the sum fixed by the policy:	根據本法或保險契約上之明示規定,保險標的全部損失時: (1)如為定值保險契約,補償限度為固定於保險契約上之金額。
第 70 條	70. Partial loss of freight Subject to any express provision in the policy, where there is a partial loss of freight, the measure of indemnity is such proportion of the sum fixed by the policy in the case of a valued policy, or of the insurable value in the case of an unvalued policy, as the proportion of freight lost by the assured bears to the whole freight at the risk of the assured under the policy.	70.運費之部分損失 根據保險契約上之明示規定,運費部分損失的補償限度,如為定值保險契約以保險契約上約定價額,如為不定值保險契約則為保險價額,按被保險人所損失的運費與保險契約所承保在危險中全部運費比例賠償。
第 71 條 第 1 項	71. Partial loss of goods, merchandise, etc. Where there is a partial loss of goods, merchandise, or other moveables, the measure of indemnity, subject to any express provision in the policy, is as follows:— (1)Where part of the goods, merchandise or other moveables insured by a valued policy is totally lost, the measure of indemnity is such proportion of the sum fixed by the policy as the insurable value of the part lost bears to the insurable value of the whole, ascertained as in the case of an unvalued policy;	71.貨物商品等之部分損失 根據保險契約上之明示規定,貨物,商品或其他動產部分損失之補償限度為: (1)當定值保險契約所承保部分貨物,商品或其他動產全部損失時,以損失部分的約定價額如同保險價額一樣,與全部保險價額按保險契約確定金額之比例部分賠償,如同不定值保險契約所確定者。

資料來源：作者整理

　　由上表 MIA,1906 有關補償金額衡量的條文可知，依第 67 條及第 68 條第 2 項之規定，被保險人於保險單中可得賠償之最高限額，或者發生全部損失後可得賠償的最高限額，於定值保險之情形即為保險單中已確定之價值（fixed by the policy），所指的也就是約定價額。再根據第 70 條有關運費保險賠償的規定，於定值保險下同樣亦是以保險單中已確定的價值為準，再依據被保險人的運費損失與保險單所承保之全部運費比例賠償；換言之，其賠償基礎仍是以約定價額為衡量。有關貨物的部分損失賠償，依第 71 條第 1 項規定在定值保險下則為以約定價值占貨物損害之價值與全部價值的比例賠償。可知定值保險下絕對是以約定價額為賠償之基礎。將第 71 條第 1 項之規定轉為計算式如下：

$$約定價額 \times \frac{貨物損害價值}{貨物全部價值}$$

在我國保險法中也有相同之規定，如保險法第 50 條第 3 項的規定：「定值保險契約為契約上載明保險標的一定價值之保險契約。」依條文的文義其實與 MIA,1906 第 27 條第 2 項之規定相同，也就是所謂定值保險契約乃是於訂立保險契約時，保險人與被保險人就保險標的的價值先行「約定」價額，而這個經約定後之價值在保險期間內都是「固定」的，再以這個約定價額投保而成為保險金額，一旦發生保險事故時，不需要再去確定當時保險標的之價值多寡，而是直接以經雙方同意的約定價額，做為計算賠償的標準。

另一種與定值保險相對應的保險契約則稱之為不定值保險契約。訂立保險契約時，保險人或被保險人以評估保險標的物之客觀市場價值後約定為保險金額，保險事故發生時，則依當時當地客觀情況估算保險標的之價值與損失金額，再參考保險金額計算理賠金額，此類保險契約即稱之為不定值保險契約（unvalued policy）。在 MIA,1906 第 28 條對不定值保險之規定為："An unvalued policy is a policy which does not specify the value of the subject-matter insured, but, subject to the limit of the sum insured, leaves the insurable value to be subsequently ascertained, in the manner hereinbefore specified."依條文之義可知，投保當時並未載明保險標的物之價值，而是於事故發生後才確定之保險契約。而所謂 "subject to the limit of the sum insured" 是指雖然保險時已經先約定保險金額，但於事故發生時若該保險標的價值低於保險金額，則保險人的賠償責任依 MIA,1906 第 81

條規定："Where the assured is insured for an amount less than the insurable value or, in the case of a valued policy, for an amount less than the policy valuation, he is deemed to be his own insurer in respect of the uninsured balance." 當發生不足額保險情形時，在定值保險情形下，被保險人對此不足額的部分視為自己承擔。

在不定值保險契約下，依 MIA,1906 第 28 條規定，保險標的之價值確認需受保險金額之限制，其實只是指保險理賠時應考慮保險金額與保險標的物的實際價值，若為不足額保險原則上發生全損時仍以保險金額為限賠償，在部分損失時則按我國保險法第 73 條第 3 項規定：「保險標的未經約定價值者，發生損失時，按保險事故發生時實際價值為標準，計算賠償，其賠償金額，不得超過保險金額。」以及第 77 條的規定概念：「除保險契約另有訂定外，保險人之負擔，以保險金額對於保險標的物之價值比例定之。」即所謂之不足額保險比例分擔理賠，其概念如圖 6-1 所示。

圖 6-1　不足額保險比例分擔示意圖

資料來源：作者自繪

在我國保險法第 50 條第 2 項規定不定值保險契約之定義與 MIA,1906 第 28 條相同，條文如下：「不定值保險契約為契約上載明保險標的之價值，須至危險發生後估計而訂之保險契約。」在財產保險實務中其實是採不定值保險為原則，定值保險卻是例外情況，主要是因為不定值保險契約於理賠時可以符合「損害補償原則」，不會使被保險人因保險契約而獲得超過其損失之利益，但是採定值保險可能事故發生當時之標的物價值已低於約定價額，所以在足額保險下若發生全損，被保險人所獲得之保險理賠金，將會超過保險標的物之實際價值，若約定價額遠高於實際保險價額者，更可能發生道德危險，此可謂定值保險單在實務理賠時之一大問題。

第二節　海上貨物保險之定值保險

國際貿易下之貨物運送可能因為貨主基於安全保障之考量，也可能是因為信用狀之要求，貨主會以該運送貨物為保險標的投保海上貨物保險。海上貨物保險因為也屬於動態保險，保險標的（貨物）會在國際間遊走，自然也可能因為不同國家之供給與需求關係，而使貨物的實際價值會因不同進、出口地點而波動，為了解決理賠時實際損失的估價困難，所以海上貨物保險絕大都是採定值保險的方式投保。

在國際貿易實務上或者在信用狀的要求下，反應於海上貨物保險實務，通常被保險人於投保時乃就商業發票（commercial invoice）上的金額再加 10% 投保，如圖 6-2 範例。

由圖 6-2 要保書的最下方保險金額（Insured Amount）欄可知，是由發票金額或信用狀金額加上某一百分比金額，依保險實務慣例的 10% 所構成，例如發票金額為美金 50,000 元，其 10% 為美金 5,000 元，所以保險金額應為美金 55,000 元。

圖 6-2　海上貨物保險要保書範例（部分）

需求保險單份數 Number of policy Required	正本_____份 副本_____份	保單編號 Policy No.		收件日期：　　年　　月　　日		
被保險人 Assured				統一編號		
受益人 Beneficiary			開狀日期 L/C Issue Date			
船　名 Vessel			開航日期 Sailing on or about			
	建造年度 Year Built-	總額位 G.R.T.-				
航　程 Voyage	自 From	到 to				
轉　船 Transhipment	於　　　　轉入 At　　　　into	含內陸運輸 Inland Transit	從 From	到 to		
運 輸 方 式 Mode of Transportation	□海運S □陸運L □空運A □郵包P 如以貨櫃裝載，請註明為□Dry Cargo □Open Top □Flat Rack □Reefer □Tank □其他 除經特別聲明或貨櫃運送外，茲保證下列貨物均裝載於艙內。 Warranted shipped under deck unless otherwise specified or containerized shipment.					
貨　名 Subject-matter insured	除經特別聲明外，茲保證上列貨物為新品。 Warranted all brandnew unless otherwise specified.					
數　量 Quantity 包　裝 Packing						
商業發票號碼或 Invoice No. Or 嘜頭及號碼 Marks & No.						
信用狀號碼 L/C No.						
保 險 條 件 Terms & Conditions	□A條款　□ALL RISKS　□WAR □B條款　□W.A.　　　□STRIKES □C條款　□F.P.A.　　 □S.R.C.C.	□陸上貨物運送保險(甲)條款　□陸上貨物運送保險(乙)條款				
發票/信用狀金額 Invoice/L/C Value	加成 Plus　　% ＋　　%　＝	保險金額 ＝ Insured Amount	賠 款 地 點 Claim if any Payable at			

資料來源：http://www.tlgins.com.tw/reportDownload.action

　　此種實務現況就國際貿易角度而言，是因為貨物在進出口時若發生了毀損滅失，損失的金額除貨物本身價值以外，尚有進出口運輸過程中必要的運費、通關等相關雜費，甚至還有預期利益喪失的考量，但這些費用及預期利益很難細分列舉，所以直接於投保時再以發票金額再加 10%做為總括含蓋上述費用及預期利益，但這個金額僅是一粗略估計，並非一精準確切的實際發生的費用以及喪失利益金額，有可能過多也有可能不及，不過既然貨主、銀行以及保險公司都可以接受，久而久之逐成爲一國際間都依循的實務慣例。

但就保險學理而言，商業發票金額可認爲是一合理客觀的買賣貨物金額，所以就是保險價額（insurable value），如果貿易條件爲 CIF 更是符合 MIA,1906 第 16 條第 3 款的保險價額規定，其規定爲：

"Subject to any express provision or valuation in the policy, the insurable value of the subject−matter insured must be ascertained as follows−− 3.In insurance on goods or merchandise, the insurable value is the prime cost of the property insured, plus the expenses of and incidental to shipping and the charges of insurance upon the whole ." 可知在英國海上保險法中有關貨物的保險價額就是以 CIF 爲標準（cost of property, insured, the expenses of and incidental to shipping）。實務上，其實不論任何的貿易條件，若再將商業發票金額加上 10% 投保而成爲保險金額時，此時應就定值保險單之概念解釋爲商業發票金額（保險價額）加上 10% 爲「約定價額」，而同時採足額保險投保，故保險金額和約定價額一樣。如圖 6-3。

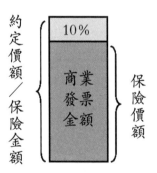

圖 6-3　商業發票金額加 10% 投保示意圖

資料來源：作者整理

　　就理論而言，這樣的實務並不是超額保險，而是定值保險契約下的足額保險，否則依保險法第 76 條之規定，保險金額超過保險標的價值之契約，無詐欺情事者，除定值保險外，其契約僅於保險標的價值之限度內爲有效；也就是當超額保險契約出現時，保險金額僅僅於保險價額的金額內有效。故若是將保險實務之商業發票金額加上 10% 投保解釋爲超額保險，豈不是指所有保險金額的 10% 都無效，不僅與實務慣例不符更是曲解了定值保險契約的意義。如圖 6-4。

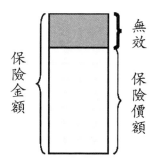

圖 6-4　超額保險示意圖

資料來源：作者自繪

　　最後一個重要觀念則是定值保險主要精神在於保險契約雙方當事人間於投保時即確定約定價值，然後再根據約定價額投保，實務上也應該都是足額保險，因爲旣然是已經「約定」價額後，似無再超額保險之必要，若被保險人擔心投保價值不夠，大可在投保時即與保險人協商，例如高關稅貨物或者運費高之特殊貨物，僅以商業發票金額加上 10% 爲保險金額恐怕不足以補償實際損失，所以可與保險人約定加 20% 甚至 25% 爲約定價額投保，只要事實如此並非詐欺，保險人也同意，就可以此爲約定保險價額，這也是理論上定值保險之「約定價額」的眞正意義，故採定值保險後，實已無必要再冒著保險金額超過約定價額部分無效的風險而超額保險。再者，若被保險人投保後考量相關費用或估計的預期利益甚高，仍感覺保險金額不足，亦可以再投保增值保險（increased value）因應，而依 ICC 第 14 條之增值保險（increased value）規定獲得補償，惟實務上投保增值保險之情形極為少見。

第 七 章‧‧‧‧‧‧‧‧

保險代位求償權

第一節　保險代位求償權之意義

　　損害補償原則為補償性保險契約的理賠最高原則，即當保險事故發生時保險人以補償被保險人實際遭受之損害為原則，使被保險人的損害得以回復至事故發生前（沒有損失之前）的狀態。相對而言，被保險人自也不能因保險事故之發生，藉由保險契約而獲得超過其損失之利益，否則將誘發道德危險。被保險人可獲得之補償範圍，在概念上就是以保險利益為限，而保險利益反應於保險標的物上就是保險價額，除了保險價額外再考慮保險契約上的保險金額後為填補最大限度。故損害補償原則除申明保險人填補之範圍，更重要的是防範不當得利的情形發生。基於此前提下，法律上乃設有禁止超額保險、複保險及共同保險的比例分攤賠償以及保險代位權等規定。損害補償原則的延伸概念如圖 7-1。

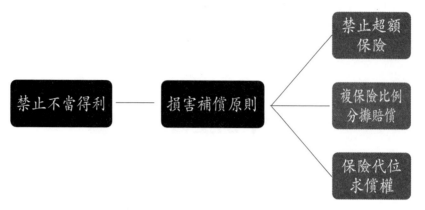

圖 7 –1　損害補償原則的延伸概念圖
資料來源：作者整理

　　代位求償權即在補償保險契約下，若保險事故是因為第三人所造成者，被保險人原則上會產生兩種請求權，一種為基於保險契約而生對保險人之保險請求權，另一種則為對第三人基於侵權行為或債務不履行的請求權。若被保險人選擇向保險人先行求償，則保險人於給付保險賠償金額後，便取得被保險人對第三人的損害賠償請求權，以及在全損情況下的殘餘物所有權。保險代位權最大的功能即在維護保險契約當事人間與應負責任之人間的法律衡平。換言之，就請求權的代位而言，保險代位權的存在不僅可以確保被保險人不因同一保險事故有兩種請求權同時存在而獲得雙重賠償，同時也讓應該負損害賠償責任的第三人不因保險制度而免除原來應負的責任。

　　保險法第 53 條規定：「被保險人因保險人應負保險責任之損失發生，而對於第三人有損失賠償請求權者，保險人得於給付賠償金額後，代位行使被保險人對於第三人之請求權；但其所請求之數額，以不逾賠償金額為限。前項第三人為被保險人之家屬或受僱人時，保險人無代位請求權。但損失係由其故意所致者，不在此限。」由此條文可知，保險代位權係屬法定代位，意即保險人於賠付被保險人後，不需要再向被保險人讓與請求權之程序，而是直接由被保險人依法移轉予保險人，以「自己之名義」逕向第三人請求損害賠償。另依條文文義也可知，保險人的代位權是「得」於給付保險金之後而取得保險代位權，而不是「應」執行保險代位權，實務上保險人可自行決定要不要進行代位求償，因為有時考量追償證據的取得，或金額不高而礙於追償成本之考量，而放棄代位追償的權利。

　　海上運輸過程中難免發生貨物毀損、滅失的情況，其原因可能是不可抗力因素，亦有可能是運送人或其受僱人的過失所造成，而於貨櫃運輸實務上亦有因貨櫃集散站之拆、併櫃過程中造成貨損，或內陸貨櫃拖車發生交通意外事故、物流倉儲期間發生貨損的情況。實務上，貨主除了依提單為運送契約之依據向運送人或相關之關係人索賠損失外，若該批貨物已投保了海上貨物運輸保險，被保險人亦可選擇根據保險契約向保險人索賠，保險人於賠付保險金後依法取得保險代位權，再向有責任之人如運送人進行求償。亦即於貨損理賠實務中，乃藉由保險代位的法理與執行，將形成貨主（被保險人）、運送人及保險人間之三角求償關係，如圖 7–.2。

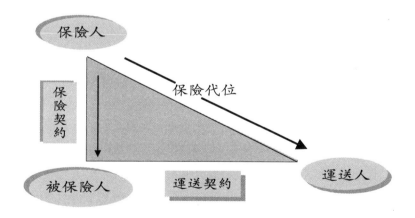

圖 7–2　貨主（被保險人）、運送人及保險人三角求償關係圖

資料來源：作者自繪

保險代位權之意義在 MIA,1906 第 79 條有詳細的規定：

79. RIGHT OF SUBROGATION

1. Where the insurer pays for a total loss, either of the whole, or in the case of goods of any apportionable part, of the subject–matter insured, he thereupon becomes entitled to take over the interest of the assured in whatever may remain of the subject–matter so paid for, and he is thereby subrogated to all the rights and remedies of the assured in and in respect of that subject–matter as from the time of the casualty causing the loss.

2. Subject to the foregoing provisions, where the insurer pays for a partial loss, he acquires no title to the subject–matter insured, or such part of it as may remain, but he is thereupon subrogated to all rights and remedies of the assured in and in respect of the subject–matter insured as from the time of the casualty causing the loss, in so far as the assured has been indemnified, according to this Act, by such payment for the loss.

由條文可知保險人之代位權可分為物上代位與權利代位兩種，分述如下：

1.物上代位

由前段條文可知，保險人取得保險標的之剩餘利益為一種權利而非法定轉讓（entitled to take over the interest of the assured……）屬於物上代位的權利。因在全損的情況下，若被保險人已獲得充分的賠償，則該保險標的若仍有殘餘利益自應屬保險人所有，否則被保險人實際所獲得的補償加上剩餘利益將超過原來未發生事故前之價值。但是此種剩餘利益之取得與否乃屬於保險人權利的行使，而並非強制性的接受；所以若保險人取得物上代位後，而必須負擔其他較重義務者，自可將該項物上代位權予以拋棄。惟於分損（Partial loss）的情況，保險人賠付分損後，僅得在其賠款金額限度內對保險標的之受損部分行使權利代位，而對於保險標的之殘餘物的所有權，則不得行使物上代位權。於第 2 項條文規定若保險人僅支付部分損失，則不能獲得保險標的之權利或剩餘利益（where the insurer pays for a partial loss, he acquires no title to the subject–matter insured, or such part of it as may remain），則為再次強調物上代位權取的之限制。

2.權利代位

第 79 條後段條文 "…subrogated to all the rights and remedies of the assured in and in respect of that subject–matter as from the time of the casualty causing the loss" 就是權利代位的規定，即指保險人於賠付後可取得對第三人損害賠償的請求權；亦可取得對與被保險人有契約關係當事人的求償權利，如因運送契約而生的請求權或對運送人之履行輔助人（受僱人、代理人），或獨立契約人（貨櫃集散站、內陸拖車、倉儲）因侵權行為而生的請求權。第 2 項後段條文也再次強調保險人得以其所賠付金額為限，行使自發生保險事故時起被保險人的一切權利（subrogated to all rights and remedies of the assured in and in respect of the subject–matter insured as from the time of the casualty causing the loss, in so far as the assured has been indemnified）。

第二節 保險代位求償權的行使要件

保險人的代位求償權是基於被保險人的請求權而來，其性質為法定移轉，不需被保險人讓與即當然取得被保險人對第三人的請求權，但該權利是否依法成立，以及可得行使之要件就保險實務而言，亦極為重要，分述如下：

1.被保險人須對第三人具備可成立的賠償請求權

保險代位權規定之主要理由乃是避免對該保險事故有賠償責任的第三人因保險制度而免責，故由保險人理賠給被保險人後代位行使該請求權。保險人代位權的權利內容，實際上與被保險人對第三人之請求權內容一致，所以不論是請求權時效期間的計算，或是求償內容均與原對第三人的請求權相同。故若是被保險人在法律上之請求權根本無法成立，保險人自無法代位，如被保險人與加害的第三人已經和解，或如海上運送人依海商法第 69 條主張免責，則保險人雖已經賠付給被保險人後，自也無法順利向第三人請求賠償。

2.須是基於保險事故發生後所取得之保險代位權

保險契約中均會約定承保範圍以及除外危險，依照保險法第 53 條的規定保險人之代位權乃在於「保險事故」發生後，並給付保險賠償後方取得代位權，此由條文的規定「被保險人因保險人『應負保險責任之損失』發生，而對於第三人有損失賠償請求權者，保險人得於給付賠償金額後，代位行使被保險人對於第三人之請求權」可知。所以如果保險人的保險給付是屬於一融通特惠性賠付（Ex gratia payment），也就是若損失發生的原因並非是保險契約所承保之事故，但保險人基於商業性因素而仍賠償予被保險人，因為並非是按保險契約的承保範圍內事故為損害賠償，而是一商業考量下的自願性賠付，則依保險法的規定保險人並無代位權。

3.必須保險人已先為賠付

保險代位法制設立的重要目的為不使被保險人因具有兩個請求權而雙重受償，故當保險人已經賠償給被保險人後，原有對於有責任第三人的請求權乃移轉至保險人，故保險人若尚未給付保險金，則並無代位權之取得，此概念於保險法第 53 條及 MIA, 1906 第 79 條均已明文規定。所以理賠實務中雖然保險事故雖已經發生，但因公證或其它調查事故原因，保險人並未取得保險代位權。然為爭取時效以確保未來保險代位權得以順利行使，保險人通常會積極要求或建議甚至協助被保險人保全其對有責第三人的賠償請求權。在理賠實務上，若保險人決定代位，會要求被保險人簽署代位求償收據（subrogation receipt），以證明已經賠償保險金給被保險人，並以保險人自己的名義提起代位求償訴訟。

4.僅適用於具補償性質之保險契約

保險契約依給付性質不同可分爲補償保險（Indemnity Insurance）與定額給付保險（Contingency Insurance）：前者保險人是依損害塡補原則，以實際損失計算保險金給付；後者則係以事先約定的保險金額，當保險契約所約定之事故發生時，則依約給付，並不需再衡量被保險人受有多少損害，且亦可能無從衡量損失，如人壽保險中的死亡保險或意外保險係按契約中表定之殘廢等級表，以保險金額的比例理賠，並非所謂「損失的補償」，此類保險契約亦稱爲非補償性之保險契約。保險代位的目的乃在於禁止被保險人獲得雙重利得，但定額給付性質的保險契約，保險人之給付是按契約的約定，非依損害塡補原則，無所謂給付是否已超過實際損害的問題，若加害人又賠償給被保險人，自也不能認爲這是雙重受償而不當得利的情況。

5.保險代位範圍以賠償金額為限

由保險代位權的理論基礎可知，其目的雖一方面爲不使被保險人雙重利得，但也不應使保險人因代位權之行使，而獲得超過其賠償金額的額外利益；所以在保險法第 53 條以及 MIA,1906 第 79 條第 2 項均有規定，保險人可行使代位的範圍僅以對被保險人「賠償金額」爲限，以避免保險人不當得利，有違保險代位權的基本涵義。實務上，在保險代位求償收據上會清楚載明保險人實際的賠償金額。

惟保險人於發生保險事故時，通常委請海事保險公證人前往公證，依保險法第 79 條規定：「保險人或被保險人爲證明及估計損失所支出之必要費用，除契約另有訂定外，由保險人負擔之。」因此，公證人的公證報告費用即所謂「證明及估計損失之費用」應由保險人負擔，故該費用乃可視為保險人處理賠案的必要理賠費用，所以筆者認為不應與實際損失合計而成為「賠償金額」向有責任的第三人代位，也就是保險法第53條所謂之「賠償金額」應指為實際損害的賠償金額，不應包括公證費用。再從另一角度而言，若沒有保險契約存在，受害人對加害人的原請求權也只於實際損失或所失利益，據此論之，現因保險契約賠償後，保險人取得之代位權是完全繼受被保險人而來，故其權利行使也應與原來的請求權內容相同，不應將保險人理賠的必要費用（公證費用）加入代位求償的請求金額中。

第三節　海上保險代位權之妨礙

保險代位制度的設立具有禁止被保險人雙重受償，與避免應負責任的第三人因保險制度免責，以及促使保險人迅速理賠等目的，而其更深層的意義乃在於避免不當得利及維護法律衡平的效果。換言之，若被保險人未保全保險代位權，使保險代位權遭破壞而無法執行時，將造成關係人間法律責任之失衡，可能使有責之第三人因而減輕責任，甚或免責；被保險人亦可能發生雙重受償的情形，致生不當得利。實務上，因被保險人之過失或對保全代位權的認知不足，未能保全對有責第三人的求償權，使保險人於賠付被保險人後無法有效行使向有責第三人求償之情形屢見不鮮，不僅影響保險人的權益，更可能使有責之第三人因保險契約而間接免除賠償責任，此即稱之為妨礙代位。

1.妨礙代位之意義與效力

妨礙代位係指保險人對第三人之請求權未受到妥善保護或被先行拋棄，造成行使保險代位權時受到影響甚或至消滅。實務上，被保險人投保僅為風險的移轉考量，對於保險代位的保全意識可能不高，甚至根本不知道，是以可能發生妨礙代位的情況。保險代位有其實質意義與衡平的效果，一旦遭受妨礙，保險代位功能即會瓦解，法律關係亦會隨之失衡。然，因保險代位係間接由被保險人處取得的權利，保險人在未完成保險給付之義務前，該項權利仍由被保險人所擁有，於此期間，被保險人若未能保全對第三人之損害賠償請求權，則保險人於給付賠款後便無法順利行使該權利。如海上貨物保險，以 CIF 為貿易條件出口之託運人（被保險人）可能不知保全代位的義務，甚或為換取低廉的運費，與運送人（即第三人）簽訂非海上運送段的免除責任契約，或事故發生後主觀認為可向保險人求償，而對運送人逕行放棄求償和解，以上種種行為不論其為故意或疏失，對保險人的代位求償均將造成損害。

被保險人逕行拋棄對第三人之請求權或未善加保護該請求權時，學者認為保險人可以基於無法求償的損失要求被保險人損害賠償[1]。主要理由為保險代位權為保險人的合理期待利益，意即保險人於給付保險理賠後，當然取得之權利，故保險人或可從「期待利益權」被侵害，於妨礙代位的範圍內，請求損害賠償。但此論點於我國保險法律並無明文規定，實務上保險人欲主張扣減理賠金額，勢將與被保險人發生爭議。

而所謂「妨礙代位之範圍」，應指在保險人理賠金額內，因被保險人之故意或過失造成保險人喪失的代位權利範圍。就海上貨物保險而言，若於載貨證券的運送航程內發生意外事故，造成貨物（保險標的物）毀損或滅失，因運送人可依據海商法規定，可主張法定免責（海商法第 69 條）、單位責任限制（海商法第 70 條），以及一年短

---

[1] 學者林群弼於其論述中參考其他學者之論點將妨礙代位之情形區分為契約成立前、後，各具不同效力，視妨礙代位之情事發生於何時，主張解除契約或被保險人該行為無效。見《保險法論》，頁 286~290。亦有學者如梁宇賢，《保險法》，頁 144~145；施文森，前揭《保險法總論》，頁 205，也是相同之看法。

期起訴期間（海商法第 56 條）等，是以保險人於理賠時考慮「妨礙代位之範圍」時，尚須考量縱使保險代位權未被破壞於行使代位權時，上述規定均可能影響向運送人的追償結果，不能期望其所賠付的金額均能全由運送人處獲得完全的補償。

我國保險法對於妨礙代位之效力並無規定，然實務上保險人則可藉由保險契約條款中，因應代位權遭受妨礙的不利影響。保險契約的條款，於不違背法律之強制規定與社會秩序善良風俗的前提下，基於契約自由若無顯失公平的情況，應可認為有效。臺灣財產保險契約中大多有訂立妨礙代位權的相關因應條款。如財產保險單參考格式及條文第 12 條與汽車保險共同條款第 16 條等，皆明示保險人可於受妨礙而未能請求之範圍內，請求被保險人返還。茲將部分保險契約中約定妨礙代位的效果整理如表 7-1 所示：

表 7-1　保險契約約定妨礙代位之效果規定表

條款名稱／條次	妨礙代位之效果
財產保險單參考格式及條文第 12 條	於受妨害而未能請求之範圍內，請求被保險人返還。
汽車保險共同條款第 16 條	於受妨害而未能請求之範圍內，請求被保險人返還。
強制汽車責任保險單條款第 23 條	保險人得請求被保險人償還保險金。
住宅及地震火險條款第 39 條	已獲得第三人之賠款，保險人得請求退還該部分之賠償。
商業火災保險基本條款第 36 條	已獲得第三人之賠款，保險人得請求退還部分之賠償。

資料來源：財團法人保險事業發展中心

綜上，不論在理論上或實務上通說認為妨礙代位後之效果應以保險人可請求損害賠償為妥。蓋被保險人於妨礙代位後，保險人不負保險賠償之主張，若不論原因或事由，一概免除保險人之責任，不免過於偏頗保險人的利益而忽略了被保險人的權益。尤其，被保險人於投保之時，僅爲透過保險做爲危險之轉嫁，對於保險代位權的認知往往不足，在此情況下，實難將因過失造成保險人代位權受妨礙的損害結果或金額完全歸責於被保險人，以免被保險人承擔了原本可能就無法代位的損失，方稱公平。

2.海上貨物保險妨礙代位之類型與效力

保險代位權遭受妨礙之情形，依其時點可歸納爲保險契約成立前與成立後，其中保險契約成立後又可再細分爲理賠前及理賠後等情況；另，尚有因被保險人之故意或過失所造成妨礙代位之情形，分述如下：

(1)保險契約成立前

託運人爲尋求低廉的運費或其他有利因素，如在貨物保險契約成立前與運送人於運送契約中簽訂免除責任之約定，當保險事故發生並賠付後，保險人執行代位權向運送人求償時，運送人便可以此免責約定拒絕保險人的代位求償。依海商法第 61 條運送人責任免除之限制規定：「以件貨運送爲目的之運送契約或載貨證券記載條款、條件或約定，以減輕或免除運送人或船舶所有人，對於因過失或本章規定應履行之義務而不履行，致有貨物毀損、滅失或遲到之責任者，其條款、條件或約定不生效力。」按條文所示，簽發載貨證券之海上運送契約下，託運人若事先簽訂免除運送人責任的條款，按此規定則該條款應爲無效。

但須注意者是，海商法第 61 條乃僅針對「件貨運送」所規定之條文，對於傭船契約的海上運送，或不適用海商法非海上運送段，則不受此條款拘束。蓋因傭船契約爲一般性的商務契約，契約雙方具有較對等的談判能力，法律上基於契約自主的原則，並不強制規定其內容，故於傭船契約下的海上貨物運送，其運送契約的內容可依託運人與運送人雙方的意思同意訂立之。故若託運人事先簽訂運送人免責條款，在不違反法律強制規定的情況下，應承認其免責約款的效力。非海上運送之免責約款概念亦同。在此情形下,保險人便無法以海商法第 61 條之規定主張此約款不具效力,當然於行使保險代位權時必遭受影響。

(2)保險事故發生後

海上貨物保險契約成立後,託運人未經保險人同意逕行拋棄對運送人的損害賠償請求權,或自行與運送人達成和解,或免除運送人的損害賠償責任等妨礙代位之情形,若事故原因係在承保範圍內,保險人仍應給付保險理賠金額,惟上述託運人的妨礙代位行為,依保險時點可分為理賠前、後,兩者不同情況下保險代位權是否被破壞,有其不同效果,詳述如下:

a.理賠給付前之妨礙代位

在此情形下,保險人因尚未為保險給付,故仍未取得保險代位權。但保險代位權仍為保險人之合理期待權益,雖尚未給付理賠金額,被保險人仍不得破壞此權利的行使。若此權利遭受侵害,除非被保險人惡意詐欺,保險人仍應依約給付保險賠款,但對於代位權遭受妨礙的範圍應可請求損害賠償。而「遭受妨礙之範圍」前已述及,應再參考如海商法第 69 條之運送人免責事項規定。故若此事故原因係屬承保範圍內,但卻是運送人的法定免責事由,如天災造成的意外事故,保險人依保險契約仍應給付保險金,惟其後當保險人執行保險代位權時,勢必將無法順利獲得自運送人的賠償。若運送人無法免責,亦應再考量海商法第 70 條的單位責任限制規定,為評估「遭受妨礙範圍」的依據。依海商法第 70 條第 2 項之規定,當託運人於載運前,若未向運送人申明貨物的價值及性質時,運送人可主張單位責任限制賠付。單位責任限制賠償指受損貨物以每件 666.67 個特別提款權(Special Drawing Right, SDR)或每公斤 2 個 SDR 分別計算,兩數值取其高者為單位責任限制的賠付金額;之後,再與實際損失比較取其低者為運送人實際應賠付的之金額,單位責任限制賠償邏輯如圖 7-3。

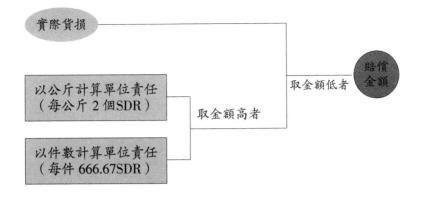

圖 7-3　單位責任限制賠償邏輯圖
資料來源：作者自繪

　　保險人取得代位權後，其追償範圍勢將受到海商法單位責任限制的規定。於 93 年度台上字第 1358 號判決與同年台上字第 1493 號判決，保險業者皆以全損賠付後，向運送人進行代位求償時，法院裁判運送人得以主張海商法所規定之單位責任限制利益，所以保險人僅能以單位責任限額獲得賠付，也就是遭受妨礙的範圍其實也應該只有單位責任限制金額而已。

　　b.保險理賠給付後之妨礙代位

　　當被保險人（貨主）已自保險人處獲得保險理賠，未經保險人同意或參與，自行與運送人簽訂和解書，不論有無自運送人處獲得賠償，均可謂爲妨礙代位之事實。若託運人自運送人處獲得賠償，則此時託運人便因同一事故取得雙重賠償，是爲不當得利，依民法第 179 條：「無法律上之原因而受利益，致他人受損害者，應返還其利益。雖有法律上之原因，而其後已不存在者，亦同。」之規定，自當返還多得之金額。若尚未自運送人處獲得賠償，雖無不當得利行爲，但其與運送人所簽訂之和解書，亦有造成保險人代位的妨礙，惟此時因保險人已經賠付，保險代位權依法已經移轉予保險人，故依民法第 118 條之規定：「無權利人就權利標的物所爲之處分，經有權利人之承認始生效力。」是以託運人與運送人所簽訂的和解書便不具效力。換言之，當保險代位權已為移轉，託運人便無權再為和解之行為，除非保險人同意，否則此處分不生效力。

因我國海商法、保險法對此情形並無規定，乃遵循代位權之法理推斷被保險人之行為無效。最高法院 86 年度台上字第 985 號判決與 93 年度台上字第 1493 號判決亦採如此之看法，承審法官認為：「保險事故發生，被保險人對第三人有損害賠償請求權者，於保險人履行其保險賠償義務後，其請求權即當然移轉於保險人，被保險人於受領保險給付之範圍內，對第三人之債權既已喪失，縱其與第三人有和解或拋棄情事，亦不影響保險人因保險給付而取得之代位權。」

c.因被保險人之過失造成之妨礙代位

於海上貨物保險的情況，被保險人因過失未能善加保全對運送人索賠的權利情況，如當運送人通知受貨人前往提貨時，若有貨損的情形，應與運送人或其委託人共同檢定，並做成公證報告以書面的形式通知運送人，同時於收貨證件上註明貨物毀損或滅失等情形；若貨損之情形並不顯著，受貨人應自提貨日起算 3 天內，以書面通知運送人。若受貨人未為上述的動作，一旦貨物經有受領，則推定運送人已完成載貨證券上之記載，交清貨物。此時，若受領權利人堅持再提出索賠，則應再舉出更有力的反證，方得順利獲償。保險人賠付後取得的保險代位權，其本質純為繼受自被保險人的權利，故若被保險人因過失，提貨時未能符合如海商法第 56 條所規定之情況，則運送人自得主張推定交清貨物，則保險人欲順利追償則必須再舉證貨損確實係運送人的運送監管期間發生。

被保險人（受貨人／貨主）於提領貨物之時該注意的行為，但若被保險人（受貨人／貨主）因自身之行為或不行為，未能保全對運送人之索賠權，即會造成保險代位的妨礙。保險人的代位權遭受妨礙後，可能無法順利追償，故保險人或可根據代位權係為合理期待利益，以侵權行為的法理，向被保險人（受貨人／貨主）請求損害賠償。惟爲保障被保險人的權益，保險人應於訂約時或於保險契約內，先行告知被保險人應負此保全代位權利的義務，清楚告知後保險人方可據以主張折扣賠付，以維當事人雙方之權利義務的衡平。

　　d.被保險人未能配合保險人之代位求償

　　被保險人於保險代位求償過程中，消極或不配合保險人追償之需求，亦爲妨礙代位的情況。蓋被保險人如無配合追償的意願或義務，保險代位權於執行時勢必發生困難，最後可能因缺乏文件或證據根本無法追償，則保險代位制度無啻虛設。我國保險法並未規定被保險人應配合協助保險人完成代位求償之相關需求或提供必要文件，是以，若被保險人於保險人代位求償期間，消極或不配合提供相關必要文件或證明，對保險人在執行代位求償權時，必會造成一定的阻礙。

　　儘管我國對於妨礙代位的情事並無直接規範，然依保險代位的法理與參考他國之相關規定，仍可針對各代位遭受妨礙的情事，逐一探討其效力。茲將海上貨物保險妨礙代位的之情形與效力彙整如表 7–2 所示。

表 7-2　海上貨物保險妨礙代位之類型與效力彙整表

妨礙代位情形			效力
保險契約訂立前	與第三人簽訂免責條款		海上件貨運送情況下，其行為無效，保險人仍可行使代位求償權
			海上傭船契約下的運送契約，其行為有效，保險人將可依被妨礙的範圍內，扣減理賠金額
保險契約訂立後	保險給付前	拋棄或免除運送人的損害賠償責任	保險人可依被妨礙的範圍內，扣減理賠金
		自運送人處獲得賠償，並簽訂和解書	
	保險給付後	拋棄或免除運送人的損害賠償責任	該行為無效，保險人仍可行使代位求償權
		自運送人處獲得賠償，並簽訂和解書	和解書無效、且被保險人不當得利，保險人仍可代位
被保險人的過失	未能善加保全對運送人索賠的權利		保險人得於代位求償權遭受妨礙的範圍內請求損害賠償
	消極或不配合保險人的追償需求		

資料來源：曾文瑞、李紀薇（2008），〈兩岸海上貨物保險代位權妨礙之效力研析〉，《保險經營與制度》，第 7 卷，第 1 期。

第八章．．．．．．．．

擔　保

一、擔保之意義

在英美一般契約法中，雙方當事人於訂約前的陳述
（representation）或允諾（Promise）；若認爲重要者可將之明訂於契
約內，而成爲契約條款（contract terms），再就條款重要性不同又可
分爲較重要的條件（condition）及次要的擔保（warranty）兩種[1]；條
件與擔保的法律效力各有不同，若契約的一方違反了契約的條件，則
受害的一方可以拒絕履行契約責任，將契約解除或終止，因爲若違反
了契約條件，係影響及契約的基礎，故受害人有權解除或終止契約。
而若違反契約擔保時，受害人僅能請求對方損害賠償，不能主張解除
契約；因擔保只是契約中一次要條款，故違反的效果並不似違反條件
般的嚴重。但海上保險契約中的擔保，已不似一般契約中的擔保；而
是提升了其法律效力，其性質已相當於一般契約中的條件，故若違反
海上保險契約中的擔保，則保險人可自違反日起解除或終止契約。因
此，在海上保險契約中關於擔保與條件二用語通常是可以互換的[2]。
擔保的定義可見於 MIA,1906 第 33 條第 1 項：「指某項承諾之擔保，
亦即被保險人不爲某特定行爲，或履行某項條件，或某特定事實情況

---

[1] 擔保之典型的例字是買賣契約法律關係上的「瑕疵擔保」，在我國民法之出
　賣人亦有瑕疵擔保的義務；故事實上，我國亦有類似 Warranty 的觀念，因此
　將之譯成擔保較爲適當。
[2] Robert Merkin, *Colinvaux's Law of Insurance*, p.119。

之確認或否定之擔保。」（means a promissory warranty, that is to say, a warranty by which the assured undertakes that some particular thing shall or shall not be done, or that some condition shall be fulfilled, or whereby he affirms or negatives the existence of a particular state of facts.）

由條文可知，擔保乃是被保險人承諾做或不做某特定事項，或完成某特定條件（fulfill）；確認（affirm）或否認（negative）某些事實之存在[3]。

二、擔保之表現方式

擔保之意義已如前述，而擔保之型態依 MIA,1906 第 33 條第 2 項區分為明示擔保（express warranty）及默示擔保（implied warranty）二種。

1.明示擔保

明示擔保係將擔保的事項，明列於保險契約上；即明示擔保必須將擔保之事項寫於保險單上，或者以其他文件附加於保險單上[4]。至於明示擔保的文字字體及書寫方式，並沒有統一規定，故欲確定何類文字才屬於擔保條件，必須自保險文字的實質意義求之[5]。所以由文字內容可以推定其為擔保的意思者，始稱為擔保。在實務上明示擔保中常有"warranted 或 warranted that"之語句；但也並非所有條款前有"warranted"語可者均為明示擔保；有些只是一個承保條款（coverage clause）或對危險之一個聲明（statement description of the risk），或是除外條款（exclusion clause）；如"warranted free of particular average"單獨海損不賠，此條款則並非明示擔保，乃表示保險人不負保險標的之單獨海損的賠償責任；與被保險人之明示擔保事項無關。因此，為了能確切分辨保單文字中何者為擔保性質，何者不屬於擔保，則應依照英國海上保險法的界說為準；使用者應加以釐

---

[3] 王衛恥，《海上保險的理論與實務》，頁 140。

[4] Arnould's, *Law of Marine Insurance and Average*, p.678。

[5] 王衛恥，《海上保險法與共同海損》，頁 327。

清以免產生混淆。MIA,1906 對明示擔保的定義規定於第 35 條如下：

(1)明示擔保得以任何足以擔保意思之文字為之。（An express warranty may be in any form of words from which the intention to warrant is to be inferred.）

(2)明示擔保應包含於保險單內，或於保險單上載明，或以其他文字附於保險單上。（An express warranty must be included in, or written upon, the police, or must be contained in some document incorporated by reference into the policy.）

(3)除非其內容完全不相同者，明示擔保不得排除默示擔保。

（An express warranty does not exclude an implied warranty, unless it be inconsistent therewith.）

故明示擔保係指以文字明確地表明於保險單上的條款，而若是明示擔保與默示擔保發生相抵觸的情況時，則默示擔保條款即不再適用。

2.默示擔保

默示擔保雖未用文字明確地表明於保險契約上，但默示擔保係依法律規定，在訂立契約時雙方當事人即應該有的共同了解。換言之，默示擔保雖不明白列示於保險單上，然契約雙方為當事人均已知道，該默示擔保實已包含於契約中[6]。依 MIA,1906 規定，默示擔保有適航性擔保及合法性擔保兩種。適航性（seaworthiness）於海上保險是一項非常重要的默示擔保，船舶的適航性不僅要求船舶能合理適應於海上航行時所有可能遭遇的海上危險，更必須包括配備，供給品、燃料、船員等均必須適當充足。法律會對適航性的默示擔保如此詳細之規訂，主因海上航行有其特殊且極高的危險性；若船舶未能具有合理的適航能力而出航，對於船舶上的人命、財產顯然缺乏保障；且船舶係由船東（被保險人）管理，若沒有適航性的默示擔保，船東極可能疏於管理船舶，引發心理危險因素增加（morale hazard），失去保險的管理危險功能。

---

[6] R. H. Brown, *Dictionary of Marine Insurance Terms*, p.430。

由 MIA,1906 第 39 條的意義可知在航程保險單（voyage policy）中，船舶於海上危險開始時，須能應付抵抗正常的海上危險；而於船舶停泊於港內時；則必須能應付抵抗正常的港灣危險；而於各不同分段航程時，則採航段理論（The doctrine of stages）[7]；即船舶必須有能力應付抵抗各個不同航段的特殊危險。

海上保險對貨物本身性質，並不要求必須具備有適航性，因為所承載貨物若屬特殊危險貨物時，乃必須於訂約前即向保險人說明，因此係屬於陳述（representation）範圍；然後保險人再依據被保險人對貨物之陳述，決定是否承保或加費承保。所以，並不要求貨物本身必須具有適航性。而於航程保單，不但船舶本身必須具備有適航性，更應要有適合裝載貨物的設備或裝置，稱之為適載貨性（cargoworthiness）；例如，載運冷凍貨物時必須在船上配備冷凍貨櫃（refrigerated container），或有足夠冷藏室才可謂之具有適載貨性。於定時保險單則並沒有對於每一階段船舶均須適航的默示擔保，但若被保險人明知其不適航而仍以不適航的船舶出航，則保險人對此不適航所致的損失不負賠償責任。

海上保險的另一項默示擔保為擔保危險應屬合法，且於被保險人的控制情形下，將以合法方式為之。即若海上保險契約中，若有法律所明白禁止的事項，則認為海上危險開始即不合法，契約自始便不生效。因為任何法律行為均必須適法，否則若違背了強制或禁止規定、社會善良風俗、公共秩序者，該法律行為應歸無效[8]。此條文對合法之解釋，應是指合於英國的法律。此規定與 MIA,1906 第 3 條第 1 項對於合法海上危險（lawful marine adventure）的規定可說是一個相呼應的條款，同時強調合法性的要求。

3.擔保之效力

MIA,1906 中的擔保為一必須確切遵守的條件，否則自違反日起

---

[7] Arnould's, *Law of Marine Insurance and Average*, p.720。

[8] Arnould's, *Law of Marine Insurance and Average*, p.361。

保險人即可解除保險責任（The insurer is discharged from liability as from the date of the breach of warranty.）。因此，不論違反擔保之事項對於承保危險是否屬重要事項（material circumstance）或被保險人有無過失，或是否被保險人已知，或損失與違反擔保間並沒有因果關係，保險人均可解除責任或終止契約。擔保之事項必須確切遵守（exactly complied），此處"exactly"必須嚴格從契約文字去解釋，不能以實質無差異去否定之。惟保險人對於在違反日前所發生因承保危險導致的保險事故，仍應負損害賠償責任。上述違反擔保之法律效果雖已明白規定，但是海上風險瞬息萬變，且世界經貿環境亦不斷在變動，故有時因為情勢變遷的結果會使原來所為了限制縮小危險之擔保變為不需要，或根本不可能再遵守。因此為了補救上述情況，MIA, 1906 第 34 條第 1 項規定了法律所允許的違反擔保事項有二種 ：(1)情勢變遷後原擔保內容已不再需要；(2)頒布新法，使原擔保之履行變成不合法。同條第 2 項規定若是擔保已經違反，則不得再抗辯於損失發生前已予以補救或履行；換言之，在違反擔保後即不得再抗辯該違反已補救或遵守，而再回復其契約效力；例如船舶發航時係不適航，隨後雖又回港修理已達適航狀況，而再度出航，不幸於中途遭遇海難而沉沒，在此情況下保險人可不賠償該損失，因為該船舶初次開航時就已造反了適航性的默示擔保，縱使其後已予以補救，也不能影響違反擔保效力。

4.擔保與特約條款

擔保主要乃係適用於海上保險，但海商法第七章中並無擔保之規定，雖海商法 126 條規定：「關於海上保險，於本章無規定者，適用保險法之規定。」而保險法也僅有特約條款可說是類似而已。特約條款主要類似於英國海上保險法之明示擔保而來；而在 ICC,2009 第 5 條中明訂有不適航及不適運的除外規定條款，故默示擔保也清楚地規定在我國保險市場使用的保險條款上。而海商法第 63 條對於適航能力的規定，係指運送契約中的適航能力，因為運送契約係載貨證券持有人及運送人間的權利義務契約，與保險並無關係。因此，適航性的默示擔保於我國並沒有法令可依據適用。擔保與特約條款兩者比較之下，我國的特約條款文字句簡短，與英國法擔保之詳實規定有很大不同。"warranty" 不僅在譯詞上不宜譯為特約條款，其在法律效果亦有極大不同，茲分述如下：

(1)英國海上保險法的擔保係區分為明示擔保及默示擔保兩種；而我國特約條款僅可說是一項類似明示擔保的條款而已，因為特約條款已排除了默示擔保的合法默示表現，也正因缺乏海上保險的默示擔保，特約條款為所有保險契約都可以特約條款予以特別約定，並非僅特別適用於海上保險。

(2)我國保險法第 67 條係指不論過去現在或將來之與有關保險契約的一切事項均得以特約條款定之，此與英國海上保險法的擔保規定相類似，但與 66 條的定義卻有矛盾之處，因保險法第 66 條顯係現在及將來事項之履行特約，但第 67 條又規定對於「過去事項」亦得特約，蓋已經過去的事實情況，並無法再追溯履行的可能，僅僅應該是對於過去之事實擔保其真實才合理，故我國特約條款若依第 66 條之規定應只是對現在及未來履行特種義務，即只有允諾的性質，然保險法第 67 條之矛盾恐為我國立法的疏失。

(3)在違反擔保時，自違反日後保險人可解除或終止契約，即自違反日起保險人始不負契約責任，但對於違反日前若發生因承保危險導致的保險事故，仍須負賠償之責。而違反了特約條款時，保險人得據以解除保險契約，使契約效力追溯自始無效，亦即依民法第 259 條規定，解除契約之後就產生了回復原狀之溯及既往不生效力的效果，故若違反特約條款之前的事故保險人已經賠償，依民法第 179 條規定：「無法律上之原因而受利益，致他人受損害者，應返還其利益。雖有法律上之原因，而其後已不存在者，亦同。」保險人仍得要求依解除契約之法理以及民法第 179 條規定，要求被保險人返還保險金。由此可知，我國違反特約條款之效力比英國違反擔保的效力更為嚴苛，這點也是保險法的特約條款與 MIA,1906 的擔保最大的不同。

三、2015 年英國保險法有關擔保之最新規定

英國海上保險法已實行一百多年，該法絕大部分條文成為海上保險之鐵則，但英國海上保險法原係利於商人法之角度規定，且當時科學與保險技術不佳，故著重於保護保險人之規範，而此可否適用於現今以消費者保險為主之發展，各方均有各種不同意見[9]。其實早於 1957 年英國即已開始進行對保險契約法檢視之工作，並提出建議方案，但不被國會所採納接受。2002 年時，一個由英國法官、律師、保險經紀人、保險公司以及少數的保險理算人，所組成之保險法律組織，其重要任務即是確實的推動必要的保險法律改革，經由該組織提出多篇有關海上保險法修正建議之研究報告後，英格蘭及蘇格蘭的法律委員會終於 2006 年開始重新審視了保險契約法[10]。

經過多次開會與協議，並進行多方面的評估，英國議會於 2015 年通過新的保險法，其中修改之部分亦影響了 MIA, 1906 之部分內容，而當 2015 英國保險法與 MIA, 1906 之法條內容有衝突時，將會適用 2015 英國保險法之規定，但與 MIA, 1906 未有衝突之部分依然會繼續適用。2015 英國保險法，是一部有關制定保險契約新規定之法律[11]，並將於 2016 年 8 月生效。該法被視為英國近 100 年以來保險法發展史上最重大的改革，其結合現代保險業的發展，對以往保險法進行了重大修改[12]。

2015 英國保險法第 10 條第 2 項對於 1906 年英國海上保險法有

---

[9] 羅俊偉（2013），〈論消費者被保險人之告知說明義務—以英國新訂法致為中心〉《消費者保護研究》，第十七期，頁 200。

[10] 謝明芳（2016），2015 年英國保險法對海上保險之影響，頁 12。

[11] Insurance Act 2015 抬頭：An act to make new provision about insurance contract;

[12] 孫珊珊（2015）〈英國 2015 年保險法修改的解讀〉《法治與社會》，2015 第 15 期，頁 252。

關擔保之規定進行了重大修改，規定當被違反之擔保已被補救後，保險契約則繼續生效。原文及翻譯如下：

2015 年英國保險法第 10 條第 2 項	
An insurer has no liability under a contract of insurance in respect of any loss occurring, or attributable to something happening, after a warranty (express or implied) in the contract has been breached but before the breach has been remedied.	被保險人違反擔保（不論明示或默示），保險人對該期間所發生之保險事故無需承擔保險責任，直到被保險人將違反擔保之情況補正完成。

對於何為可補救之擔保在第 6 項中也有清楚之規定，擔保要求於某一可確定的時間內完成（或不完成）某事，或必須履行某條件，或發生（不發生）某情況之事件，但被保險人無法滿足此要件時之擔保違反，屬於可以補救知擔保 [13]。然若是被保險人之擔保違反是因情勢變更，該契約終止擔保條款之適用時、因任何後來法律規定，認定該擔保條款為違法、以及保險人就擔保條款知違反為放棄權利主張者，保險人不得以被保險人違反擔保，尚未補救而不負擔其保險責任，此規定與 MIA,1906 第 34 條有關違反擔保之違反寬免為相似之規定，儘管如此，2015 保險法第 10–(7)–(b)已規定刪除 MIA,1906 第 34 條之規定。

綜言之，在 2015 新保險法中被保險人即使違反了擔保，但若在違反擔保前所發生之保險事故或被違反之擔保已補正完成後，保險人皆須負責其保險人責任，保險人僅在被保險人違反擔保，契約終止時不需對這段期間所生之保險事故負責，此點與過去 MIA, 1906 所規定之違反效果不同。

---

[13] Insurance Act 2015 10–(6)A case falls within this subsection if—
    (a)the warranty in question requires that by an ascertainable time something is to be done (or not done), or a condition is to be fulfilled, or something is (or is not) to be the case, and
    (b)that requirement is not complied with.

第3篇

2009 年英國協會貨物
保險條款逐條釋義

第九章　ICC,2009 之承保範圍

第十章　ICC,2009 之除外條款

第十一章　ICC,2009 之保險期間

2009年英國協會貨物保險條款逐條釋義

　　ICC,2009 年版之 ICC（A）、（B）、（C）三套條款與 1982 年條款一樣各有 19 條條款，而且三套條款中除了第一條危險條款不同以外其餘都一樣。將 ICC,2009 條款結構列，如表 1。

　　ICC,2009 延續 ICC,1982 的以條款簡單口語化英文（plain English）的本質而修訂，甚至更加落實於新條款中，如將許多條款用語改現代實務慣用的用語（modernization of language），相信國際社會的認同度應該會比 ICC,1982 更高。根據表 1 整理可知，ICC,2009 共區分為五大區塊，即承保範圍、除外危險、保險期間、理賠事項以及其他等五類，而其他類中包括了保險權益、減少損失、避免遲延以及法律與慣例等條款。第一區塊條款是第 1 條至第 3 條的「承保範圍」（Risks Covered），其中以第 1 條最為特殊，因為 ICC,2009 A, B, C 三套條款間唯一的差別就是第 1 條，其餘 18 條的條款規定都一樣。在承保範圍的規定中 A 條款是「概括式」承保，B 條款與 C 條款是採「列舉式」承保，而 B 條款與 C 條款之列舉承保危險項目又以 B 條款比 C 條款多，也就是 B 條款承保範圍比 C 條款大。

　　第 2 條是規定發生共同海損及海難救助時，保險人應負賠償責任的條款，但第 2 條的承保概念是採負面表列方式，即除了因除外危險第 4 條至第 7 條所造成的共同海損及海難救助保險不負賠償責任之

表 1　ICC,2009 條款結構表

條款內容之分類	條次／條款名稱	
Risk Covered（承保範圍）	第 1 條	Risks（危險）
	第 2 條	General Average（共同海損）
	第 3 條	Both to blame Collision Clause（雙方過失碰撞條款）
Exclusions（除外事項）	第 4 條	
	第 5 條	
	第 6 條	
	第 7 條	
Duration（保險期間）	第 8 條	Transit（航程）
	第 9 條	Termination of Contract of Carriage（運送契約終止）
	第 10 條	Change of Voyage（變更航程）
Claims（理賠事項）	第 11 條	Insurable Interest（保險利益）
	第 12 條	Forwarding Charges（轉運費用）
	第 13 條	Constructive Total Loss（推定全損）
	第 14 條	Increased Value Clause（增加價值）
Benefit of Insurance（保險權益）	第 15 條	
Minimising losses（減少損失）	第 16 條	Duty of Assured（被保險人的義務）
	第 17 條	Waiver（放棄）
avoidance of delay（避免遲延）	第 18 條	
Law and practice（法律與慣例）	第 19 條	

資料來源：作者整理

外，其餘任何原因所造成的共同海損及海難救助保險人均會理賠。第3 條其實是一個責任保險條款，承保貨主（被保險人）基於運送契約下的雙方過失碰撞條款所產生的補償責任，保險人願意代為抗辯以及負責賠償。

第 2 區塊條款是「除外事項」，由第 4 至第 7 條組成，第 4 條在 ICC,1982 的條款中稱為一般除外不保條款（General Exclusions Clause），(A)條款共計有 4.1 至 4.7 款等七項除外危險，(B)與（C）條款則有 4.1 至 4.8 款等八項除外危險。ICC,2009 大體上對於第 4 條僅僅為文字上都修改，除外事項規定的內容並無結構性改變，惟 ICC,2009 已經將條款名稱（General Exclusions Clause）刪除。第 5 條為有關船舶適航性（seaworthiness）以及運送工具適運性（fitness）的規定，主要概念是若被保險人於裝載時明知該船舶不適航，或者裝櫃時明知該貨櫃或運送工具不適運，則保險人對此不適航或不適運所造成的貨損不負賠償之責。第 6 條在 ICC,1982 是戰爭險（又稱兵險）除外不保條款（War Exclusion Clause），第 7 條在 ICC,1982 是罷工險除外不保條款（Strikes Exclusion Clause）。這兩條條款在 ICC,2009 除了將條款名稱刪除外，第 6 條並無改變，而第 7 條為因應美國 911 恐怖攻擊所延伸的保險問題，將「恐怖活動」的定義重新釋義，並將恐怖行為擴大到含有政治、意識形態或宗教動機等行為。惟這兩條條文雖是除外不保條款，但係屬於可以再附加承保的條款；也就是再多繳些保險費後，則可以分別以協會戰爭險條款（Institute War Clauses, Cargo）及協會罷工險條款（Institute Strikes Clauses, Cargo），再將戰爭兵及罷工或恐怖攻擊等危險予以承保。

第三區塊條款為保險期間之規定，分別由第 8 條至第 10 條所組成。第 8 條是保險期間規定的核心條款，分成 8.1 至 8.3 三款。其中 8.1 規定保險標的物在正常運輸過程中的保險效力開始與終止；8.2 則規定當保險標的物在最終卸貨港後，運送脫離正常運輸過程時的保險效力規定。8.3 則規定當被保險人無法控制的情況下如發生偏航（deviation）、遲延（delay）、強制卸貨（forced discharge ）、重新裝船（reshipment）與轉船（transhipment），運送人行使自由航行權等行為時，該保險仍繼續有效。第 9 條規定在被保險人無法控制的情況下，運送契約於保險單所載預定目的地以外的地點被終止，或者貨物因其他原因運送被終止，而不能依原正常運送過程將貨物送達原預定目的地時保險契約效力的問題。第 10 條為變更航程條款，主要是規定被保險人主動變更航程後保險的效力問題，ICC,2009 在第 10 條中除將 "Held Covered" 這個專有名詞明文化外，也增列了 10.2 規定當被保險人或其受僱人於開始運送時不知將變更航程時的保險效力問題。

第四區塊條款為理賠事項條款，是由第 11 條第 14 條所組成。第 11 條規定被保險人於求償時必須具備保險利益的規定，同時也規定例外的 "lost or not lost" 情形。第 12 條是當保險事故發生時，保險標的物需要轉運至原目的地或其他目的地時的轉運費用賠償規定。第 13 條規定保險事故發生時被保險人以推定全損求償的標準規定，第 14 條為增值條款，規定保險標的物價值增加之後，若有第 2 張增值保險出現，或本身就是增值保險時的保險賠償問題。

最後 5 個條款分別為第 15 條之保險權益條款，本條在 ICC,2009 中幾乎重新改寫 ICC,1982 的內容，以更貼近條款內容的真義，主要為規定本保險的權益運送人或其他關係人不得享有，也明訂被保險人的範圍包括受讓人。第 16 條及第 17 條同為「減少損失」組內之兩條款，第 16 條為與英國海上保險法規定類似的損害防阻規定，第 17 條為明訂任何人的損害防阻行為都不應被認為接受委付或放棄委付。第 18 條為規定在被保險人可以控制的情況下都應避免延誤條款，最後的第 19 條為準據法條款，規定保險條款乃依據英國之法律及慣例。

第九章

ICC,2009 之承保範圍

第一節　危險條款

ICC,2009 第 1 條是保險人承保範圍的規定條款，三套條款各計有 19 條條款，其中唯一不同的也只有第 1 條與第 4 條。茲將 ICC,2009 第 1 條在(A)、(B)及(C)條款之規定列如表 9-1。

表 9-1　ICC,2009(A)、(B)及(C)第 1 條

條款	內容
ICC,2009(A)	Risks 1. This insurance covers all risks of loss of or damage to the subject-matter insured except as excluded by the provisions of Clauses 4, 5 ,6 and 7 below.
	危險 1.除下列第 4、5、6 及 7 條除外規定以外，本保險承保被保險標的物一切滅失或毀損之危險。

ICC,2009 (B)	Risks 1. This insurance covers, except as excluded by the provision of Clauses 4, 5, 6 and 7 below, 　1.1 loss of or damage to the subject−matter insured reasonably attributable to 　　1.1.1 fire or explosion 　　1.1.2 vessel or craft being stranded grounded sunk or capsized 　　1.1.3 overturning or derailment of land conveyance 　　1.1.4 collision or contact of vessel craft or conveyance with any external object other than water 　　1.1.5 discharge of cargo at a port of distress 　　1.1.6 earthquake volcanic eruption or lightning, 　1.2 loss of or damage to the subject−matter insured caused by 　　1.2.1 general average sacrifice 　　1.2.2 jettison or washing overboard 　　1.2.3 entry of sea lake or river water into vessel craft hold conveyance container or place of storage, 　1.3 total loss of any package lost overboard or dropped whilst loading on to, or unloading from, vessel or craft.
	危險 1. 本保險除了第4、5、6及7條之除外規定外，承保以下事故 　1.1 合理歸因於下列事故造成保險標的物的毀損或滅失 　　1.1.1 火災或爆炸 　　1.1.2 船舶或駁船的擱淺、觸礁、沉沒或傾覆 　　1.1.3 陸上運送載具的翻覆或出軌 　　1.1.4 船舶碰撞或船舶、駁船或其他運輸載具與水以外之任何物體的觸撞 　　1.1.5 於避難港時之卸貨 　　1.1.6 地震、火山爆發、雷擊 　1.2 下列事故直接造成保險標的物的毀損或滅失 　　1.2.1 共同海損犧牲 　　1.2.2 投棄或海浪掃落 　　1.2.3 海水、湖水、河水進入船舶駁船之船艙、貨櫃，或儲存處所 　1.3 於船舶或駁船裝貨、卸貨時整件掉落或落海之全損

	Risks
	1. This insurance covers, except as excluded by the provision of Clauses 4, 5, 6 and 7 below,
	1.1 loss of or damage to the subject—matter insured reasonably attributable to
	1.1.1 fire or explosion
	1.1.2 vessel or craft being stranded grounded sunk or capsized
	1.1.3 overturning or derailment of land conveyance
	1.1.4 collision or contact of vessel craft or conveyance with any external object other than water.
	1.1.5 discharge of cargo at a port of distress,
	1.2 loss of or damage to the subject—matter insured caused by
	1.2.1 general average sacrifice
ICC,2009 (C)	1.2.2 jettison.
	危險
	1. 本保險除了第 4、5、6 及 7 條之除外規定外，承保以下事故
	1.1 合理歸因於下列事故造成保險標的物的毀損或滅失
	1.1.1 火災或爆炸
	1.1.2 船舶或駁船的擱淺、觸礁、沉沒或傾覆
	1.1.3 陸上運送載具的翻覆或出軌
	1.1.4 船舶碰撞或船舶、駁船或其他運輸載具與水以外之任何物體的觸撞
	1.1.5 於避難港時之卸貨
	1.2 下列事故直接造成保險標的物的毀損或滅失
	1.2.1 共同海損犧牲
	1.2.2 投棄

資料來源：作者整理

　　ICC,2009 的 A 條款為「概括式（All Risks）」的承保，而 B 條款與 C 條款則稱為「列舉式（named perils）」的承保。概括式的承保範圍指的是保險單只概括地對承保的危險敘述，而非屬於除外不保事項的危險事故，則自然地在承保範圍之內。因此，危險事故發生時，保險人若要主張不負賠償責任，則要證明發生危險的原因屬於除外不保事項之內，否則就要負賠償責任。我國海商法第 129 條規定：「保險人對於保險標的物，除契約另有規定外，因海上一切事變及災

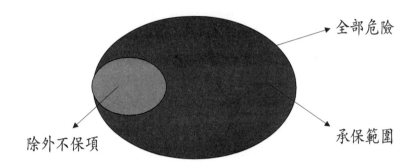

全部危險

除外不保項

承保範圍

圖 9-1　概括式承保概念圖

資料來源：作者自繪

害所生之毀損滅失及費用，負賠償責任。」亦同樣為概括式承保的規定。「概括式（All Risks）」承保範圍概念如圖 9-1

　　保險理賠實務上有時因保險人為顧及賠付後保險代位權可以順利執行，而要求被保險人須先行取得相關證明如短卸或破損報告，才可以申請理賠。但就(A)條款概括式承保的概念，被保險人其實只要證明損害是發生於保險期間，事故發生後也立即通知保險人，則應可以申請理賠。至於事故證明文件並非(A)條款索賠的必要舉證文件，保險人除非能證明事故非保險期間發生、事故非承保危險、被保險人不具保險利益等事項，否則保險人理論上應負保險給付之責。航運實務上若被保險人（貨主）提貨後發現貨損，頂多只能依海商法第56條規定以書面通知運送人，或除非貨櫃場於拆櫃時立即開立異常報告以釐清責任，否則一旦貨主提貨後，又進一步要求運送人出具事故證明，實務上非常困難，也可謂是強人所難。綜言之，依保險人責任是「契約責任」也是「結果責任」的法理，保險理賠人員若嚴格要求投保(A)條款的被保險人出具運送人或倉儲、櫃場之事故證明文件方可申請理賠的做法，可能已曲解概括式承保之義，恐生爭議。

所謂列舉式的承保範圍，即是在保險契約中將承保的危險一一列舉，故列在除外不保事項內的危險，固然保險人不須負賠償責任，而即使不在除外不保項目內，若同時也不在承保範圍內的危險項目，保險人應當也不需要負賠償責任。因此，危險發生後，被保險人必須要證明發生危險的原因是在承保範圍之內才能獲得賠償。其承保範圍概念如圖 9-2。

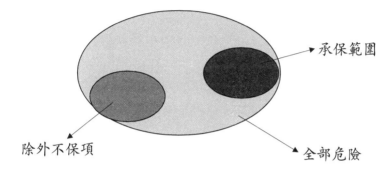

圖 9-2　列舉式承保概念圖

資料來源：作者自繪

由 ICC,2009（A）條款第 1 條對於承保範圍的規定在解釋上分為兩段邏輯，第 1 個思考邏輯是（A）條款原則上是承保所有的事故（covers all risks of loss of or damage to the subject-matter insured），第 2 個思考邏輯是逆向思考，即若是除外條款第 4 至第 7 條所造成的保險標的物的毀損滅失，保險人就不須理賠。所以欲了解（A）條款的承保範圍有那些，反而應該是先去了解除外不保的規定有那些，也就是只要不是除外不保（第 4，5，6，7 條）之規定事項所造成的事故，就是保險人的承保範圍。

由於（A）條款的承保範圍採負面表列，涵蓋了大部分的危險事故，故實務上常延續 ICC,1963 的 All Risks 概念，將（A）條款稱之為「全險條款」，但其實當年 ICC,1963 改成 1982 年的新條款，除為了將條款簡明化外，其中一個重要原因則是雖然 "All Risks" 本來就是

「概括式的保險」概念，但是在國內翻譯時這個名稱容易讓被保險人混淆甚至誤解，將「All Risks（概括式的保險）」與「all risks（所有的危險）」兩者劃上等號，造成只看外表名稱後，以為不論任何事故所造成保險標的物之毀損滅失保險人都會賠償的謬誤，後來英國倫敦保險人協會在 1982 年推出新條款，ICC,1982(A) 條款逐準備取代 ICC,1963 的 All Risks，以避免誤解。ICC,2009 仍延續此概念將概括式承保的條款以(A) 條款命名，故實務上實在不宜再將(A) 條款以「全險條款」概略稱之。至於 ICC,2009(A) 條款的第 4 條則於往後章節詳述釋義。

ICC,2009(B) 及 (C) 條款是採列舉式承保概念，也可稱為正面表列，兩張保險單的承保範圍如第三篇表 1 所示。其中 (B) 條款比 (C) 條款多出的承保事故為 1.1.6 earthquake volcanic eruption or lightning（地震、火山爆發、雷擊）、1.2.2 washing overboard（海浪掃落）、1.2.3 entry of sea lake or river water into vessel craft hold conveyance container or place of storage（海水、湖水、河水進入船舶駁船船艙、貨櫃，或儲存處所）以及 1.3 total loss of any package lost overboard or dropped whilst loading on to, or unloading from, vessel or craft（於船舶或駁船裝貨、卸卸時整件掉落或落海之全損）等四種。故實務上投保應用時如果貨物性質較擔心濕損，如紙卷、電子零組件等，若遭遇水濕即有嚴重損害的貨物，則至少應投保(B) 或(A) 條款，若貨物特性沒有運送過程的莫名毀損疑慮，也不擔心偷竊短少等問題，如大宗物資，則或許可以考慮投保(C) 條款即可。不過貨物種類品項眾多無法一一列舉說明，惟除了信用狀已經規定應投保的險別外，根據貨物特性與危險需求再考量不同險別的承保範圍，據以決定投保何種條款方為最佳危險管理策略。

ICC,2009(B) 條款與 (C) 條款就承保範圍的描述概念並無不同，且都僅承保因保險事故所造成之「滅失與毀損（loss of or damage to）」，並沒有把因保險事故所造成的額外費用（expense）承保在內，主要原因是除了明訂只承保標的物之毀損、滅失外，至於若發生了額外費用原則上也可自其他條款中獲償，如第 2 條的共同海損與救助費用、第 12 條的轉運費用、第 16 條的損害防阻費用等。然而條款內除明訂列舉出的保險事故所造成的損害負賠償責任外，也同時再明訂 "except as excluded by the provision of Clauses 4, 5, 6 and 7 below "（除了第 4、5、6 及 7 條之除外規定外）之除外規定，解釋條款時應再考慮若因第 4、5、6 及 7 條所造成的列舉範圍內事故時，保險人仍然不予理賠，如保險標的物是因戰爭引起火災造成毀損。雖然火災是承保事故，但其是因為戰爭所造成，故依主力近因概念，戰爭（除外事故）為保險標的物毀損主力近因，故保險人仍不負賠償之責。因此，條款解釋時應在此列舉式承保條款上再加上這個限制條件，以確認、判斷保險人的理賠責任。

另外，就承保事故主力近因原則適用方面，不論是 ICC,2009（B）條款或(C)條款都把承保範圍分成兩組。條款內 1.1 所規定的主力近因適用是「可合理歸因於（attributable to）」的承保概念，亦即只要貨損原因與列舉的承保事故具有因果關係，不論是造成損失的直接原因或間接原因，保險人都需負賠償之責，如火災灌救後造成貨物濕損，雖然在 ICC,2009(C)不承保水濕的損害，但為該濕損與火災具有因果關係，所以保險人仍應理賠；而條款 1.2 所規定的主力近因是適用「直接造成（caused by）」的承保概念，故只有在承保範圍裡所列的事故原因是造成損失的直接原因時，保險人才需要賠償，如貨損是共同海損犧牲或被投棄等原因造成，保險人才負賠償責任，不需再考慮造成貨損的間接原因。由兩者比較之下可知，「直接造成（caused by）」的規定已縮限被保險人可以索賠的範圍，而「合理歸因（attributable to）」的規定，被保險人於索賠時只要提出貨損原因與事故之事實具有因果關係，保險人就應負損害賠償之責，否則就應舉證貨損原因是除外事故所造成才可主張拒賠。將(B)條款與(C)條款之列舉承保事故詳述如下：

1.1.1 fire or explosion（火災或爆炸）

本承保事故同時列舉於(B)條款及(C)條款中。因本款是採合理歸因（attributable to）的承保概念，所以只要保險標的物的毀損或滅失原因可合理歸因於火災所引起的，均在承保範圍。換言之，不論保險標的物在船舶上或倉庫或任何運輸工具，只要是在保險航程範圍內，造成毀損或滅失是因火災直接造成，或火災間接的熱氣影響損失（heating damage）均為承保範圍；甚至為了防阻火災擴大或滅火之損害亦應包括在內。惟若是保險標的物因化學變化或本質引起的自燃造成毀損，則將被認為是除外條款 4.4 款的因保險標的物固有瑕疵或本質引起（caused by inherent vice or nature of the subject matter insured），保險人不負損害賠償責任。

所謂爆炸，在 1984 年 Commonwealth Smelting Ltd. v. Guardian Royal Exchange Assurance 一案中法官定義為：因急速的化學或核反應，或是瓦斯、壓力下的蒸氣爆出所造成的大聲且劇烈的事件。不論保險標的物是否直接因爆炸所發生的損失都屬承保範圍，即使是因為其他鄰近物品發生爆炸，使保險標的物造成擠壓的損害，也屬於爆炸的承保範圍。

1.1.2 vessel or craft being stranded grounded sunk or capsized （船舶或駁船的擱淺、觸礁、沉沒或傾覆）

本承保事故也同時列舉於(B)條款及(C)條款中。擱淺、觸礁、沉沒或傾覆為傳統海上危險事故（perils of the seas）。早期保險實務中有必要區分擱淺與觸礁之不同，因為 F.P.A.保單中並不承保擱淺但卻承保觸礁，但自 ICC,1982 版後都已經將兩者承保在內。所謂擱淺是指船舶與水底的物體意外接觸並繼續擱置一段時間而無法前進之狀態；觸礁則指船舶擦過沉沒在水中的礁岩物體或其他阻礙物；沉沒指船舶失去浮力及航行能力，而令船體全部沉入水底或大部分沉沒於水平面下的狀態；傾覆則指因意外事故造成船舶失去重心而翻覆[1]。實務上應注意的是，雖然 ICC,2009(C) 條款不承保海水侵入船艙造成的貨物濕損，但若是因船舶沉沒或傾覆造成濕損，在(C)條款下仍可以本款獲得賠償。

在 S.G 保單中以 "perils of the seas" 涵蓋所有因海上惡劣氣候造成的損害，包括因惡劣氣候造成甲板上的保險標的物被海浪掃落，或船艙中因惡劣氣候造成的貨物互相碰撞損害。但 ICC,2009(B) 條款及(C)條款僅特別將擱淺、觸礁、沉沒或傾覆造成的貨損列舉為承保範圍；實務上，當船舶發生擱淺或觸礁事故後，貨物卸下時其實很難判斷損害滅失究竟是因不當裝載或是船舶擱淺、觸礁所直接造成的，為避免舉證爭議，只要保險標的物毀損、滅失的原因可合理歸因於承運船舶的擱淺、觸礁、沉沒或傾覆，均為保險人的承保範圍。依本款的規定若船舶觸礁後進水造成海水濕損，雖濕損非直接因船舶觸礁造成，但仍與船舶觸礁有合理因果關係，則不論是(B)條款或(C)條款，保險人均應理賠；抑或保險標物損失原因是因為船舶擱淺當時造成貨物在船艙內彼此碰撞造成，或甲板上貨物掉落損害，保險人依此款均應負損賠償之責。

1.1.3 overturning or derailment of land conveyance （陸上運送載具的翻覆或出軌）

貨物保險為航程保險單，為了配合國際複合運送的保險需求，保險航程可以自最短的「港到港（port to port）」，依不同的國貿條件的危險負擔移轉規定，而將保險航程約定成為「港到戶（port to door）」或「戶到港（door to port）」或「戶到戶（door to door）」等不同模式，因此自 ICC 的 1982 年版開始就列舉了有關陸上運送的承保事故，至 ICC,2009 本款仍然存在。所謂陸上運送載具之翻覆

---

[1] 許曉民，《海的危險事故》，國立台灣海洋學院航海學會，民 74 年，頁 5–23、5–29、5–31。姚玉麟，《海上保險名詞釋義》，航貿圖書出版社，頁 501、507。

（overturning），包括卡車、貨櫃拖車等均屬之，而 "overturning" 也專指陸上運輸工具因意外事故的翻覆，與前述 1.2.2 的 "capsized" 為船舶的傾覆在概念上仍有不同。而 "derailment" 則是指任何軌道運輸工具的出軌意外事件，在美國盛行的複合運送或稱陸橋運送（land bridge service），經常是以雙層列車將自遠東開往美國西岸卸下的貨櫃運往東岸或美國內陸點，故若不幸運送過程中因火車出軌造成保險標的物的損害，即可依此款獲得賠償。本款另有一點應注意的是，假若貨物放置於車站月台準備裝載運送，若被意外出軌的列車壓毀，因為尚未裝載於列車上，故不屬於本款之列舉事故範圍內，保險人應可主張不負保險責任。

1.1.4 collision or contact of vessel craft or conveyance with any external object other than water（船舶碰撞或船舶、駁船或運輸載具與水以外之任何外在物體的觸撞）

本款亦為傳統的海上運輸風險，由條款文義可知，只要可合理歸因於不論是船舶與船舶之間的碰撞（collision），無論該船舶是在航行、錨泊、或是繫泊的狀態；或載運保險標的物船舶、駁船或其他運輸載具與「水」以外的外在其他物體，如碼頭、防波堤、橋式起重機（gantry crane）的觸撞（contact），所造成的保險標的物直接或者間接造成的毀損或滅失保險人均應理賠。另由於本款除了將船與船之間的碰撞或與其他物體的觸撞均列為承保事故外，對於船舶的定義也涵蓋了一般運送船、駁船或其他運輸載具都屬於本款的運送工具。所謂其他「運輸載具（conveyance）」這個名詞分別出現在 ICC,2009 的第 1.1.3 land conveyance、第 1.1.4 款（本款）、第 5.1.2 款 unfitness of container or conveyance……、第 8.1 項…immediate loading into or onto the carrying vehicle or other conveyance for the commencement of transit、第 8.1.1 款 completion of unloading from the carrying vehicle or other conveyance in……、第 8.1.2 款 completion of unloading from the carrying vehicle or other conveyance in……、第 8.1.3 款……elect to use any carrying vehicle or other conveyance or any container…等。在解釋適用時 "conveyance" 從上述條款之內容與文義並非專指船舶，尤其第 8 條之航程保險期間約定亦可包括陸運過程，故 "conveyance" 一詞在第 8 條中更不會是只有指船舶，第 5.1.2 條之 "unfitness of conveyance" 也指的是船舶以外的運輸載具不適運。綜上，本款所謂「contact（觸撞）」亦應可適用於陸上運送過程的卡車或運輸工具的意外事故觸撞如車禍，所造成直接或間接的保險標的物損害。

所謂「水以外的外在物體（external object other than water）」，已非常清楚排除海上惡劣氣候（heavy weather）所造成的保險標物損害，如巨浪衝擊甲板上貨櫃，造成櫃內貨物擠壓變形，或甚至貨櫃因巨浪衝擊後破裂，造成櫃內貨物損失等損害均非保險人的賠償範圍。

1.1.5 discharge of cargo at a port of distress（於避難港時之卸貨）

船舶航行時發生海難，往往請求救助支援駛往避難港，船舶上的貨載也將依貨主的意思再安排接駁船退運回原來起航港，或者轉運至原目的港。因此在避難港中將會產生卸貨、暫時儲存、以及轉運費用。在 ICC,2009 的第 12 條將承保保險標的物因保險事故發生後的避難港卸貨、儲存以及轉運等「額外費用」；而本款乃是承保合理歸因於避難港卸貨時所發生的直接或間接「損失」，兩者承保的內容仍有不同。本款之適用依字義規定僅僅只在於「避難港卸貨」的貨損，至於在避難港中因暫時儲存或重新裝船所造成的實質損害，或原來正常目的港的卸貨損失，均不是本款的承保範圍。惟若被保險人因自己無法控制的強迫卸貨造成貨損，應可以第 8.3 項的規定下獲得賠償，條款內容詳見第 8 條的說明。

因本款同時出現於 ICC,2009（B）、及 (C) 條款，原則上若提貨時發現貨物有毀損情況，則應先舉證乃是承保的事故所造成，故被保險人若要以此條款索賠，須先證明貨損是在避難港卸貨時發生，但就航運實務而言，除非在避難港卸貨當時發生損害後立即公證或是開立證明，否則等到提貨時發現貨損，被保險人或保險人其實都極難判定損失是不是發生於避難港卸貨當時。

1.1.6 earthquake volcanic eruption or lightning（地震、火山爆發、雷擊）

本款只出現在 ICC,2009 的(B)條款，也就是(C)條款並沒有列舉此項危險事故，所以這款是兩套條款間之差異之一。1980 年代以後為複合運送的興起，反應之於 ICC,1982，遂出現了涵蓋內陸運送或倉儲期間可能發生的地震、火山爆發、雷擊等危險事故。本條款適用時應再配合保險航程而決定保險人是否應負保險責任。如出口貨物航程若是以 from shipper's warehouse 開始起保生效，若於貨櫃集散站併櫃或儲放期間或在裝船期間，保險標的物因為地震而掉落毀損則被保險人將可依此款的承保規定獲得賠償。反之，若保險單是以 port to port 為保險航程，則在貨櫃集散站儲放期間因尚未開始併櫃，故保險尚未生效，縱使保險標的物因地震而毀損，保險人亦無須負損害賠償責任，其他如火山爆發或閃電雷擊的解釋與適用亦是同樣的邏輯，惟閃電雷擊的損害並不需與惡劣氣候有關，只要損失與閃電雷擊間具有合理因果關係即可。

若地震或火山爆發發生於海上，極容易引發海嘯，可能造成船舶傾覆或沉沒，或者海嘯摧毀港埠設施、倉棧、岸邊穀倉或油槽等設施，因此造成保險標的物之毀損，則因為是合理歸因於地震或火山爆發所引起的直接或間接損害，保險人仍應負賠償責任。

1.2.1 general average sacrifice （共同海損犧牲）

自 1.2 項開始主力近因原則的適用為「直接造成（caused by）」，故保險標的物之毀損、滅失必須是因共同海損行為後的共同海損犧牲方為保險人的承保範圍；換言之，若共同海損不成立則也不會產生共同海損犧牲，更不應將損失列為本款而求償。至於共同海損行為後所發生的共同海損費用，或者經理算師計算後的應分攤共同海損分擔額，則依 ICC,2009 第 2 條之規定獲償，詳見第 2 條之說明。依英國海上保險之規定及理賠實務之慣例，保險人對於共同海損犧牲的賠償為先賠償被保險人全數的損失（犧牲），而不是先由被保險人向其他受益關係人請求分擔後，保險人僅賠償其自行應分擔部分，所以共同海損犧牲的索賠程序與單獨海損之賠償是完全相同的。

1.2.2 jettison or washing overboard （投棄或海浪掃落）

本款在 ICC,2009（B）條款與（C）條款不同，即（B）條款比（C）條款多列了一款「washing overboard（海浪掃落）」。所謂 "jettison" 亦為傳統海上事故的一種，會發生貨物投棄的原因可能是該貨物有危害船

圖 9-3 半貨櫃船
資料來源：作者提供

舶航行安全之虞，或產生異味、惡臭等，使船長下令將貨物自船舶上投棄於海。若該投棄動作後宣布共同海損，則保險標的物直接因投棄的損失，將被列為共同海損犧牲，由所有利害關係人共同分擔；反之，若沒有宣布共同海損，則該投棄損失則歸類為單獨海損，再依保險條款的規定由保險人負保險賠償之責。實務上須注意者是，若該投棄是被保險人的惡意行為，或如（B）條款及（C）條款除外的第 4.7 款規定之任何人的不法行為導致之損失，保險人仍然可以主張不負保險責任。惟會發生投棄損失的貨物一定是放置於甲板運送的貨物，且船上具有起重設備的船舶，以目前貨櫃為主流運輸方式而言，除非半貨櫃船本身裝有裝卸櫃之起重機設備，如圖 9-3，否則全貨櫃輪在技術上絕不可能發生投棄之損失。

所謂 "washing overboard" 指船舶於海上航行中遭遇暴風雨，船舶在持續不斷的巨烈搖晃下，使得貨物自甲板上翻落海中，依 ICC,

2009（B）條款第 2.2.2 款規定，可自保險人處獲得賠償。惟依此款的承保概念，被保險人必須舉證貨物是因被海浪掃落後產生的損失，若僅是因為纜繩繫固不當，或船舶航行時船身傾斜造成貨物掉落都不屬於海浪掃落。實務上，除非船長於航行時記載明確且提供給貨主做為向保險人求償的證明，否則被保險人將很難舉證貨物落海究竟是甲板裝運時繫固不當，或是海浪掃落所造成，對投保（B）條款之被保險人較為不利。

1.2.3 entry of sea lake or river water into vessel craft hold conveyance container or place of storage （海水、湖水、河水進入船舶、駁船之船艙、貨櫃，或儲存處所）

本款為水溼危險，也僅僅規定在（B）條款，（C）條款並未列舉此款危險。對於列舉式危險的解釋除了確認保險的範圍外，也應該嚴格探求條款真意，故雖然本款列舉了 sea（海水）、lake（湖水）以及 river（河水）三種不同水濕危險，但並未列舉 rain（雨水），也就是當保險標的物濕損時，公證人或保險人首先需確認濕損原因，可能是海水，當然也可能是雨水或湖、河水，最簡單的判斷方式可以硝酸銀（silver nitrate）進行鹽分測試，確認濕損貨物的水分是否有海水成分，再判斷運送航程是否經過湖區或內河航運，做為判斷水濕的原因。由於（C）條款中並未列舉此危險事故，故除了因第 1.1 項列舉事故以及共同海損犧牲或投棄所造成的水濕外，保險均不負濕損之責。

本款所列舉的三種發生水濕的地點非常廣，舉凡船舶、駁船、船艙、運送工具，貨櫃，或儲存處所都包括在內，亦即不論是海上航行、內河航行、湖區航行的水侵入了運輸工具或儲存保險標的物之處所，如颱風來臨後造成河水暴漲使貨櫃集散站淹水造成貨物濕損，都屬於保險人應賠償的責任。換句話說，若貨物發生海水、河水、湖水濕損之地點不在船舶、駁船、船艙、運送工具、貨櫃、或儲存處所，如岸邊等待裝載的貨物濕損，則因不在運輸工具也不在儲存處所內，保險人也不負保險責任。但若發生此類情形，被保險人只要呈現承保範圍內的濕損即可求償，而保險人除非取得記錄完整之文件，否則要舉證非在運輸工具或儲存處內發生濕損，恐怕有極大的困難。

1.3 total loss of any package lost overboard or dropped whilst loading on to, or unloading from, vessel or craft（於船舶或駁船裝貨、卸貨時整件掉落或落海之全損）

本款僅規定在(B)條款，(C)條款並未列舉此款危險，又稱為掉落損失（sling losses）。本款承保的損失只有保險標的物的全損（total loss），當然全損的範圍除了實際全損（actual total loss）外，也包括推定全損（constructive total loss），而發生全損的「情況」必須是在裝貨或者卸貨時「整件」掉落或落海。換言之，若全損並非發生在裝貨或卸貨當時，又或全損的原因不是「整件」掉落，均不是本款列舉事故的範圍，保險人都可以對該損失主張不負保險責任。至於整件的定義應於當時貨物運輸的實際情況而論，如貨櫃整櫃掉落、或吊運棧板貨物整個棧板掉落、或整批貨物掉落其中一獨立貨件，該獨立貨件的全損等都應是整件的概念。另外，本款危險事故不論是船舶或者是駁船的裝、卸貨都屬之，故如於特殊之中流作業卸貨方式時整件掉落全損，也是本款的承保範圍。最後，將本款危險事故歸納整理可知，被保險人若欲以本款列舉之事故求償必須符合下列四要件：

(1)時間：裝貨或是卸貨當時發生。

(2)地點：於船舶或駁船之裝卸作業。

(3)事故：整件貨物掉落或落海。

(4)損失：全損（包括實際全損及推定全損）。

第二節　共同海損

一、共同海損之意義

ICC,2009 第 2 條的條款名稱是 "General Average"，所以將條款名稱翻譯為「共同海損」，但其實第 2 條內容不僅規範了保險人對於共同海損的責任，也規範了保險人對於海難救助的賠償責任規定，故嚴格而言，本條款應該是「共同海損與海難救助」。ICC,2009 之 (A)、(B) 及 (C) 條款都是相同的規定。條款內容如表 9-2。

表 9-2　ICC,2009 第 2 條共同海損

ICC,2009 第 2 條	General Average 2. This insurance covers general average and salvage charges, adjusted or determined according to the contract of carriage and/or the governing law and practice, incurred to avoid or in connection with the avoidance of loss from any cause except those excluded in Clauses 4, 5 , 6 and 7 below.
	共同海損 2. 本保險承保依據運送契約及或有關適用法律與慣例所理算或認定之共同海損與施救費用，而其發生係為了避免或有關避免除以下第 4、5、6 及 7 條除外條款之任何原因所致之損失。

資料來源：作者整理

共同海損是一個極為古老的海事制度，在古代羅得法（Rhodian Law）中明文規定貨物因為了減輕船貨載重而被投棄的損失，應由全體分擔，故共同海損制度的形成，乃因事故發生時的「損失分攤」問題而起，而為了全體利益所犧牲的個體損失，應由全體關係人分攤補償之公平概念，則為共同海損制度最基本理念。共同海損制度經過多年來的演變，與法院之解釋裁判，對於何謂「共同海損行為」已慢慢

發展其概念上之定義與必要的成立原則。將我國海商法第 110 條、英國海上保險法及約克安特衛普規則的規定，綜合歸納得認定爲共同海損損失（General Avarage Loss）之成立要件爲：

1.必須在海上航行中遭受意外事故。

如我國海商法第 110 條指共同海損，謂在「船舶航程期間」所發生者。係共同航程中因海「難」所生之損害與費用，無「難」即無共同海損，故通常之船舶折舊及船員薪資之支出等，對船舶所有人而言固爲損害，但非基於「危難」而生。

2.須爲共同海損行爲「直接」引起的犧牲或費用。

如我國海商法第 110 條及英國海上保險法第 66 條第 1 項均有共同海損損失必須是直接（directly）由於共同海損行爲所致之規定。

3.須爲「額外」的犧牲或費用。

即共同海損行爲所產生之犧牲或者費用，必須是異常性的、非正常性的性質。所謂額外犧牲或費用，乃排除正常航行中所必須消耗或花費的費用，如正常船員薪資。2004 年約克安特衛普規則 Rule A 中亦爲相同之規定，對共同海損的犧牲與費用的認定必須爲具有額外或非常性質（extraordinary），在 Black Law Dictionary 中所謂 "extraordinary" 係指在通常之外的、超過平常的程度。

4.該爲了共同安全之處置需爲「故意」並「自願」的行爲。

我國海商法第 110 條即有「爲求共同危險中全體財產之安全所爲故意及合理處分」之規定。相同概念亦見於 2004 年約克安特衛普規則之 Rule A（There is a general average act when, and only when, any extraordinary sacrifice or expenditure is intentionally and reasonably made or incurred for the common safety for the purpose of preserving form peril the property involved in a common maritime adventure.）。

5.船、貨等財產須有保存的效果。

若共同海損行爲後並無財產受到保存，則可能爲船舶沉沒之全損，無保存後的分擔價值，自也沒有分擔共同海損的問題，此由海商法第 111 條之規定：共同海損以各「被保存財產價值」與共同海損總額之比例，由各利害關係人分擔之。可知，需有保存之事實方有分擔的計算；惟保存財產價值的多寡則非所問。

共同海損起源早於海上保險，在海上保險尚未問世之前，共同海損的分攤及補償方法就已存在，故其成立條件與分攤制度並不因共同航程之關係人是否有投保海上保險而有所改變，此海事制度與海上保險契約乃是兩獨立制度。惟在海上運送過程中，貨主、船東爲求貨物與船舶的安全，往往爲其財產或運送責任投保海上保險，當海上事故發生時，可將損失轉移給保險人承擔，以確保自身財務經營的安全。所以本來跟海上保險是沒有任何關係，但因爲海上保險契約中，已將承保危險所引起的共同海損損失，納入保險理賠範圍，所以兩者間才會產生關聯。依 MIA,1906 規定共同海損損失概念圖如圖 9-4。

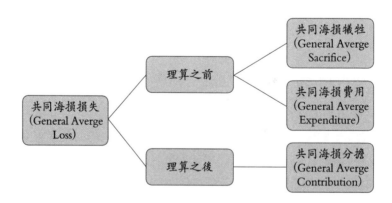

圖 9-4　共同海損損失概念圖

資料來源：作者自繪

1.共同海損犧牲（General Average Sacrifice）

指為了船、貨共同安全或順利完成航程而犧牲掉的財物，在1994與2004年約克安特衛普規則有關共同海損犧牲的規定如表9-3。在我國海商法則於第113條分別規定船舶、貨物及運費之共同海損犧牲之補償額規定，籠統涵蓋共同海損犧牲。

表 9-3　約克安特衛普規則共同海損犧牲規定表

1994 及 2004 年 約克安特衛普規則	共同海損犧牲項目
Rule 1	貨物投棄（Jettison of Cargo）
Rule 2	為共同安全的財產犧牲 （Loss or Damage by Sacrifices for the Common Safety）
Rule 3	撲滅船舶上的火災（Extinguishing Fire on ship board）
Rule 4	切除殘餘物（Cutting away Wreck）
Rule 5	故意擱淺（Voluntary Stranding）
Rule 7	為浮起船舶造成之機器及鍋爐的毀損 （Damage to Machinery and Boilers）
Rule 8	減輕擱淺船舶重量的費用及損失（Expenses lightening a Ship when Ashore, and Consequent Damage）
Rule 9	使用貨物、船舶上的材料、給養品供作燃料 （Cargo, Ship's Materials and Stores Used for Fuel）
Rule 12	卸貨造成之貨損（Damage to Cargo in Discharging, etc.）

資料來源：作者整理

2.共同海損費用（General Average expenditure）

指為了船、貨共同安全或順利完成航程而支出的額外費用。在1994與2004年約克安特衛普規則有關共同海損犧牲的規定如表9-4。在我國海商法則於第114條分別規定了避難港費用，進出避難港期間，船員薪津、給養及其他費用，墊付資金之佣金，共同海損損失額的利息以及替代費用等五種共同海損費用。

表 9-4　約克安特衛普規則共同海損費用規定表

共同海損費用項目	1994 年約克安特衛普規則	2004 年約克安特衛普規則	2004 年對 1994 年版之修改說明
替代費用（Additional Expense; Substituted Expense）	Rule F	Rule F	無修改
救助報酬（Salvage Remuneration）	Rule 6	Rule 6	僅於若救助報酬係由一關係人（如船東）代其他關係人（如貨主）支付者，才將救助報酬列入共同海損之計算。
避難港費用（Expenses at Port of Refuge etc.）	Rule 10	Rule 10	無修改
進出避難港期間，船員薪津，給養及其他費用（Wages and Maintenance of Crew and other expenses bearing up for and in a Port of Refuge etc.）	Rule 11	Rule 11	船舶在避難港停留期間的船員工資和給養，不再認入共同海損。
臨時修繕（Temporary Repairs）	Rule 14	Rule 14	以在裝貨港、停靠港或避難港進行臨時修理的費用，與最終進行永久修理的費用合計，超過若在裝貨港、停靠港或避難港進行永久修理所需費用的差額為限。
墊付資金之佣金（Provision of Funds）	Rule 20	————	刪除船東墊付共同海損費用之 2% 佣金
共同海損損失額之利息（Interest on Losses made good in General Average）	Rule 21	Rule 21	取消共同海損損失補償利息之固定利率，改採用浮動利率計算利息。

資料來源：整理自張桂華，《我國海商法共同海損率之再修正芻議——以約克安特衛普規則為中心》，頁 23-23。

3.共同海損分擔（general average contribution）。

所有共同海損事件中之相關利益人應該分擔的數額即為共同海損分擔，實務上通常以「共同海損分攤」金額表示，以避免與海商法第

112條之「共同海損分攤價值（general average contributory value）」混淆。

　　共同海損分攤額之計算原則上，乃是以共同海損犧牲及共同海損費用依據各利害關係團體的共同海損分攤價值所計算出，至於共同海損分攤價值的認定，則依以各財產於航程終止時地或放棄共同航程時地之實際淨值加上共同海損補償額（made good）；也就是航程終止時之被保存財產價值加上共同海損犧牲的補償額，海商法第112條所規定的概念即為此。三個名詞間之關係詳見於海商法第111條，可以下列公式表示：

$$\frac{\text{共同海損損失（犧牲＋費用）}}{\text{船舶分攤價值＋貨物分攤價值＋運費分攤價值＋}\\ \text{其他財物分攤價值}} = \text{共同海損分攤比例（R）}$$

R × 貨物分攤價值　　＝　貨物分攤額
R × 船舶分攤價值　　＝　船舶分攤額
R × 運費分攤價值　　＝　運費分攤額
R × 其他財物分攤價值　＝　其他財產分攤額

貨物分攤額＋船舶分攤額＋運費分攤額＋其他財產分攤額＝共同海損損失

資料來源：徐當仁、曾文瑞，初學者海上保險基礎理論與實務，頁 IV-8。

二、共同海損與海上保險

　　保險契約在其承保原則下，賠償被保險人之共同海損犧牲、費用及分攤。換言之，發生共同海損後，在不同之保險契約下，不同的保險人將承擔不同被保險人因共同海損所致之犧牲，額外之費用，以及將來共同之海損分攤之理賠責任。保險人不僅承保對共同海損之犧牲、費用和分攤，在貨物保險之理賠實務上，還常代墊共同海損保證金（General Average Deposit）或簽發擔保函（General Average Guarantee），並代表被保險人處理共同海損理算事宜，使得原應由船、貨和運費各方之間進行之共同海損理算，經由保險契約及代位求償之法理，已經轉變成由船舶保險人與貨物保險人之間進行共同海損理算，保險人對被保險人之理賠正式結案，則需到共同海損理算結束後才完成。就保險理論而言，保險人賠付共同海損損失之二大基本原則如下：

1.必須是保險契約所承保之危險造成之共同海損損失。

保險人理賠時通常是依主力近因原則確認是否爲保險責任，共同海損損失的理賠自也不例外。若是因承保事故所引起的共同海損，保險人就有義務賠償相關的共同海損損失，故主力近之判斷後若非承保事故所引起的共同海損，則保險人並無賠償的義務。如在英國海上保險法第 66 條第 6 項規定，不在承保範圍之事故所造成的共同海損，保險人並無賠償共同海損失及分攤的責任。

2.共同海損分攤之理賠須受不足額保險（Under Insurance）之限制。

英國海上保險法第 73 條規定第 1 項規定，保險人對於已付或應付之共同海損分攤，若負責分攤的保險標的物，係以全部分攤價值投保，則以分攤價值的全數賠償；但如果並非以全部分攤價值投保，則保險人所賠付之金額，則需按不足額比例賠償。故在賠付與共同海損分攤時，如果被保險人的分攤價值（Contributory Value）低於保險金額時，則爲不足額保險，於理賠時應適用不足額保險的「比例分攤」原則。

在貨物保險中當船東宣布共同海損後，被保險人可能發生共同海損犧牲及共同海損分攤。但就貨主而言，不會有共同海損費用存在。故依保險契約條款的約定，共同海損損失可以分成二種情況獲得補償：

1.共同海損犧牲

被保險人發生共同海損犧牲時，因犧牲爲財產之直接毀損，原即屬於保險人的承保範圍，故可以直接自保險人處獲得賠償，保險人於賠償共同海損犧牲後，再行使代位求償權（subrogation right）向其他應負責分擔之共同冒險的關係人，要求支付共同海損分攤。MIA,1906第66條第4款後段規定："in the case of a general average sacrifice, he may recover from the insurer in respect of the whole loss without having enforced his right of contribution from the other parties to contribute."共同海損實務中其實乃是向共同海損基金（General Average Fund）請求分攤。故共同海損犧牲，保險人應先賠償被保險人全數的損失，無須由被保險人先向其他受益關係人分擔，其索賠程序與單獨海損之賠償是完全相同的。

2.共同海損分攤

被保險人如並未於共同海損行為中遭受損害，反而因其他共同航程關係人的犧牲而保全其財產安全，則在此情況下被保險人有必須分擔共同海損分攤的責任，依MIA, 1906第66條第5規定（Subject to any express provision in the policy, where the assured has paid, or is liable to paid, a general average contribution in respect of the subject insured, he may recover therefore from the insurer.）。

由此條文可知，除保單另有明示外，保險人需依保險契約規定，賠償被保險人已支付（has paid）或有責任（liable to paid）承擔的共同海損分攤。所謂已支付乃指共同海損發生後，被保險人已先提供共同海損保證金（General Average Deposit）者即為已付。如共同海損實務中，船東將會先向貨主收取共同海損保證金，確保將來收取共同海損分攤之債權，於收到共同海損保證金後，將簽發共同海損保證金收據，註明所收取之保證金金額及其占共同海損分攤價值之預估比例，貨主收到收據後連同保險單交給保險人請求歸墊。倘若尚未繳付保證金，至理算報告做出後，被保險人應分攤的金額即為有責任之應付金額。故依本條款文義無論為已付或應付金額，保險人均有賠償被保險人共同海損分攤之責。

在貨櫃運送貨物的多樣化及關係人繁多的特性下，共同海損分攤之計算並非短時間內可以完成，故通常於貨主提貨時，保險人會簽發共同海損擔保函（General Average Guarantee）予船東，共同海損擔保函並無固定格式，但一般而言擔保函中會承諾二項義務：一為保險人將來願意給付共同海損，救助費用或其他特別費用的分攤額，以代替立即交付保證金；其二為承諾將提供理算師所要求的貨物有關的詳細資料、價值及貨物狀況。

再根據 MIA,1906 第 73 條規定，保險人對於共同海損分攤的賠償，乃係以保險標的物之分攤價值與保險金額兩者之比例為標準。條文中規定計算保險金額時，若有單獨海損應自原保險金額中扣除，因為單獨海損本來就是保險人應賠償的範圍，將之扣除後才係實際上保險人應對共同海損負責賠償的上限金額，如此對保險人而言方屬公平。故若保險金額大於分攤價值，保險人即按被保險人應支付的共同海損分攤全數賠償；然若保險金額小於分攤價值，則為不足額保險，保險人僅能依照分攤價值與保險金額之比例與全數應支付的共同海損分攤相乘積賠償。

在 ICC,2009 第 2 條規定中，保險人承保為了避免損失發生或擴大，依據運送契約規定或政府法律及習慣，所成立的共同海損費用與救助費用，保險人願付賠償之責，且依條文規定，除了因保險契約中之第 4 至第 7 條除外不保危險所產生的共同海損犧牲與費用外，保險人皆有賠償責任。此條文與 MIA,1906 第 66 條第 6 項之規定，保險人對於共同海損僅賠償承保危險所生者，在理賠邏輯上並不相同。貨物保險條款相較於英國海上保險法規定，保險人的賠償責任相對較為沉重，然因為英國海上保險法並不反對貨物保險條款中，有不同的規定，故應將其視為與英國海上保險法不同的特別約定，關於共同海損之理賠應優先適用貨物保險條款的規定。

故保險理賠時，貨物保險條款(B)及(C)係採列舉式承保，其承保共同海損的概念與英國海上保險法相同。因此，只要不在承保範圍內的危險事故造成的共同海損損失，保險人自不負保險賠償之責；而若是除外不保事故造成的共同海損損失也不理賠，自無疑義。然而貨物保險條款(A)因是採概括式承保，故理論而言，發生共同海損的原因只要不是除外之危險，保險人均應賠償其共同海損犧牲或共同海損分攤。再根據 MIA,19062 第 66 條第 6 項規定前語「除非保險契約另有明示規定外（In the absence of express stipulation）」，可知英國海上保險法雖規定僅賠償承保範圍內的共同海損損失，但基於契約自由，亦同意保險契約有不同之規定，故貨物保險條款(A)即為一典型與其不同的規定。整體而言，貨物保險條款(A)之規定與英國海上保險法比較下，保險人的賠償責任較為沉重，然而我國實務上均採用協會貨物保險條款，故應將此條款視為與英國海上保險法不同的特別約定，只要共同海損發生的原因，不是第 4 條至第 7 條之除外不保危險所引起，保險人皆須負擔共同海損損失的賠償責任。

　　ICC,2009 第 2 條有關共同海損的賠償，可說是 MIA,1906 第 66 條之補充，明確規定共同海損理算應適用的法律。故在理算之依據規定方面，發生共同海損時，貨主（被保險人）對於共同海損之理算並無法控制，保險人明文接受依照運送契約規定，或國際實務慣例之共同海損理算，賠償貨主（被保險人）應負擔的共同海損犧牲，以及共同海損分攤及救助費用分攤。保險契約中載明共同海損依運送契約規定，或政府法律或相關慣例理算，此條款一般稱為「外國理算條款（The Foreign Adjustment Clause）」。該條款的主要用意乃在於，當此條款訂定於保險契約時，表示保險人同意共同海損的理算依照外國之法律與慣例，保險人的責任自應受外國理算條款之拘束。實務上，運送人會在載貨證券中明訂發生共同海損時的理算依據及適用，一般而言，乃為約克安特衛普規則，然若沒有明文規定，則依據航成終止地的法律理算。

三、海難救助與海上保險

ICC,2009 第 2 條的內容除了保險人對共同海損的賠償外，另有救助費用的賠償規定，其實海難救助與共同海損一樣都屬於海事制度問題，不論有無保險契約存在，若海難因救助而保存財產，受救助者都應該給付救助報酬給施救者（對受救助者而言則稱之爲救助費用），而因爲 ICC,2009 第 2 條承保了貨主應負擔之救助費用，故與海上保險產生了關聯。救助費用根據 MIA,1906 第 65 條之規定爲：

1. Subject to any express provision in the policy, salvage charges incurred in preventing a loss by perils insured against may be recovered as a loss by those perils.
2. "Salvage charges" means the charges recoverable under maritime law by a salvor independently of contract. They do not include the expenses of services in the nature of salvage rendered by the assured or his agents, or any person employed for hire by them, for the purpose of averting a peril insured against. Such expenses, where properly incurred, may be recovered as particular charges or as a general average loss, according to the circumstal1ces under which they were incurred.

由 MIA,1906 第 65 條可知救助費用係指獨立於契約以外之救助人，依海事法規定所能獲得賠償的費用。如我國海商法第 103 條規定：「對於船舶或船舶上財物施以救助而有效果者，得按其效果請求相當之報酬。」即爲典型海事法規定下的救助費用。但若施救行爲後未能成果挽救財貨，則依條文文義施救者就不能請求報酬，即是「無效果即無報酬（no cure no pay）」原則。英國海上保險法所規定的救助費用之認定並不包括被保險人或其代理人（agent）或受僱人（employ），爲了避免保險單所承保的危險所發生屬於救助性質的費用。因為若是被保險自己或其代理人、受僱人等所發生之避免損害發生的相關費用，將視情況而歸類區分為單獨費用或共同海損。

　　海洋環境污染防止觀念日益高漲，因為救助報酬的計算是以救助勞務終了後財產交付時地之價值（property saved which attaches at the time and place where the salvage services terminate）為基準，再考慮施救成本、施救難易程度等因素決定救助報酬的百分比，故殘餘價值愈低，救助報酬就會愈低。所以，施救人面對油輪或化學船等遭遇海難時，不僅考量施救困難與成本，而其殘餘獲救價值過低，恐怕施救行為後之報酬將不符成本，而不想進行救助造成海洋環境的污染，被避免海洋環境污染，1989年海難救助公約乃採納 Lloyd's Open Form of Salvage Agreement（1980）中有關海洋環境污染海上救助的觀念，受救助船若為油輪或載有危險易污染品之輪船，則若施救人的施救行為可以避免發生環境污染，或對環境保護有所幫助貢獻者，根據1989年海難救助公約第13條第1項b款對於法定救助報酬之考量基準中，將能避免發生環境污染的救助行為，可以視其技能與努力（the skill and efforts）請求救助報酬，如此規定當可較無環境損害之虞的單純救助船、貨之報酬為高；並再於第14條規定即使救助不成功，但對環境的損害有防止或者減輕時，施救人亦可以申請特別補償（Special Compensation）以補償該救助作業所發生的費用，以其所支付之費用30%為標準，惟亦可視當時情況將特別補償提高至實際費用的100%，此即「無效果也可能有報酬」的觀念原則。條文如下：

International Convention on Salvage 1989　Article 14: Special compensation

1. If the salvor has carried out salvage operations in respect of vessel which by itself or its cargo threatened damage to the environment and has failed to earn a reward under Article 13 at least equivalent

to the special compensation assessable in accordance with this Article, he shall be entitled to special compensation from the owner of that vessel equivalent to his expenses as herein defined.

2. If in the circumstances set out in paragraph 1, the salvor by his salvage operations has prevented or minimized damage to the environment, the special compensation payable by the owner to the salvor under paragraph 1 may be increased up to a maximum of 30% of the expenses incurred by the salvor. However, the Tribunal, if it deems it fair and just to do so and bearing in mind the relevant criteria set out in Article 13 paragraph 1, may increase such special compensation further, but in no event shall the total increase be more than 100% of the expenses incurred by the salvor."

我國海商法第 103 條第 2 項規定：「施救人所施救之船舶或船舶上貨物，有損環境之虞者，施救人得向船舶所有人請求與實際支出費用同額之報酬；其救助行為對於船舶或船舶上貨物所造成環境之損害已有效防止或減輕者，得向船舶所有人請求與實際支出費用同額或不超過其費用一倍之報酬。」即為與 1989 年海難救助公約相類似之規定。將海商法第 103 條有關救助費用之邏輯概念如圖 9–5 所示。

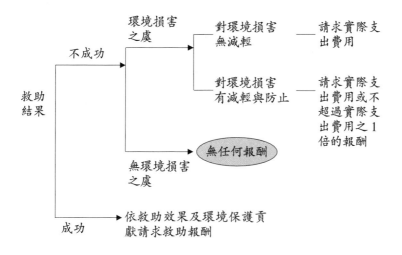

圖 9-5　海商法第 103 條救助報酬概念圖
資料來源：作者自繪

　　就 ICC,2009 第 2 條而言，不論是基於海商法所產生的救助費用還是基於救助契約所產生的救助費用，都應屬於條款的承保範圍。海商法第 103 條應再注意的地方，有關救助報酬負擔之人於第 1 項是「船舶」及「船舶上的財物」（即貨物等），但第 2 項有關環境污染救助時，則僅僅只有規定為「船舶所有人」。然而，實務上在船舶與貨物都共同獲救的情形下，按照救助公約或救助契約的規定或約定，船舶並沒有幫貨主代付救助報酬的義務，因此，施助人必須分別向船東與貨主收取救助報酬。所以若海難事故發生後船東宣布共同海損，貨主在處理完與救助人之間的救助擔保（Salvage security）之後，還要再提供給船東共同海損擔保（General Average security），此時就依 ICC,2009 第 2 條之規定由保險人簽具救助擔保函及共同海損擔保函給運送人。

　　基於 1994 年約克安特衛普規則第 6 條 a 項前段之規定，救助報酬的產生，只要是為保全航行中財產的共同安全，不論是基於契約或其他方式（under contract or otherwise），均可認為共同海損費用，但 2004 年約克安特衛普規則則除了船東代墊的救助費用外，其餘均不納入共同海損費用理算。1989 年海難救助公約第 13 條第 1 項 b 款所額外增加之救助報酬，可以列入共同海損費用的計算，但是依第 14 條所可請求之特別補償則不能列入共同海損。綜上，一旦宣布共同海損後，於 1994 年約克安特衛普規則下救助報酬將成為共同海損費用的一種，透過共同海損的理算，貨主所支付的共同海損分擔額中將會分攤到一部分救助費用，當然最後也就轉嫁到貨物保險人承擔了。

第三節　雙方過失碰撞責任

ICC,2009 為貨物保險條款，所承保的保險標的原則上應只有「貨物」，也就是說所有可以運送的有形物品，不論是固態或液態如機器設備、化學品、油品等都可以成為保險標的。但本條款卻極為特殊，所承保的是被保險人（貨主），基於運送契約下的雙方過失碰撞責任條款，對船東應負責的賠償責任，所以嚴格而言，乃是一責任保險條款。ICC,2009 第 3 條在(A)、(B)及(C)條款都是相同的規定，條文如表 9–5。

表 9-5　ICC,2009(A)、(B)及(C)第3條

條款	內容
Both to Blame Collision Clause	3. This insurance indemnifies the Assured, in respect of any risk insured herein, against liability incurred under any Both to Blame Collision Clause in the contract of carriage. In the event of any claim by carriers under the said Clause, the Assured agree to notify the insurers who shall have the right, at their own cost and expense, to defend the Assured against such claim.
	3. 本保險賠償於承保的危險下，被保險人依運送契約之任何「雙方過失碰撞條款」下所發生的責任。當運送人依據該條款要求賠償時，被保險人通知保險人後，保險人得以自己的成本或費用，為被保險人對該求償抗辯。

資料來源：作者整理

一、運送契約下的雙方過失碰撞

　　所謂船舶碰撞，通說是指兩艘以上船舶，於水面爲直接或間接的接觸，而致損害之謂[2]。就我國「海商法」規定，船舶碰撞乃指船舶在海上或者與海相通的可航水域發生接觸造成損害的事故。觀其要旨爲碰撞須發生在海上或與海相通的可航水域。蓋海商法上之船舶碰撞雖無地點的限制，但仍需須在海洋或與海相通之河川、湖泊上，此由海商法第 1 條「本法稱船舶者，謂在海上航行，或在與海相通之水面或水中航行之船舶。」及第 94 條規定「船舶之碰撞，不論發生於何地，皆依本章之規定處理」可知[3]。

　　實務上，當船舶發生碰撞發生後，在求償之前首先必須先判定碰撞發生的原因以及雙方船舶的過失比例。雙方當事人再依對方的過失比例求償自己船舶的損害，如 1910 年船舶碰撞國際公約

---

[2] 曾國雄、徐當仁，《海商法》（下）〈海上危險與海上保險〉，頁 253。
[3] 張慈民，《船舶碰撞責任與保險理賠之研究》，頁 7。

（International Convention for the Unification of Certain Rules of Law in regard to Collison, 1910）第4條第1項規定 "If two or more vessels are in fault the liability of each vessel is in proportion to the degree of the faults respectively committed. Provided that if having regard to the circumstances, it is not possible to establish the degree of the respective faults, or if it appears that the faults are equal, the liability is apportioned equally." 由條文可知，當船舶碰撞後雙方責任碰撞所造成之物的傷害，乃是各按自己的過失比例承擔損害賠償責任，若不能判定過失程度時，則平均負其責任，即所謂交叉責任（cross liability）。此規定在我國海商法第97條規定：「碰撞之各船舶有共同過失時，各依其過失程度之比例負其責任，不能判定其過失之輕重時，各方平均負其責任。」為相同概念規定。當然，若只有一方之過失則，過失人應負全部賠償責任，若為不可抗力的原因，則各自承擔自己之損失，在我國海商法第95條及第96條均有明文，自不待言。

然當船舶碰撞後除可能造成兩造船舶的損害外，雙方船舶上所裝載的貨物當然也有可能會發生毀損；而按海商法的規定，受損的貨物所有權人若向裝載貨物的船舶求償，該承運的運送人將會依海商法第69條第1款規定或海牙規則第4條第2項(a)款之規定主張法定免責[4]。惟此款規定在2010年生效的鹿特丹規則（國際海上或部分海上貨物運送契約；Convention on Contract for the International Carriage of Goods Wholly or Party by Sea）中已將其刪除，本船之運送人欲以航行過失之法定免責機會將會減少，極有可能僅賠償單位責任限制部分。

---

[4] 海商法第69條第一款：因下列事由所發生之毀損或減失，運送人或船舶所有人不負賠償責任：一、船長、海員、引水人或運送人之受僱人，於航行或管理船舶之行為而有過失。海牙規則第4條第2項(a)款：Neither the carrier nor the ship shall be responsible for loss or damage arising or resulting from: (a) act, neglect, or default of the master, mariner, pilot, or the servants of the carrier in the navigation or in the management of the ship;

　　不論運送人主張免責，或者主張單位責任限制賠償，貨主則再將不足部分向對方船運送人依侵權行為請求賠償，對方船舶的運送人依1910 年船舶碰撞國際公約第 4 條第 1 項或商法第 97 條之規定，必須賠償給貨主的損失。在此結果下，對方的船舶運送人除了將對船舶損害求償外，再加上賠償給貨主的損失（以其他費用名義），依過失比例向承運該貨物的運送人求償，故使得原可主張法定免責的運送人將「間接」負擔貨物的損害。在此情況下，運送人為了貫徹原可主張的法定免責利益規定，乃在運送契約上規定「雙方過失碰撞條款」（Both to Blame Collision Clause），該條文大意是指當船長碰撞後，因雙方過失之交叉求償後，若遇到被對方船舶求償關於「本船」貨物的損失責任時，貨主承諾「補償」運送人因此而發生的賠償損失[5]。此時貨主不但損失了貨物，還要承擔運送人基於運送契約的雙方過失碰撞條款的求償責任。

　　舉例說明依雙方過失碰撞責任條款，若有 A、B 兩船發生碰撞，A、B 兩船之過失比例分別為 80% 及 20%，若 A 船的損失 2,000 萬，

---

[5] Both to Blame Collision Clause：If the （carrying） Ship comes into collision with another ship as a result of the negligence of the other ship and any act, negligence or default in the navigation or the management of the carrying Ship, the Merchant undertakes to pay the Carrier or, where the Carrier is not the owner and in possession of the carrying Ship, to pay to the Carrier as trustee for the owner and/or demise charterer of the carrying Ship, a sum sufficient to indemnify the Carrier and/or the owner and/or demise charterer of the carrying Ship against all loss or liability to the other or non-carrying ship or her owners insofar as such loss or liability represents loss of or damage to, or any claim whatsoever of the Merchant, paid or payable by the other or non-carrying ship or her owners to the Merchant and set-off, recouped or recovered by the other or non-carrying ship or her owners as part of their claim against the carrying ship or her owner or demise charterer or the Carrier. The foregoing provisions shall also apply where the owners, operators, or those in charge of any ship or ships or objects, other than, or in addition to, the colliding ships or objects, are at fault any ship or ships or objects, other than, or in addition to, the colliding ships or objects, are at fault in respect to a collision, contact, stranding or other accident. 邱展發，《海運提單實務》，頁 282，財團法人張榮發基金會。

A 船所承運的的貨物損失（貨主丙）120 萬，B 船的損失 1,276 萬。A 船貨物的貨主丙，因法定免責事由，無法向 A 船之運送人求償，但可向 B 船運送人以侵權行為求償其損失 120 萬 × 20%（B 船之過失比例）= 24 萬。B 船於賠付貨主丙後，將此 24 萬賠償金列為其他損失連同自己船舶的損失向 A 船運送人求償（1,276 萬+24 萬）× 80%（A 船之過失比例）= 1,040 萬。

故在此 1,040 萬中有 19.2 萬（24 萬×80%）為 A 船運送人間接賠付給貨主丙，致使 A 船完全無法享有法定免責事由的利益，乃在運送契約訂立雙方過失碰撞條款，依此條款要求丙應對 A 船運送人負責人賠償 19.2 萬元。船舶碰撞後關係人之損失求償如圖 9-6。

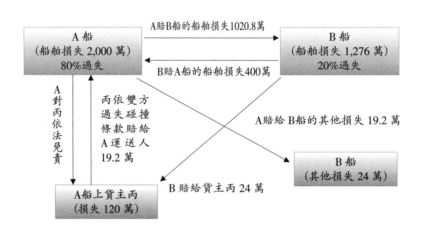

圖 9-6　雙方過失碰撞條款下損失分擔圖

資料來源：作者自繪

由上敘述可知，1910 年船舶碰撞國際公約對船舶碰撞之共同侵權行為人對財物之損害為各船舶依其過失程度之比例負「分別責任」，而非「連帶損害賠償」責任。然而美國法中並未如 1910 年關於船舶碰撞國際公約之「分別責任」，而是以過失比例各 50%，或以連帶損害賠償責任的概念賠償全額損失。故當本船與他船碰撞而雙方均有過失時，依美國法之概念，本船對船上所運送貨物因碰撞後造成損害，雖因「船員航行上之過失」而得以免除責任，但對方船對本船運送之貨物之損害，則因負「連帶損害賠償」責任關係，需賠償本船運送之貨物之全部損害。他船於賠償本船運送之貨物之全部損害後，其與本船間仍得依共同侵權行為人「連帶損害賠償」責任之「比例分擔」原則，請求本船賠償其原應依其過失應分擔之部分責任。造成本船對本船運送之貨物之損害原得免責之部分卻需因此賠付予他船所有人。故國際海運界乃藉由海上貨物運送契約之「雙方過失碰撞條款」，要求當本船之貨物所有人基於共同侵權行為人「連帶損害賠償」責任之原則，要求他船負全責時，致使本船對其運送貨物之損害，需對他船負共同侵權行為之分擔責任時，貨物所有人應負責補償其因此所產生的損失。

綜言之，「雙方過失碰撞條款」之所以受到國際海運業廣泛使用，係因海上貨物運送人於訂立海上貨物運送契約時，無法確知何時會適用美國法，或其他國家法律與美國法一樣並未採取 1910 年關於船舶碰撞國際公約之情形，故為保險起見均於其海上貨物運送契約預先置入「雙方過失碰撞條款」。[6]

二、ICC, 2009 雙方過失碰撞條款

當船舶發生碰撞後，由上例可知貨主丙的損失原為 120 萬元，雖依侵權行之損害向 B 船求償得 24 萬元，但卻又被 A 船運送人依運送契約的雙方過失碰撞條款賠償 19.2 萬元；換言之，貨主丙最後的補償只剩下 4.8 萬元，也就是 24 萬元的 20%。惟若貨主丙投保海上貨物保險，則除了原 120 萬元可依保險契約獲償外，經由保險代位程序及交叉求償後，A 船運送人仍然會向貨主丙依求依運送契約的雙方過失碰撞條款求償 19.2 萬，為使貨主不會因此受到不利益，貨物的保

---

[6] 黃正宗，《我國我國海商法船舶碰撞法律規範研究》，頁 4-12。

險人乃在 ICC 1982 Clause 3 中明訂，這種情形下貨主（即被保險人）所應補償給運送人的損害，則依條款之承保規定轉由保險人負擔。同時，被保險人（貨主丙）遭受求償時應通知保險人，而保險人則在認爲有必要的情況下，會以自己的費用（at their own cost and expense）對運送人提出抗辯（defend the Assured against such claim）。

ICC,2009 第 3 條相較於 ICC,1982 年版，除了條款用字簡明實務化外，如將 "contract of affreightment" 變更爲 "contract of carriage" 、 "underwriters" 改爲易懂的 "insurers" ，以及將 "shipowners" 改以 "carriers 外，將 1982 年版的「extended to indemnify（額外補償）」概念，直接刪除 "extended" 一詞，使條款文義解釋時將變成是保險承保的基本損失一種情況，而非額外補償，但不論如何 ICC,2009 之更改並不影響保險人的責任。

ICC, 2009 於本條新增 "in respect of any risk insured herein, against liability incurred under any Both to Blame Collision Clause in the contract of carriage." 主要是爲澄清說明本條款的事故原因必須與第 1 條承保之危險有因果關係連結；換言之，若非承保事故所造成的船舶碰撞，被保險仍然無法依第 3 條獲得賠償。又 ICC,2009 將 1982 年版的「such proportion of liability（碰撞責任百分比）」改爲「liability incurred under any Both to Blame Collision Clause in the contract of carriage（基於任何運送契約內之雙方過失碰撞責任條款產生的責任）」，依 ICC,2009 第 3 條的文義當指在任何（any）運送契約下的雙方過失碰撞責任條款，均爲 ICC,2009 第 3 條所認可代爲貨主補償的條款。

第十章 •••••••••

ICC,2009 之除外條款

第一節　一般除外條款

　　ICC,2009 第 4 條至第 7 條，一共 4 個條款是屬於保險人的除外責任。第 4 條在 ICC,1982 稱之爲一般除外條款（General Exclusion Clause），但在 ICC,2009 中則將條款名稱刪除，內容分別於 4.3、4.5、4.6 及 4.7 等款稍有修改，但整體除外條款規定事項並無結構性改變。ICC,2009（A）、（B）及（C）三組條款除（B）與（C）條款的第 4.7 款之規定（A）條款沒有以外，其餘內容均相同。ICC,2009 第 4 條規定如表 10–1。

表 10-1　ICC,2009 第 4 條

條款	內容
ICC,2009 (A)	4. In no case shall this insurance cover 　4.1 loss damage or expense attributable to wilful misconduct of the Assured 　4.2 ordinary leakage, ordinary loss in weight or volume, or ordinary wear and tear of the subject-matter insured 　4.3 loss damage or expense caused by insufficiency or unsuitability of packing or preparation of the subject-matter insured to withstand the ordinary incidents of the insured transit where such packing or preparation is carried out by the Assured or their employees or prior to the attachment of this insurance (for the purpose of these Clauses "packing" shall be deemed to include stowage in a container and "employees" shall not include independent contractors) 　4.4 loss damage or expense caused by inherent vice or nature of the subject-matter insured 　4.5 loss damage or expense caused by delay, even though the delay be caused by a risk insured against (except expenses payable under Clause 2 above) 　4.6 loss damage or expense caused by insolvency or financial default of the owners managers charterers or operators of the vessel where, at the time of loading of the subject-matter insured on board the vessel, the Assured are aware, or in the ordinary course of business should be aware, that such insolvency or financial default could prevent the normal prosecution of the voyage This exclusion shall not apply where the contract of insurance has been assigned to the party claiming hereunder who has bought or agreed to buy the subject-matter insured in good faith under a binding contract 　4.7 loss damage or expense directly or indirectly caused by or arising from the use of any weapon or device employing atomic or nuclear fission and/or fusion or other like reaction or radioactive force or matter.
	4. 本保險不承保下列事項： 　4.1 歸因於被保險人的故意行為所致之毀損滅失或費用。 　4.2 保險標的物之正常的滲漏、正常的失重或失量，或正常的破損。 　4.3 因保險標的物的不充足或不適當包裝或整備，以足夠承受正常運輸過程中之意外事故，所引起的毀損滅失或費用。此種包裝或整備為由被保險人或其受僱人於保險開始生效前已完成為限（貨櫃內貨物的積載亦視為是本款所謂的包裝，受僱人不包括獨立契約人）。

	4.4 因保險標的物之固有瑕疵或本質所引起的損害或費用。 4.5 因延遲所致的損害或費用，即使該延遲之發生是由承保之危險所致者亦同（依上述第2條可以賠付的費用不在此限）。 4.6 當保險標的物裝載於船舶當時，若被保險人已知或依正常業務程序被保險人應知道，該破產或債務糾紛將會妨礙正常航行時，則由於船舶所有人、經理人、租船人或船舶營運人之破產或債務糾紛所直接造成之毀損滅失或費用。 本款不適用於保險契約已經轉讓給已購買或已同意購買本保險標的物的善意受讓人求償人。 4.7 任何使用原子反應裝置物，或核子分裂及或融合或其他類似反應，或放射性之武器等直接或間接所造成之毀損滅失或費用。
ICC,2009 (B)、(C)	4.7 deliberate damage to or deliberate destruction of the subject−matter insured or any part thereof by the wrongful act of any person or persons
	4.7 任何人之不法行為導致保險標的物或任何其他部分的惡意損壞或破壞。

資料來源：作者整理

　　保險契約中除了載明承保範圍外，除外不保事項亦是重要內容。所謂除外不保事項指保險契約中，基於法律、核保、保險經營技術與安全的考量，針對某些特定危險事故、損失及費用類型、財產予以明示於除外不保的條款。換言之，除外不保事項為與承保範圍相反之條款，主要為限制或修正澄清保險人的保險責任，常見者為不保之危險、不保之損失、不保之財產及不保之區域等類別。在英國海上保險法第55條中亦明文規定法定除外不保事項，主要包括被保險人的故意行為（willful misconduct）、遲延（delay）、正常破損（ordinary wear and tear）、正常的滲漏（ordinary leakage and breakage）、保險標的物之固有瑕疵或本質（inherent vice or nature of the subject−matter insured）、蟲蛀鼠咬（rats or vermin）、非海上危險造成的機器損失（any injury to machinery not proximately caused by maritime perils）等。ICC, 2009第4條雖係源自於MIA, 1906第55條的法定規範內容，但因航運現況及環境不同並非所有法定事項皆移入，如在 19 世紀公衛環境不佳，常見蟲蛀鼠咬，尤其碼頭倉庫中更是鼠類四處出沒橫行，肆虐可食用之貨物，也常毀損貨物，故實務上在無法徹底消滅鼠患之下，則視爲經常性且不可避免的損害。然而後期的船舶建造及倉庫的建材均有防阻鼠害之作用，且同時鼠類亦無昔日之猖獗，甚至已不常出現，故並未將其納入貨物保險條款中除外。表 10-2 爲 MIA, 1906 與 ICC, 2009 關於除外不保項目的規定彙整。

表 10-2　MIA,1906 與 ICC,2009 之除外規定比較

除外危險	MIA, 1906	ICC, 2009		
		(A)	(B)	(C)
被保險人之故意行為 （willful misconduct of assured）	55-(2) (a)	4.1	4.1	4.1
正常滲漏（ordinary leakage）	55-(2) (c)	4.2	4.2	4.2
正常破損（ordinary breakage）	55-(2) (c)	–	–	–
正常失重（ordinary loss in weight）	–	4.2	4.2	4.2
正常耗損（ordinary wear and tear）	55-(2) (c)	4.2	4.2	4.2
正常失量（ordinary loss in volume）	–	4.2	4.2	4.2
包裝或整備不當 （improper packing or preparation）	–	4.3	4.3	4.3
貨櫃內之積載不當 （improper stowage in containers）	–	4.3	4.3	4.3
固有瑕疵或本質 （inherent vice or nature）	55-(2) (c)	4.4	4.4	4.4
遲延（delay）	55-(2) (b)	4.5	4.5	4.5
運送人之破產或財務糾紛 （insolvency or financial default）	–	4.6	4.6	4.6
惡意破壞 （any person deliberate damage）	–	–	4.7	4.7
核子武器（nuclear weapons）	–	4.7	4.8	4.8
鼠咬蟲蛀（rats and vermin）	55-(2) (c)	–	–	–
非海上危險造成的機器損壞（any injury to machinery not proximately caused by maritime perils）	55-(2) (c)	–	–	–

資料來源：作者整理自林慧珊，《2009 年協會貨物保險條款增修因素之研究》，頁 82。

　　ICC,2009（A）第4條共列舉了7款不保危險，而（B）及（C）條款第4條則列舉了8款不保危險。條款中有關主力近因原則適用的條款用語分別有"caused by"、"arising from"以及"attributable to"等三種，就保險理賠角度而言，不同的條款用語於保險人理賠時確認損失與意外事故的關係時將有所不同。"arising from"爲起因於某事故之概念，而"caused by"則爲直接因某事故所造成的概念。當保險契約的除外事項以"arising from"某事故時，在一個連續事件中，若其中有一事故是除外危險，保險人只須證明損失是因連續的事故其中之一爲此除外事項時，即可稱之爲損失之發生與此除外事故具因果關係，而主張拒賠。

　　另，保險條款中"caused by"適用嚴格的主力近因原則，指當被保險人請求理賠時，必須舉證其貨物毀損滅失主要係由承保危險所直接造成，而此時保險人必須舉證該貨損並不是由承保危險所直接造成，或是造成貨損原因是屬除外不保事項，方可主張拒賠。就主力近因原則之適用而言，"arising from"之範圍較"caused by"爲廣，故若"arising from"置於除外事故，與"caused by"比較之下，"arising from"對保險人主張拒賠時較爲有利；反之，若"arising from"置於承保範圍之條款內，則相對"caused by"而言，對被保險人的求償有利。

　　至於"attributable to"之概念可稱之爲「合理歸因於某原因」，除外事項以"attributable to"某事故時，如"attributable to willful misconduct of the Assured"，即當事故發生若合理歸因於被保險人的故意行爲，雖該惡意行爲非直接造成損害，保險人依然可以主張不負賠償責任。

ICC,2009 第 4.1 款

條款	譯文
loss damage or expense attributable to willful misconduct of the Assured	歸因於被保險人的故意行為所致之毀損滅失或費用

　　本款在三套條款中規定都相同。被保險人的故意行為在保險學理論中即稱為道德危險（moral hazard），指因為被保險人的不法行為故意使保險事故發生，意圖領取保險賠償。道德危險除了違法外，也破壞了可保危險要件中「損失不確定性」原則，故保險人當然予以除外。本款在 ICC,2009（A）之解釋為保險人的故意行為所造成之損害不賠；換言之，保險人承保被保險人之重大過失與一般過失所致之損失，亦承保被保險人的受僱人或代理人（servants or agents）之故意或過失所致之損失；此與 MIA,1906 第 55 條第 2 項第 (a) 款規定邏輯相同。其規定為 "The insurer is not liable for any loss attributable to the willful misconduct of the assured, but, unless the policy otherwise provides, he is liable for any loss proximately caused by a peril insured against, even though the loss would not have happened but for the misconduct or negligence of the master or crew;"（保險人對被保險人故意行為產生之損害不負責任。但除保險契約另有約定外，對承保危險事故有接近因果關係原因所產生之損失，縱該損失如無船長或船員之惡意行為或過失不致於發生，保險人仍應負責。）

　　故 ICC,2009 之（A）條款對被保險人之使用人或代理人故意產生之損失，原則上，保險人應負責任。

　　但是因為 ICC,2009（B）以及（C）條款是列舉式承保，且在第 4.7 中亦比（A）條款增列了「任何人之不法行為導致保險標的物或任何其他部分的惡意損壞或破壞」，由 4.1 及 4.7 款之規定可知，ICC,2009（B）以及（C）條款卻排除了被保險人之故意及其受僱或代理人（servants or agents）及其他任何人之故意行為產生之損失。因此，被保險人若

投保 ICC,2009（B）或（C）條款，欲排除 4.7 款之除外不保規定，使與 ICC,2009 之（A）條款第 4 條相同時，則必須再附加「協會故意損害條款（Institute Malicious Damage Clause）」，以利萬一除了被保險人之故意行為所造成的貨損可獲得保險人之賠償。

在海上貨物保險中，被保險人除了個人物品（Personal Effects）的託運是自然人外，通常是國際貿易的賣方或者是買方的公司法人，就貿易信譽角度言，都希望貨物如期如數安全抵達，以維商譽或順利進口銷貨，所以道德危險情況較為少見。

2.ICC,2009 第 4.2 款

條款	譯文
ordinary leakage, ordinary loss in weight or volume, or ordinary wear and tear of the subject–matter insured	保險標的物正常的滲漏、正常的失重或失量或正常的破損

本款所列示出不論是液態貨物的滲漏、重量或容量減少，或是貨物本身的自然破損，均以運輸過程中必然發生，如運送過程中因航程緯度高低，溫度自然變化造成液態貨物蒸發（evaporation）致使失量或失重。由於既然是航程中必然（正常）發生的原因，即非不可預料之事故，屬於保險學理中不可保之危險原則，故保險人自可對此正常的滲漏、正常的失重或失量，或正常的破損主張不負保險責任，特在 ICC 條款中明文除外。故理賠時保險公證人丈量實際損失時，必將總損失重量扣減必然發生的正常失量損失，方為被保險人之實際損失。實務上為避免舉證的困擾及爭議，保險人亦經常以自負額概念，做為「正常」失重、失量的標準，如在保險契約中訂立一固定百分比正常耗損門檻，如約定保險標的物的 0.5%以內之量差為正常失量，必須由被保險人自己承擔損失；反之，若超過 0.5%的丈量量差，則視為意外事故所造成，保險人則賠償以總損失重量扣減 0.5%後為實際賠償損失。

3.ICC,2009 第 4.3 款

條款	譯文
loss damage or expense caused by insufficiency or unsuitability of packing or preparation of the subject-matter insured to withstand the ordinary incidents of the insured transit where such packing or preparation is carried out by the Assured or their employees or prior to the attachment of this insurance (for the purpose of these Clauses "packing" shall be deemed to include stowage in a container and "employees" shall not include independent contractors)	因保險標的物的不充足或不適當包裝或整備，使其不足以承受正常運輸過程中的意外事故，所引起的毀損滅失或費用。此種包裝或整備為由被保險人或其受僱人於保險開始生效前已完成為限（貨櫃內貨物的積載亦視為是本款所謂的包裝，受僱人不包括獨立契約人）

　　本款主要規定保險人主張除外損失的原因有兩個部分，一者為保險標的物開始運送前的包裝或整備不當，另一者為貨櫃內堆載不當引起的貨損。長久以來，保險人了解不良的包裝將會提升貨物發生毀損的機會，故要求被保險人至少應有適當的包裝材質、強度可以抵抗搖晃、及正常運送途中的運送危險，但若被保險人未做好適當之損失預防措施，所造成的損失，保險人不負任何賠償責任。條款中所謂"packing"除了貨物本身包裝外，也包括在「貨櫃」的堆載（include stowage in a container）。而"preparation"乃為防止貨物運輸途中之事故發生的運送前整備。"preparation"應考慮整個運送及地理等外部條件，如裝、卸港或轉運港的設施，以及航程中是否需防污、防水、防熱等準備措施及程度；調查收貨地氣候風土，是否屬熱帶或多溼地；若將接續一段長距離之內陸運送，則應加強避震措施等均屬於貨物之整備（preparation）。

　　就貨櫃內積載不當（poor stowage）而言，依條款規定必須符合兩項條件，即以該櫃內堆載是在保險效力開始之前（prior to attachment of this insurance）或由被保險人或其受僱人（employees）所為者，只要其中有一個條件成立，則堆載不當就會被視為是包裝不

足或不當，其因此造成的損失就會被列爲除外不保項目。櫃內積載不當及保險人責任分析詳如表 10-3 所示。

表 10-3　ICC,2009 第 4.3 條櫃內積載不當與保險責任分析表

	保險生效前	保險生效後
被保險人或其受僱人之堆載不當	可視爲積載不當	可視爲積載不當
貨物由其他第三人堆載不當	可視爲積載不當	不可視爲積載不當

資料來源：作者整理

　　而受僱人之概念並不包括獨立契約人（independent contractors），如專門負責併櫃的貨櫃集散站經營業。實務上，貨櫃集散站乃受貨櫃船公司或海運貨物承攬運送業（ocean freight forwarder）的委託而進行拆、併櫃之業務，也不受運送人直接指揮與監督，故爲一獨立契約人角色，更非貨主（被保險人）之受僱人。

4.ICC,2009 第 4.4 款

條款	譯文
loss damage or expense caused by inherent vice or nature of the subject-matter insured	因保險標的物之固有瑕疵或本質所引起的損害或費用

　　固有瑕疵（inherent vice）之除外規定不僅同時出現於 ICC,2009 的 (A)、(B) 及 (C) 條款，也在 MIA,1906 第 55 條規定，以及 1963 年、1982 年的貨物保險條款均有規定。所謂保險標的之固有瑕疵乃指保險標的物本身即已存在損害，而非受外界原因所引起的損害，如二手機器本身即已存在缺陷，或皮革製品在裝船前放置於含水分木板，造成皮革產品含水過多而腐壞。而本質（nature）所引起之損失，概念上與固有瑕疵原因仍有些許不同，若保險標的本身的自然特

性所引起的損害即為本質所引起的損失。如水果常溫下自然腐爛，煤或魚粉自燃（spontaneous combustion）、鋼鐵製品氧化等均屬之。

另，本款所除外者乃是保險標的物因固有瑕疵或本質所直接造成（caused by）的毀損滅失及費用，但若是其他貨物固有瑕疵或本質所引起的保險標的物損失，則保險人仍應負保險賠償之責。

5.ICC,2009 第 4.5 款

條款	譯文
loss damage or expense caused by delay, even though the delay be caused by a risk insured against（except expenses payable under Clause 2 above）	因延遲所致的損害或費用，即使該延遲之發生是由承保之危險所致者亦同（依上述第 2 條可以賠付的費用不在此限）

延遲除外條款除了在 ICC,2009 明定除外不保之外，也是 MIA,1906 所舉例的法定除外事故。實務上造成貨物遲延到達的原因，極大的比例是船舶發生海難事故，或者偏航或者船舶失去航行能力等。惟本款已清楚規定縱使造成遲延的原因是承保危險事故造成，保險人依然不負損害賠償責任；如承運船舶發生碰撞後貨物因安排轉運而遲延到達目的地，該貨物也因此價值貶損，在此情況下，保險人可以第4.5 款的遲延除外拒賠該損失。

保險人將直接因遲延所造成的損失或費用除外之原因，為該損失或費用通常是生命周期短或有市場性的保險標的物，因遲延抵達而造成市場價值喪失，如當季的電子產品，或因進口商因貨物遲延到達而造成違約罰款。因為保險人核保主要是以當時保險標的之價值以及航程來擬訂保險費率，通常不考慮事後違約的問題，故承保當時並未評估此危險因素，且該違約罰款或市場價值的喪失，都存有無法衡量與客觀評估的問題，並不符合可保危險要件之「損失可衡量」原則，故保險人將遲延所造成之損失及費用賠償責任予以除外。

條款最後亦規定，若依 ICC,2009 第 2 條之規定下符合海難救助

或共同海損條件下的費用項目，保險人仍應負保險賠償責任。主要原因乃是該遲延所造成的費用若可以符合救助費用或共同海損費用，則該遲延所造成的費用已轉變成救助費用或共同海損費用，故依保險條款之規定，保險人仍應理賠。

6.ICC,2009 第 4.6 款

條款	譯文
loss damage or expense caused by insolvency or financial default of the owners managers charterers or operators of the vessel where, at the time of loading of the subject-matter insured on board the vessel, the Assured are aware, or in the ordinary course of business should be aware, that such insolvency or financial default could prevent the normal prosecution of the voyage This exclusion shall not apply where the contract of insurance has been assigned to the party claiming hereunder who has bought or agreed to buy the subject-matter insured in good faith under a binding contract	當保險標的物裝載於船舶當時，若被保險人已知或依正常業務程序被保險人應知道，該破產或債務糾紛將會妨礙正常航行時，則由於船舶所有人、經理人、租船人或船舶營運人之破產或債務糾紛所直接造成之毀損滅失或費用。本款不適用於保險契約已經轉讓給已購買或已同意購買本保險標的物的善意受讓人求償人。

　　本款主要將貨主（被保險人）與運送契約有關係的人如船東、管理人、傭船人或營運人等，因財務糾紛所引起保險標的毀損、滅失或費用予以除外。例如早期中東石油輸出國因共同限制石油出口，造成油價飆漲而獲取暴利，而中東又大部分物資不論是民生用品或奢侈品都仰賴國外進口，在消費能力增加情況下，進口物資數量自然也大幅增加，某些營運船東為謀取利益紛紛加入營運行列，但是這些船公司不但素質不好，更因近視短利而非以永續經營的態度營運，故經常造成貨損或積欠港口費用、代理費用等，債權人為求保全債權得以獲償，只好向法院申請扣船強迫船東出面解決。在此情況下，若仍未能順利解決債務問題，即馬上面臨船舶被拍賣，而其上貨載則變成無人

照料或安排轉運的情況，貨主除了自行安排轉運或當地尋求買主售出外，別無他法，因此也造成了損失。惟保險人認為因運送人債務問題造成貨損並非海上意外事故的概念，故予以除外。

本款之規定旨在鼓勵被保險人（貨主）對運送人之選擇須應審慎選擇信譽良好的運送人。由於本款之主力近因概念是採 "caused by" 用語，有別於 ICC,1982 以 "arising from" 的概念，故貨損原因必須是因船舶所有人、經理人、租船人或船舶營運人之破產或債務糾紛所直接造成的毀損滅失或費用，保險人方可主張拒賠。本款所規定的關係人為船舶所有人、經理人、租船人或船舶營運人，文義上並不及於其他的獨立契約人破產或財務糾紛，故如貨櫃集散站、倉庫、內陸拖車運送人的財務糾紛所致之貨物毀損滅失或費用，保險人仍將予以承保。

ICC,2009 於本款對 ICC,1982 做了大幅度的更動，亦即除了主力近因是採 "caused by" 概念，其相對縮限了過去用 "arising from" 保險人之拒賠空間；另也參考 1983 年之協會貨物貿易條款（Institute Commodity Trades Clauses, ICTC, 5/9/83）(A)條款中 4.6 款的觀念，增列了「當保險標的物裝載於船舶當時，若被保險人已知或依正常業務程序被保險人應知道，該破產或債務糾紛將會妨礙正常航行時……」條款文字，主要乃是讓裝船前或當時不知道運送人其相關人有財務問題，且該破產或債務糾紛將會妨礙正常航行的被保險人免於因此條款而遭拒賠的不利情況。

又為了保護善意第三人，條款又增列「本款不適用於保險契約已經轉讓給已購買或已同意購買本保險標的物的善意受讓人求償人」，即凡在保險契約已經轉讓的情況下，或已購買或同意購買保險標的物之善意不知情保險請求權人，其保險權益不受影響。

7.ICC,2009（B）、（C）第 4.7 款

條款	譯文
deliberate damage to or deliberate destruction of the subject–matter insured or any part thereof by the wrongful act of any person or persons	任何人之不法行為導致保險標的物或任何其他部分的惡意損壞或破壞

　　本款首先必須注意的是只有規定在(B)及(C)條款，也就是在(A)條款中並沒有列為除外。在運送實務上貨損發生原因很多，有如天災、過失造成的意外事故、甚至正常的耗損等，由4.1之規定可知若是被保險人之故意行為，保險人一定會以道德危險主張拒賠，但若是非被保險人本人之故意行為造成貨損，由於（A）條款並沒有除外，所以只要不是被保險人本人之故意行為，縱使是其受僱人，保險人仍然應該理賠；至於（B）及（C）條款因4.7之除外規定，任何人的故意破壞行為所造成之貨損，包括被保險人的受僱人、運送人之履行輔助人、獨立契約人或其它第三人保險人都不負賠償責任。再依本款之 "…destruction of the subject–matter insured or any part thereof…" 規定可知，損失範圍包括全損或部分損失都不予賠償。

　　最早的S.G.保單當中承保船長與海員對於船舶所有人或傭船人所為之惡意行為（barratry），然此項規定應無法適用於貨物保險；而1963年版被保險人投保 W.A.或 F.P.A.條款時，會以加保罷工險之方式來附加承保惡意損害之危險，然此危險並未見於1982年及2009年版之罷工險條款當中。實務上，倫敦保險市場為使有此危險需求投保(B)及(C)條款之被保險人得以轉嫁危險，也推出了「malicious damage clause（惡意毀損條款）」，以附加條款方式承保任何人惡意破壞造成之毀損，換言之，被保險人只要加附額外保險費，可將原4.7款之任何人惡意行為毀損之除外危險再附加承保，可謂是對不願意投保(A)條款之被保險人之另一危險管理之策略選擇。內容如下：

1/1/82（FOR USE ONLY WITH THE NEW MARINE POLICY FORM）

Malicious Damage Clause

（For use with Institute Cargo Clause（B）or（C））

In consideration of an additional premium, it is hereby agreed that Clause 4.7 of the Institute Cargo Clauses id deemed to be deleted and further that this insurance covers loss of or damage to the subject–matter insured caused by malicious acts vandalism or sabotage, subject always to the other exclusions contained in this insurance.

8.ICC,2009（A）第 4.7 款，ICC,2009（B）、（C）第 4.8 款

條款	譯文
loss damage or expense directly or indirectly caused by or arising from the use of any weapon or device employing atomic or nuclear fission and/or fusion or other like reaction or radioactive force or matter.	任何使用原子反應裝置物，或核子分裂及或融合或其他類似反應，或放射性之武器等直接或間接所造成之毀損滅失或費用。

　　本款應是所有除外危險中實務上發生最少的情況。1986 年於蘇聯發生車諾比（Chernobyl）核子反應爐事件（nuclear reactor），該事故被認為是歷史上最嚴重的核子電廠事故，也是國際核事件分級表（International Nuclear Event Scale）中唯一的第七級事件，其所釋放出的輻射線劑量是投在廣島的原子彈的 400 倍以上，約造成兩千億美元的損失[1]。核能輻射之損害不僅會損及運送途中的貨物，對於其他儲存中的貨物亦會造成影響。故本款規定將任何使用原子反應裝置物，或核子分裂及或融合或其他類似反應，或放射性武器等直接或間接所造成之保險標的物毀損或發生額外費用予以除外，只要因使用核子或類似武器所產生直接或間接的損害均不在承保範圍之列。

　　本款之所以除外主要也是因為不符合保險學理中可保危險的要

---

[1] 維基百科，http://zh.wikipedia.org/zh–tw。

件，保險危險要件中有一「危險單位之損失不能同時發生」原則，即當意外事故發生時，不能使絕大多數危險單位同時受損，也就是所謂之巨災危險，不僅破壞了保險理論的損失分散概念，也可能是保險人無法承擔該巨災損失而失卻清償能力。故面對巨災危險保險人通常都先予以除外，而在評估危險後，在可行情況下，以附加方式爲有條件承保，如颱風洪水險、地震險等均屬之。因此，本款之原子反應裝置物，或核子分裂及或融合或其他類似反應，或放射性武器等所造成之損失必然是一個巨災損失，故保險人明訂除外不保。

第二節　不適航及不適運條款

不論是船舶不具適航性或載貨工具不具適載性，都有可能造成承運貨物之毀損，因此保險條款中特別將船舶不具適航性或載貨工具不具適載性之保險問題規定於第 5 條。詳如表 10-4。

表 10-4　ICC,2009 第 5 條

條款	譯文
5.1 In no case shall this insurance cover loss damage or expense arising from 　5.1.1 unseaworthiness of vessel or craft or unfitness of vessel or craft for safe carriage of the subject-matter insured, where the Assured are privy to such unseaworthiness or unfitness, at the time the subject-matter insured is loaded therein 　5.1.2 unfitness of container or conveyance for the safe carriage of the subject-matter insured, where loading therein or thereon is carried out prior to attachment of this insurance or be the Assured or their employees and they are privy to such unfitness at the time of loading. 5.2 Exclusion 5.1.1 above shall not apply where the contract of insurance has been assigned to the party claiming hereunder who has bought or agreed to buy the subject-matter insured in good faith under a binding contract. 5.3 The Insurer waive any breach of the implied warranties of seaworthiness of the ship and fitness of the ship to carry the subject-matter insured to destination.	5.1 本保險不承保因下列事故所引起的損害或費用： 　5.1.1 當保險標的裝載時，被保險人明知該載運船舶或駁船不適航，或載運船舶或駁船不適載保險標的。 　5.1.2 被保險人或其受僱人，於保險生效前明知該貨櫃或運輸工具不適載運保險標的而裝載。 5.2 上述 5.1.1 除外規定不適用於該保險契約已經轉讓予已買入或已同意買入此批保險標的物之善意受讓人之索賠。 5.3 保險人放棄任何違反載運船舶應具備適航能力及適載運送保險標的物至目的地之默示擔保。

資料來源：作者整理

1 船舶適航性及適載性之意義

　　所謂船舶適航性是指船舶應具有抵抗正常之自然風浪能力，並於船舶航行中配置適當之設備、海員，輔以合適維持其設備與海員於良

好狀況之方法，以及配置具有航海技術與良好資格之船長等[2]。我國海商法第 62 條第一項規定：「運送人或船舶所有人於發航前及發航時，對於下列事項，應爲必要之注意及措置：一、使船舶有安全航行之能力。二、配置相當海員、設備及供應。三、使貨艙、冷藏室及其他供載貨物部分適合於受載、運送與保存。」

由上述規定可知，船舶之適航性應具備下列能力，分別爲：1.於船舶實體構造上須能抗拒預定航程所可能預見之危險（此爲狹義的船舶適航性定義）；2.配置相當的船長及海員，包括配置適任及充足數額之船員（指運送人或船舶所有人必須證明其對船員之選任以盡相當的注意，並應對其執行職務期間，做適當監督）；3.配置相當之設備及船舶之供應，以及 4.提供具有適載能力的貨艙、冷藏室及其他供載運的部分等能力。

聯合國國際貿易法委員會於 2008 年 12 月 11 日通過，並於 2010年生效之「聯合國全程或者部分海上國際貨物運輸公約（United Nations Convention on Contracts for the International Carriage of Goods Wholly or Partly by Sea），簡稱鹿特丹公約。」該公約第 14 條規定運送人於海上航程中應盡之特定義務（Specific obligations applicable to the voyage by sea），其中規定運送人於發航前及發航時與海上航程途中，應就下列事項爲相當必要之注意：(a)使船舶具有且保持適航性；(b)適當地配置船舶之船員、設備及供應，且在全程之航程途中維持此等船員、設備及供應於良好之狀態；(c)使貨艙、冷藏室及船舶所有供載運貨物之其他部分，以及由運送人所提供之貨櫃能適合

---

[2] Henry Campbell Black, M. A. "A warranty of seaworthiness means that the vessel is competent to resist the ordinary attacks of wind and weather, and, is competently equipped and manned for the voyage, with a sufficient crew, and with sufficient means to sustain them, and with a captain of general good character and nautical skill." *Black Law Dictionary*, 1968, p.1518.。

並安全地收受、運送及保存貨物[3]。

由條文規定可知，運送人不僅於發航前及發航時須使船舶具有適航能力，並擴大其責任範圍至海上航程途中，運送人就該船舶仍須使其具備且維持適航能力，就本公約之規範條文而言，其立法精神與1978年漢堡規則較為接近。

適載性（cargoworthiness or fitness）或稱船舶、運輸工具之適載能力；指運輸工具上若有裝載貨物，則除須妥善且合適裝載外，該船舶尚須具備運送該貨物安全抵達目的地之能力。Robert H. Brown 對於船舶適載性之解釋為「船舶合理且適合載運被保險之貨物（The vessel is reasonably suitable and fit to carry the cargo insured）」。我國海商法第 62 條第 1 項第 3 款亦為有關船舶適載性之規定。

2.ICC,2009 之船舶適航性及適載性規定

在海商法概念中船舶的適航性及適載性都是屬於運送人不可轉嫁之義務，就運送人或運送契約而言，船舶適載性之規定已被納入於廣義之船舶適航性規定當中，亦即若船上之貨物如超載或裝載不當，以致船舶無法應付預定航程中所面臨之危險事故等襲擊，即該船舶即不具適載性。但是就海上貨物保險而言，船舶適航性的問題與適載性的問題是兩種不同之規定。就 ICC,2009 第 5.1 款之內容而言，其區分為 5.1.1 有關船舶適航性之規定，以及 5.1.2 有關運輸工具適載能力之規定。換言之，5.1.1 所規範之範圍為載運之船舶應具有適航性與適載

---

[3] Article 14 Specific obligations applicable to the voyage by sea

The carrier is bound before, at the beginning of, and during the voyage by sea to exercise due diligence to:

(a) Make and keep the ship seaworthy; (b) Properly crew, equip and supply the ship and keep the ship so crewed, equipped and supplied throughout the voyage; and (c) Make and keep the holds and all other parts of the ship in which the goods are carried, and any containers supplied by the carrier in or upon which the goods are carried, fit and safe for their reception, carriage and preservation.

性，而 5.1.2 則是規範其所裝運保險標的物之貨櫃應具有安全適載之
情況。原則上若貨損是因爲此不適航或不適運所造成，保險人可以依
此條款主張拒賠。但此舉證責任在於保險人，亦即保險人若要主張此
條除外不保之事項，需舉證貨損原因是因船舶不適航或運輸工具不適
運造成，才能主張拒賠。ICC, 2009 第 5.1.1 款於有關船舶之適航性則
仍維持原 ICC, 1982 第 5.1 款之規定，且將「受僱人」排除於裝船時明
知船舶不適航之適用規定。蓋船舶是否具適航能力除了是法律問題外，
更是專業之技術認定問題，故實務上被保險人（貨主）對於託運船舶
是否適航已不可能知情，其受僱人更不可能知道，故 ICC, 2009 將
「受僱人」一詞刪除，當更爲貼近實務。

　　然對於貨櫃或運輸工具之適載性方面，於 ICC, 2009 第 5.1.2 款
則清楚規定僅於被保險人或其受僱人於保險生效前裝入此不適載之貨
櫃或運輸工具，且於裝櫃時已知此不適載情形時，保險人方可以免
責。就保險人之角度而言之，欲依第 5.1 款之規定而主張拒賠，須提
出兩項舉證，其一爲舉證被保險人或其受僱人於保險標的物裝船時，
明知該載運船舶或貨櫃不具適航性或適載性，仍將保險標的物裝載上
船；其二爲保險人須舉證該保險標的物之毀損、滅失或費用係由於船
舶或貨櫃之不適航或不適載所致者，亦即該等損失係與船舶或貨櫃之
不適航與不適載有相當之因果關係所導致，保險人才能夠不負賠償責
任。惟實務上，保險人欲完成此兩項舉證實非易事。

　　再以被保險人（貨主）角度言之，貨主將承運之貨物交由運送人
運送，對於裝運貨物之船舶是否具備適航性並無從得知。就航運實務
觀察而言，貨主在全櫃運送（Full Container Load，簡稱 FCL）時因
貨主自行裝櫃、併櫃後交予貨櫃集散站裝載上船，由於該裝櫃作業係
由貨主自理，因此貨主對於該貨櫃之櫃況以及是否具有安全裝運貨物
之能力應能清楚了解。但是實務上於貨櫃場提領空櫃時，除非當場檢
查櫃況時發現櫃損，並於貨櫃交接單（Equipment Interchange
Receipt，簡稱 E.I.R.）已註記櫃損，否則保險人難以舉證被保險人或

其受僱人知情，但既然已經發現櫃損，也應該會要求換櫃，故再換櫃後之 E.I.R.上自不會註記。反之，若貨主係以 LCL（Less Container Load）之方式交由貨櫃併裝業者併櫃後裝運上船，由於貨主僅將貨物交送併裝業者併裝，貨櫃係由併裝業者提供，因此，貨主根本無從得知該裝運貨櫃之櫃況如何，若由於該貨櫃不適運而致貨物之毀損、滅失等情事發生，亦為貨主所不樂見。綜上，不論貨主係屬自行裝櫃抑或是併櫃之方式交送海上運送人為運送行為，保險人皆很難舉證被保險人明知運載貨物之船舶不具適航性，或被保險人及其受僱人明知該載運之貨櫃、運輸工具不具適載能力。

ICC,2009 第 5.2 款規定有關船舶不適航之除外規定，並不適用於該保險契約已經轉讓予已買入或已同意買入此批保險標的物之善意受讓人的索賠。此為 1982 年版所沒有的規定，主要目的當為保護不知情的善意受讓保險契約之第三人，以維公允。

ICC, 2009 第 5.3 款中仍維持保險人放棄適航性及船舶適載性之默示擔保（implied warranties of seaworthiness of the ship and fitness of the ship），因貨物被保險人並無法擔保載運船舶之適航能力，而要求被保險人負其違反效果顯失公平，故保險人聲明放棄任何違反擔保之權利。就第 5.3 款與第 5.1.1 款呼應對照之下，雖然保險人已經放棄適航性及船舶適載性之默示擔保，但若被保險人裝船時明知該船不適航或不適運，保險人仍然可以對此主張解除責任（discharge liability），故因不適航或不適運而引起之貨損，保險人不負賠償之責。

第三節　戰爭及罷工除外條款

戰爭危險及罷工危險所造成的損失，通常可能發生巨災損失，故在保險條款中予以除外。不過戰爭危險及罷工危險雖然在標準條款中除外，但仍然可以附加險的方式再予保險，即投保協會貨物戰爭險條款（Institute War Clauses（cargo）），以及協會貨物罷工險條款（Institute Strike Clauses（cargo））。故與前述第 4 條及第 5 條之絕對除外不保不同。

1. 戰爭險除外條款

ICC,2009 第 6 條之內容即為戰爭危險除外之條款，本條款是自 1963 年的「捕獲與扣押免責條款（Free of Capture and Seizure Clause，簡稱為 F.C.&S）」演變而來，ICC,2009（A）、（B）以及（C）條款有一個部分不同，即（A）條款中將海盜（piracy）排除在除外危險之外，而（B）及（C）條款則沒有把海盜危險排除於除外危險，又（B）及（C）條款也沒有列舉海盜行為造成之毀損列為承保範圍，故（A）條款承保海盜危險，而（B）及（C）條款則將海盜危險除外不保。條款之內容詳如表 10–5。

表 10-5　ICC,2009 第 6 條

	原文	譯文
ICC(A)	6. In no case shall this insurance cover loss damage or expense caused by 6.1 war civil war revolution rebellion insurrection, or civil strife arising there from, or any hostile act by or against a belligerent power 6.2 capture seizure arrest restraint or detainment（piracy excepted）, and the consequences thereof or any attempt threat 6.3 derelict mines torpedoes bombs or other derelict weapons of war.	6. 本保險不承保下列事故所致的毀損、滅失或費用： 6.1 因戰爭、內戰、革命、叛亂、顛覆，或其引起之內亂或任何因交戰國或其對抗之敵對行為。 6.2 因捕獲、扣押、拘留、禁制或扣留（海盜除外），以及這些行為或意圖為前述行為所引起的結果。 6.3 遺棄的水雷、魚雷、炸彈或其他遺棄的戰爭武器。
ICC(B) ICC(C)	6. In no case shall this insurance cover loss damage or expense caused by 6.1 war civil war revolution rebellion insurrection, or civil strife arising there from, or any hostile act by or against a belligerent power 6.2 capture seizure arrest restraint or detainment, and the consequences thereof or any attempt threat 6.3 derelict mines torpedoes bombs or other derelict weapons of war.	6. 本保險不承保下列事故所致的毀損、滅失或費用： 6.1 因戰爭、內戰、革命、叛亂、顛覆，或其引起之內亂或任何因交戰國或其對抗之敵對行為。 6.2 因捕獲、扣押、拘留、禁制或扣留，以及這些行為或意圖為前述行為所引起的結果。 6.3 遺棄的水雷、魚雷、炸彈或其他遺棄的戰爭武器。

資料來源：作者整理

　　本條款之除外其實在實務上很少出現，其中的專有名詞也很難清楚釐清其義，如內戰（civil war）、革命（revolution）、叛亂（rebellion）、顛覆（insurrection）等，在概念上應只是程度上不同，而泛指反政府的暴力行動；不過就保險而言，因為都是除外危險，所以似乎問題也不大。就拘留（arrest）而言，依 Arnonld 之解釋是指保險標的物的主權國家為其政治目的，暫時強占船舶或貨物，而非司法上的扣押。依 MIA,1906 保單解釋規則（rules for construction of policy）第 10 條之規定： "The term 'arrest, etc., of kings, princes ,and peoples' refers to political or executive acts, and does not include a loss caused by riot or by ordinary judicial process" 可知爲海上保險裡所提到的扣押，指的是政治上或行政命令上的行爲，不包含暴動與司法上的扣押所造成的損失。

　　海盜危險因亞丁灣（Gulf of Aden）海域索馬利亞海盜猖獗，已經成了國際間的航運與保險話題。海盜之定義依 MIA,1906 保單解釋規則（rules for construction of policy）第 8 條之規定包含乘客的叛變行爲，與來自岸上暴民的攻擊（The term "pirates" includes passengers who mutiny and rioters who attack the ship from the shore），但此定義與傳統中以海上劫掠爲生的海盜概念有所不同。海盜在海上是屬於強迫且暴力的搶劫，不論搶劫者是否是從船外、水手或是乘客登上船，基本的要素是用暴力奪取船舶以及貨物。故海盜危險不僅指海上之搶奪造成的毀損、滅失，也包括陸上暴民的武力攻擊，也包含船上海員或乘客所爲的搶奪行爲。若船舶停泊於碼頭或被固定在錨位時，小偷是用非強迫行爲登上甲板偷竊，則不屬於海盜，因在此情況下有關海盜定義之「暴力行爲」是不存在的。

　　「扣押（seizure）」一詞概念上爲不論是否爲合法授權，只要是用武力強制奪取均可稱之。在 2002 年 Bayview Motors Ltd vs. Mitsui 一案中，汽車船自日本運往多明尼加，到達後多明尼加海關卻強行將汽車占爲己有，被保險人遂將損失向保險人求償，但保險人卻以扣押爲除外危險爲由拒賠。最後法官引用 1883 年 Cory vs. Burr 的裁判，認爲所謂扣押合理的解釋是包括任何不論是法律授權或者是無法反抗的強迫強制占有，而本案僅是海關人員的基於個人利益的非法強占，故不適用於扣押之概念，故保險人應賠償此損失。

　　第 6.3 款所規定的「遺棄（derelict）」的水雷，魚雷，炸彈或戰爭武器等，在解釋條款時的重點乃在於「遺棄」，故上述這些戰爭武器均指戰爭結束之後被還遺留在海域裡的戰爭用武器。條款規定雖然戰爭已經結束，但若保險標的物被遺棄的水雷，魚雷，炸彈或戰爭武器等造成毀損，滅失或費用，依本款予以除外不保。

2.罷工險除外條款

罷工險除外條款可追溯至 1930 年協會貨物保險條款第 9 條罷工暴動與民眾騷擾條款（Strikes, Riots and Civil Commotions Clause, S. R. & C.C. Clause）。其乃是由捕獲扣押免責條款（F.C. & S. Clause）中抽出而另行制訂的條款。直至 1963 年第 13 條、1982 年第 7 條以及 2009 年版都有相同之條款出現，只是不同年代之版本間有進行微幅的修改。ICC,2009 年第 7 條即是罷工危險除外不保之規定，條款內容如表 10-6。

表 10-6　ICC,2009 第 7 條

7. In no case shall this insurance cover loss damage or expense 7.1 caused by strikers, locked-out workmen, or persons taking part in labour disturbances, riots or civil commotions 7.2 resulting from strikes, lock-outs, labour disturbances, riots or civil commotions 7.3 caused by any act of terrorism being an act of any person acting on behalf of, or in connection with, any organisation which carries out activities directed towards the overthrowing or influencing, by force or violence, of any government whether or not legally constituted 7.4 caused by any person acting from a political, ideological or religious motive.	7. 本保險不承保下列之毀損、滅失或費用： 7.1 直接因罷工者、停工者或參與工潮，暴動或民眾騷擾人員所致者。 7.2 因罷工、停工、工潮、暴動或民眾騷擾之結果引起者。 7.3 直接因任何代表人或有關組織，採取以武力或暴力方式，藉以任何恐怖主義行為直接推翻或影響，不論其是否為合法成立之任何政府組織。 7.4 直接因任何人政治、意識形態或宗教動機行為所致者。

資料來源：作者整理

由本條之規定可知，第 7.1 條中所除外者是因為參與罷工的人，參與停工的人，以及參與工潮，暴動或民眾騷擾的「人員」所「直接造成（caused by）」的損失。而第 7.2 條則規定除外的是因為罷工等「事件」所引起的損失，由於條款用語是以「resulting from」故是指

只要是因為罷工、停工、工潮、暴動或民眾騷擾等事件所直接或間接引起的損害或費用都除外不保。如原運送目的港因發生罷工或類似事件，貨物被迫轉卸載於替代港，等到罷工結束後，被保險人（貨主）則必須將貨物自該替代港再轉運至原來之目的港，貨物雖然沒有因此罷工而受損，但卻也因此產生額外轉運費用，保險人仍不負保險責任。

　　新修訂之 7.3 款內容特別明確解釋其恐怖主義之定義為「任何人代表任何組織或與任何組織連結所為之行為，而其執行之行動係以武力或暴力為手段之恐怖主義行為，以達到推翻或影響任何政府為目的。」本款之增訂乃為統一國際使用 ICC 時對於恐怖主義之一致性解釋，避免爭議。7.4 款亦為 ICC,1982 所沒有之規定，條文規定任何因意識形態或宗教上之動機者（person acting from a ideological or religious motive）所致之毀損、滅失或費用不負賠償責任。故就 ICC, 2009 第 7.4 款與 ICC, 1982 第 7.3 款比較下，兩者主要之差異在於 ICC, 2009 明確解釋本款之「行為」為「具政治動機、意識形態與宗教動機」，而 ICC, 1982 僅規定了「政治動機」一詞。本款之規定讓除外不保的範圍不在只侷限只有政治動機者所致，而是擴大至任何懷有意識形態或宗教上之動機者所致之保險標的物毀損、滅失或費用之情況皆適用之。

　　有關於「民眾騷擾（civil commotions）」的意義，指則指群體性的聚集行為行為所造成保險標物的損害。所謂「暴動（riots）」其實與民眾騷擾也極為類似，國外學者 Susan Hodges 認為所謂暴動人數不得少於 3 人，有共同的目的（common purpose），並著手於共同的目的的實施，這群人彼此相互支援，必要時會運用武力來消除那些反對他們達到共同目的的阻力；故不論是武力與暴力，不僅僅是用來達成共同的目的，同時也是用來展示警告他人的合理決心與勇氣[4]。

---

[4] Susan Hodges, *Law of Marine Insurance*, p.347。

第十一章 · · · · · · · · ·

ICC,2009 之保險期間

第一節　航程條款

　　海上貨物保險為航程保險單，即保險期間規定原則是以保險契約所約定的定點開始生效，直到送達保險契約所約定的定點卸貨完成後保險終止。保險期間為保險理賠時非常重要的規定，因為縱使保險事故發生，但若不是在保險期間內，被保險人依然無法獲得賠償。ICC,2009 第 8 條即為有關航程保險期間的規定，不論是(A)、(B)或(C)均是相同之規定。條款內容詳列如表 11-1。

表 11-1　ICC,2009 第 8 條

條款	內容
ICC,2009 第 8 條	8.Transit Clause 8.1 Subject to Clause 11 below, this insurance attaches from the time the subject−matter insured is first moved in the warehouse or at the place of storage (at the place named in the contract of insurance) for the purpose of the immediate loading into or onto the carrying vehicle or other conveyance for the commencement of transit, continues during the ordinary course of transit and terminates either 8.1.1 on completion of unloading from the carrying vehicle or other conveyance in or at the final warehouse or place of storage at the destination named in the contract of insurance, 8.1.2 on completion of unloading from the carrying vehicle or other conveyance in or at any other warehouse or place of storage, whether prior to or at the destination named in the contract of insurance, which the Assured or their employees elect to use either for storage other than in the ordinary course of transit or for allocation or distribution, or

8.1.3 when the Assured or their employees elect to use any carrying vehicle or other conveyance or any container for storage other than in the ordinary course of transit or

8.1.4 on the expiry of 60 days after completion of discharge overside of the subject–matter insured from the oversea vessel at the final port of discharge, whichever shall first occur.

8.2 If, after discharge overside from the oversea vessel at the final port of discharge, but prior to termination of this insurance, the subject–matter insured is to be forwarded to a destination other than that to which it is insured, this insurance, whilst remaining subject to termination as provided in Clauses 8.1.1 to 8.1.4, shall not extend beyond the time the subject–matter insured is first moved for the purpose of the commencement of transit to such other destination.

8.3 This insurance shall remain in force (subject to termination as provided for in Clauses 8.1.1 to 8.1.4 above and to the provisions of Clause 9 below) during delay beyond the control of the Assured, any deviation, forced discharge, reshipment or transhipment and during any variation of the adventure arising from the exercise of a liberty granted to carriers under the contract of carriage.

8.1 依下列第 11 條規定，本保險自被保險標的物於保險契約中載明之倉庫或儲存處所內，為了即裝上或裝進運送車輛或其他運輸工具，並開始以運送為目的之第一次移動時開始生效。並於正常之運輸過程中繼續有效。
上述至下述情形之一時終止：
8.1.1 於本保險契約所載之目的地最終倉庫或儲存處所，自運送車輛或其他運輸工具完全卸載。
8.1.2 在未送達最終目的地預定倉庫前，被保險人將保險標的運至其他任何被保險人或其受僱人用作正常運輸過程以外的儲存或分配、分送之倉庫或儲存處所內，自運送車輛或其他運輸工具完全卸載。
8.1.3 被保險人或其受僱人選擇使用任何運送車輛工具或其他運輸工具或任何貨櫃內，進行正常運輸過程以外的儲存。或
8.1.4 保險標的在最終卸貨港自海船上卸貨完成後六十天。
上述情形，先發生者保險契約即為終止。

8.2 若保險標的於最終卸貨港自船舶卸載完畢後，於本保險失效之前，將保險標的運往本保險契約所載明以外之目的地時，則本保險之效力，除仍受 8.1.1 至 8.1.4 規定之限制外，於保險標的物為了運往其他目的地時之第一次移動時終止。

8.3 本保險之效力，除依 8.1.1 至 8.1.4 之規定而終止，及第 9 條終止條款之規定外，在下列情形仍繼續有效；被保險人無法控制之遲延、重新裝船或轉船、由於運送人行使依運送契約中之自由航行權，而對航程所做的任何變更。

資料來源：作者整理

1. ICC,2009 第 8.1 款

ICC,2009 相較於 ICC,1982 而言，改變最多的部分莫過於第 8 條。依 ICC, 1982 第 8 條規定，保險於保險單所承保的貨物為了運送

的目的而離開保險單所載明地點的倉庫或處所時開始生效。保險單上所「記載列明」的倉庫或儲存場所，此地點可能為港口的海關倉庫，亦可為出口商的內陸倉庫，換句話說，若保險單記載為內陸地名，且該處所亦有被保險人所使用之倉庫，則保險單的效力自貨物離開被保險人倉庫時即開始生效。若保險單上所載地點為裝貨港地名，則保險單效力自貨物離開被保險人於裝貨港倉庫或離開裝貨港海關倉庫時，保險單才開始生效。故海運實務之 CY（FCL）運送時，係由出口商（託運人）自行裝櫃，若貿易條件是由出口商投保時，一旦於裝櫃過程中發生意外事故，因為尚未以運送目的而離開倉庫，故保險人並不須負裝櫃時的損害賠償之責，而傳統的商業火險亦未承保因裝櫃造成的之貨物毀損滅失，且若又非委外裝櫃時，被保險人將可能造成求償無門的窘境。

現今國際物流過程中經常出現將貨物先送運至物流中心進行流通加工，再裝櫃出口的情形，但是對於物流貨物運往流通加工之途中，就 ICC,1982 的條款邏輯，因為已經脫離了正常運輸過程，故 ICC, 1982 並不承保。縱使貨主於保險單中特別將航程擴大投保以 "From shipper's warehouse" 為條件，亦無法獲得保險人之理賠，因為若僅是為了物流或加工目的，如運至物流中心重貼標籤、重新組裝、包裝等，雖然已離開保險契約所載明的倉庫或儲存處所，但都不是「以運送之目的運送」，故保險仍未生效。在此情況下，貨主仍應再自行投保內陸運輸保險，承保「非運送為目地」的內陸段危險，雖然加工過程可透過商業動產流動保險轉嫁委託簡單加工時的危險，但同樣亦造成物流過程的分割投保問題[1]。

---

[1] 商業動產流動保險乃是貨物運輸保險跟商業火險的結合，於動產會在不同儲存地點有運送且有暫存的情況（具商業營利性質、非私人），都可以用商動險來承保，轉嫁風險。商業動產流動保險主要承保物流貨物於正常運輸途中、正常運輸途中之暫時停放，以不超過七天為限、修理保養期間、操作使用期間、委託他人加工處理期間等風險。

　　針對以上兩項問題，ICC,2009 的 8.1 款中除了仍保留必須「以運送爲目的之運送」爲保險生效原則外，特別將保險生效「動作」提前到保險契約載明的倉庫或儲存處所內，爲了將保險標的物以運送爲目的立即裝載於運送工具之「第一次移動」開始。但並不包括爲了運送而裝載前的儲存，或倉庫內暫存區的儲存。條款中所謂「first moved（第一次移動）」在海上運輸實務上可能的情形爲使用堆高機將貨物於倉庫門口空地開始搬運時的動作，或從倉庫內部貨架、棧板或貨堆上利用堆高機開始將貨物放置於出口貨櫃內或貨車上的動作。若爲高樓式倉庫者，則所謂「第一次移動」應爲從某特定樓層搬運開始的動作。惟因爲國際貿易貨物種類繁多，裝運流程與模式也各有不同，故如何判斷何謂條款中的第一次移動，應以該事實而予以認定爲宜。

　　另條款中所謂 "for the purpose of the immediate loading into or onto the carrying vehicle or other conveyance for the commencement of transit"，除了就條款字面解釋是爲了立即裝上或裝進運送車輛或其他運輸工具，並開始以運送爲目的之第一次移動時開始生效。就貨櫃運輸實務而言，應指保險標的物於倉庫內堆高機將該貨物自倉庫內貨架取下，並堆載於貨櫃或貨車上，且該裝櫃動作係要以立刻運送爲目的而爲之裝櫃或裝貨，方屬條款所規定的概念。由上述 ICC,2009 規定可知，不論貨主是以 CY 於貨主自己倉庫裝櫃，抑或是 CFS 之運送模式於貨櫃集散站併櫃期間，只要符合以運送爲目的之裝載所進行的第一次移動過程，即算是保險期間開始生效。ICC,2009 此新增規定擴大保險期間的結果當可解決貨主於貨物運送過程中裝櫃與裝貨之貨損危險，而此危險亦恰是所有傳統險種如海上運輸保險、火災保險、商業動產流動保險的承保危險缺口。茲將 ICC,2009 與 ICC,1982 有關保險期間開始生效的規定比較如表 11–2。

表 11-2　保險期間生效規定比較表

保險契約效力 開始之規定第	ICC, 1982	ICC, 2009	說明
第 8.1 款	貨物離開倉庫或儲存地點開始運送時，保單始生效。	自被保險標的物於保險契約中載明之倉庫或儲存處所內，為了立即裝上或裝進運送車輛或其他運輸工具，並開始以運送為目的之第一次移動時開始生效。	將保險效力提早至以運送為目的，為立即裝入運送車輛或其他運輸工具之第一次移動為瞬間保單效力生效點。

資料來源：作者整理

　　ICC,2009 第 8.1 款將保單生效動作「提前」之規定影響，就國際貿易而言，若買賣雙方約定貿易條件為出口商必須安排海上保險的情況，投保 ICC,2009 當比 ICC,1982 更為有利。2000 年版國際貿易條件中出口商應投保之貿易條件整理如表 11-3。

表 11-3　出口商應投保的貿易條件

貿條件通用代號	內容	名稱
CIF	Cost, Insurance and Freight	運保費在內
CIP	Carriage and Insurance Paid to	運保費付訖
DAF	Delivered at Frontier	邊境交貨價
DDU	Delivered Duty Unpaid	輸入國稅前交貨
DES	Delivered Ex Ship	目的港船上交貨
DEQ	Delivered Ex Quay	目的港碼頭交貨
DDP	Delivered Duty paid	輸入國稅迄交貨

資料來源：作者整理

　　相對於進口商而言，若貿易條件約定「貨交運送人價」之 FCA（Free Carrier…（named place））條件，或「運費付至目的地價」之 CPT（Carriage Paid to（…named place of destination））條件者，

由於此二項條件規定貨物危險負擔之移轉時點在於當貨物交付第一運送人或貨櫃場時危險負擔移轉予買方，故以 CFS 進口情況言之，若投保 ICC,2009，當出口商將貨物送交至貨櫃場時，危險負擔即已經移轉，故於貨櫃集散站併櫃過程中的損害，進口商即可向保險人申請理賠。相對於採 FOB 貿易條件，貨物必須越過船舷後危險負擔移轉的規定，若貨物損害發生時裝櫃期間，由於保險利益尚未移轉，雖然 ICC,2009 已包含裝櫃時的危險，但若逕行賠付給買方恐仍留有爭議。故採 FCA 及 CPT 之貿易條件進口商，若投保 ICC,2009 條件者較投保 1982 年版 ICC 條款，將可減少理賠爭議更為有利。

保險契約之終止規定，依 ICC,2009 第 8.1 之規定共有四種情況，分別為：

1.於本保險契約所載之目的地最終倉庫或儲存處所，自運送車輛或其他運輸工具完全卸載。

2.在未送達最終目的地預定倉庫前，被保險人將貨物運至其他任何被保險人或其受僱人用作正常運輸過程以外的儲存或分配、分送的倉庫或儲存處所，自運送車輛或其他運輸工具完全卸載。

3.被保險人或其受僱人選擇使用任何運送車輛工具或其他運輸工具或任何貨櫃內，進行正常運輸過程以外的儲存。

4.保險標的在最終卸貨港自海船上卸貨完成後六十天。

ICC,1982 第 8.1.1 條規定貨物「運達」被保險人於保險單上所載明之倉庫或儲存場所時。所謂「貨物送達被保險人倉庫時」（on delivery to consignee's warehouse ），意指送交受貨人或其他受託人可以處置地點，如倉庫內、倉庫屋簷下、露天倉庫或至少應為倉庫或儲存所的附屬場所。如同保險單效力開始情況，保險單效力終止的地點可為海關倉庫，亦可為被保險人（或實際受貨人）的內陸倉庫，全視保險單記載而定。

但實務上，"delivery to"一字之中文譯詞可能為「運達」，亦有譯為「交付」，此兩者意義與解釋大相逕庭，其最主要差異與爭議在於是否包含「卸貨期間（自卡車或櫃內卸下，及擺放完成）」貨物所遭受的毀損或滅失。即在理賠實務上，貨物是送達到倉庫門口時，保險單就終止，或是必須待貨物完全卸下後，保險效力才是終止，實務上存有爭議。依保險法第 54 條規定：保險契約之解釋，應探求契約當事人之真意，不得拘泥於所用之文字；如有疑義時，以做有利於被保險人之解釋為原則。然為避免爭議，實務上或可建議於保單中加入以下 wording: "safely deposited in the warehouse at destination named herein." 改善安全卸載疑慮；亦可以在保險單上以加註或批單外加蓋車縫章的方式來補充，後來所增的條款內容則為被優先適用。

針對此實務問題，ICC,2009 之修改為 "on completion of unloading form the carrying vehicle or other conveyance in or at the final warehouse or place or storage at the destination named herein." 依條款之義解釋為自運送車輛或其他運輸工具「完全卸載」至本保險契約所載之目的地最終倉庫或儲存處所。可知 ICC,2009 明確將保險契約效力終止往後延伸至保險標的完全卸載完畢止，承保範圍包括卸貨動作之危險，顯然擴大保險人保險期間至保險標的卸貨完成時，對貨主極為有利，亦解決 ICC,1982 中 "delivery to" 條款解釋的爭議。

ICC,2009 第 8.1 之規定對保險人理賠責任之認定而言，因保險生效期間已較 ICC,1982 提前至在倉庫內為了運送目的之立即裝載的第一次搬運開始，故被保險人於索賠時應對貨損是發生於 "first moved" 期間負舉證責任，蓋是否發生於保險期間本來就應是被保險人索賠時的舉證內容。為確保被保險人理賠權益，建議於廠區或倉庫內部加設監視攝影機，監控倉庫內部裝卸貨情形，以利萬一裝貨時發生貨損，可做為舉證索賠依據。再就有關意外事故是否發生於保險期間之認定，則應同時就保險航程與運輸模式考量，列如表 11-4 如下：

表 11-4　ICC,2009 第 8.1 款保險期間判定表

	保險航程自出口地內陸倉庫開始	保險航程自港口倉庫開始
CY 運送模式	若貨損發生於內陸倉庫裝櫃時，若符合第一次移動概念，出口商均可索賠。	若貨損發生於內陸倉庫裝櫃時，因事故發生時保險尚未生效，保險人無理賠責任。
CFS 運送模式	若貨損發生於內陸倉庫裝上卡車時，若符合第一次移動概念，保險人應該理賠給出口商。若貨損發生於貨櫃集散站併櫃時，因為在保險航程內，保險人應該理賠給出口商。CIP 條件下則因危險負擔已經移轉，保險人應該理賠給進口商。	若貨損發生於內陸倉庫裝上卡車時，因事故發生時保險尚未生效，保險人無理賠責任。若貨損發生於貨櫃集散站併櫃時，若符合第一次移動概念，保險人應該理賠給出口商。CIP 條件下則因危險負擔已經移轉，保險人應該理賠給進口商。

資料來源：作者整理

　　ICC,2009 第 8.1.2 款，原則上與 ICC,1982 規定文義相同，只是將條款字句結構改變，並且呼應了第 8.1.1 款有關「完全卸載」之新規定，即 ICC,2009 之 8.1.2 與 ICC,1982 之 8.1.2 之規定僅在於將 "on delivery to" 改為 "on completion of unloading from"，並將條次簡化，其餘並無不同。條款中所謂的「未到達最終目的地預定倉庫前」，乃指未到達原目的地前之其他地點的倉庫，也可能指的是已到達原目的地，但為原目的地預定倉庫以外的倉庫。所謂的「儲存」，指的是正常運輸途中必要儲存行為「以外」的儲存，因為若是「必要」的儲存行為，則是屬於正常運輸途中過程的一環，保險契約的效力將不會終止。保險契約之所以將「儲存」與「配銷」的行為不納入承保範圍之內，完全是因為「儲存」與「配銷」的危險與「運輸」不同，已經不屬於保險人原先所預估的危險，必須另做考量與評估。所以當被保險人將保險標的物在該「儲存」或「配銷」之倉庫卸載完成後，保險契約的效力即行終止；亦即，在儲存及等待配銷期間，該保險標的就不再受保險的保障。

ICC,2009 對於保險契約之終止新增規定："8.1.3 when the assured or their employees elect to use any carrying vehicle or other conveyance or any container for storage of the subject-matter insured"，即若被保險人或其受僱人將保險標的放置於任何運送工具或貨櫃內，保單效力亦將終止。本條款那將原來 ICC,1982 之保險契約終止情況增設一個規定，即原條款僅規定運抵「倉庫」時或船舶卸貨完成後六十天尚未提貨之終止規定，實務上若提貨後進倉前，跳脫正常運輸過程時，若將保險標的儲存於貨櫃上，則將出現舊條款規定之空窗。故此新增條文同時排除六十天之適用，以及避免過去貨主故意不將保險標的卸櫃，以免保險期間終止的漏洞。

惟依此新增條款規定，造成保險契約終止情況，必須是正常運送過程「以外」之情況，被保險人或其受僱人將保險標的放置於任何運送工具或貨櫃內；換言之，若該情況是屬於正常運輸過程，保險人仍不得主張契約終止。原則上，此新增規定爲對被保險人增加一項限制，若有此類情況發生且因此而發生貨損，保險人自可依條款主張保險期間已終止而拒賠。惟實務上大概僅有低單價貨物，若將進倉儲放其成本相對過高時，方有可能不進倉而儲放於貨櫃內。

ICC,2009 第 8.1.4 款與 ICC,1982 之規定並無不同，規定保險標的在最終卸貨港自海船上卸貨完成後六十天，保險契約終止。條款中所提到之六十天的期限是由貨物自「海船卸貨完成後」起算，而非船舶到港後六十天。而所謂的「海船（overseas vessel）」指的是能越洋行駛的船舶，因此，當貨物卸入駁船（craft）時，此六十天的期限已經開始起算，如香港之中流作業先將貨櫃自海船上卸入駁船，則由拖船將無動力駁船拖運至碼頭卸櫃，在此情況下，六十天之起算點仍爲貨物卸入駁船時開始。另外，雖然被保險人提貨時已經超過卸貨完成後的六十天，依規定保險契約已經終止，但若是被保險人能夠舉證證明事故是發生於保險終止之前，如海水水濕造成，則保險人仍應負保險責任，此乃終止的法律效果爲自終止之日起契約往後終止，但不影響契約終止前的保險效力或保險請求權。

　　茲將 ICC,2009 與 ICC,1982 有關保險期間開始生效之規定比較列如表 11–5。

表 11–5　保險期間終止規定之比較表

保險契約的終止	ICC,1982	ICC,2009	說明
第 8.1.1 款	運達至保單所載明之目的地之最終倉庫或儲存處所。	於本保險契約所載之目的地最終倉庫或儲存處所，自運送車輛或其他運輸工具完全卸載。	ICC, 1982 規定運達到倉庫即終止， ICC, 2009 則規定自運送工具完全卸載後，保單效力才終止。
第 8.1.2 款	所保貨物運達至保單所載目的地以外之任何其他倉庫或儲存處所而為被保險人用作正常運輸過程以外之儲存、分配或分送。	在未送達最終目的地預定倉庫前，被保險人將保險標的運至其他任何被保險人或其受僱人用作正常運輸過程以外的儲存或分配、分送之倉庫或儲存處所內，自運送車輛或其他運輸工具完全卸載。	條款規定原則不變，如同第 8.1.1 之規定，只是將運達的規定改自運送工具完全卸載後，保單效力才終止。
第 8.1.3 款	無	被保險人或其受僱人選擇使用任何運送車輛工具或其他運輸工具或任何貨櫃內，進行正常運輸過程以外的儲存	本款為 ICC, 2009 所新增。
第 8.1.4 款	所保貨物在最終卸貨港自海船上卸貨完成後 60 天。	保險標的在最終卸貨港自海船上卸貨完成後 60 天	條款規定不變，僅修改「所保貨物」為「保險標的」。

資料來源：作者整理

2. ICC,2009 第 8.2 款

　　第 8.2 款所規定的是被保險的航程有所變更的情況，依條款之義指若保險標的自最終卸貨港卸載後，但在第 8.1 條所規定的保險契約

效力終止前，如果被保險人選擇將保險標的運往原定目的地以外地點，則保險契約效力在保險標的物為了運往其他改變後目的地時第一次移動時終止，此類情形如貨主臨時將貨物轉賣給其他貨主，或臨時變更儲存在原目的地以外倉庫，例如貨物於高雄港卸貨後，最終目的地原應運至台南科學園區倉庫，但因已被轉賣至屏東大發工業區而將被改運往屏東交貨，因此依條款的規定，當貨物準備離開高雄港運往屏東，於港區倉庫內為了裝載運送的第一次移動時，保險契約的效力即行終止。

　　保險人於訂立保險契約時，即就約定承保範圍，根據被保險人所明示或習慣上可得推知之為危險進行評估，進而擬訂保險費。契約成立後，保險人估定的危險，以不再更動為原則；換言之，除經當事人同意外，在保險契約有效期間內，應維持約定時的危險條件，即與保險人所承擔危險有關各項要素，不得有所變更。倘發生航程變更的情事，此與保險人預先評估而同意承擔之危險已有不同，因此，保險契約效力即受影響。所謂變更航程，依 MIA,1906 第 45 條的規定指開始航程後，船舶之目的地自保險單所載明之目的地任意變更（Where, after the commencement of the risk, the destination of the ship is voluntarily changed from the destination contemplated by the policy）。貨物保險為航程保險單，ICC,2009 之 8.2 條乃變更最後目的地，在概念上亦與 MIA,1906 第 45 條之 Change of Voyage 規定極為類似，但 MIA,1906 第 45 條所規定者乃是海上航行的目的港變更，但本款是最後的內陸目的地變更，前者適用於海上保險航程，後者適用於含陸上目的地之保險航程，然兩者在法律效果上則都是開始往變更目的地出發時，保險契約即告終止。因此，雖然 MIA,1906 第 45 條所指者為海上航行的航程，但時至今日，ICC,2009 所保險的航程有可能包括 "door to door" 的整體運送過程，故只要被保險人變更原來的目的地，與 MIA,1906 的變更航程所規定的概念其實相同。故當被保險人變更航程後，保險人將自被保險人開始變更航程時即解除責任（the insurer is discharged from liability as from the time of change）。故依上段舉例，保險航程原因運到台南科學園區，但臨時轉運到屏東大發工業區，很明顯被保險人已經改變原目的地，因此 ICC,2009 於本款規定，保險契約效力在保險標的物爲了運往其他改變後目的地時之第一次移動時終止，雖然與 MIA,1906 第 45 條的終止保險契約時間不同，但與 ICC,1982 之規定確是相同，ICC,2009 爲配合第 8.1 款的修改規定，故將終止契約的概念與第 8.1 款一樣，不論如何，ICC,2009 可謂是一契約特別規定，對於被保險人的變更航程規定應優先適用。

ICC,2009 將「正常運輸過程」之概念縮限在倉庫內的第一次搬移動作決定，如前所述應係呼應第 8.1 款的規定。事故發生時保險人雖可自第一次搬動保險標的物時主張保險契約終止，似對保險人有利，但舉證責任應在於保險人，應同時舉證貨損是於開始運往其他目的地時發生，以及卸船後的第一次移動是爲了開始運往其他目的地，方可以主張保險契約已終止而不負保險責任。但實務上保險人並非實際運送人，對於貨物運送過程不可能全程掌握，故將會有舉證上之困難。

3. ICC,2009 第 8.3 款

第 8.3 款所規定者爲另一危險改變的情況。實務上，因被保險人（貨主）於託運後保險標的即交由運送人監管運送，因此若運送人於運送期間某些特殊行爲造成運輸航程危險有所改變，則產生保險契約的效力是否應該隨危險改變而終止的問題。ICC,2009 第 8.3 款規定，當貨主無法控制的情況下（beyond the control of the Assured），若發生運輸危險變更的情況，仍然可以允許保險單效力繼續有效（Remain in force）。此類情況包括被保險人無法控制之遲延（Delay）、偏航（Deviation）、強制卸貨（Forced discharge）、重新裝船（Reshipment）、轉船（Transhipment）或船東或傭船人行使運送契約（Contract of carriage）所賦予之權利而對航程所做之任何變更（Variation of adventure）。茲就危險變更之情況敘述如下：

(1)被保險人無法控制之遲延

保險契約上所承保之航程，不僅應於適當的期間內發航，且在航程進行中，亦應以合理的速度繼續航程，若有不合理的遲延發生，原預定的航程時間定會往後延長，即可謂為航程危險變更。故保險人對於不合理的遲延所引起的損失及費用均不負責任。惟航程的進行通常係由船長指揮、控制，故於大部分情況下，被保險人通常無法知悉或控制航程進行的情況，若因此而拒絕理賠，對被保險人而言似乎過於嚴苛，故現今保單條款皆有規定，若產生被保險人無法控制之遲延，保險契約的效力不因此而失效。

(2)偏航

所謂「偏航（Deviation）」，係指船舶並未完全放棄完成保單所載之航程，而係自願地、無正當原因地偏離所指定的航線。而此處所指定的航線，除保險契約另有規定，係依經驗及習慣所可得推定之最安全、直接、快速的由二端地點的航行路線[2]。由於偏航可能導致危險變更，故只要有偏離航道事實，保險契約效力即告終止。依 MIA, 1906 第 46 條之規定，保險人於船舶偏航之時起，即解除對保險的賠償責任（The intention to deviate is immaterial; there must be a deviation in fact to discharge the insurer from his liability under the contract）。然而，實務上貨主對於船舶的指揮與管理無權利干涉，船舶偏航自非被保險人（貨主）所能控制的危險變更。故 ICC,2009 規定若被保險人因無法控制之偏航造成的保險標的之毀損、滅失，保險人仍須負擔賠償責任。

(3)強迫卸載、重行裝船或轉船

航運實務中卸載、重行裝船及轉船將會影響航程危險，尤其在裝卸機具不良或轉運港區環境設備不好的地方卸載、裝船及轉船。就保險危險估算而言，危險增加自然應加收保險費，此乃指開航前被保險

---

[2] Arnould, *Law of Marine Insurance and Average*, p.322.

人已知且必要的卸載、重行裝船及轉船,此類情形也是屬於投保險的告知(disclosure)問題;若投保當時未能將此必要的轉船情況告知保險人,則屬告知義務的違反,依我國保險法第 64 條的規定,保險人可以主張解除契約。

但若卸載、重行裝船及轉運是被保險人無法控制的情況,且在原正常航程中也不應發生轉船的情形,則 ICC,2009 規定保險契約的效力將繼續有效,惟前提是船舶開航後發生被保險人不知或無法控制的卸載、重行裝船及轉船而言。

(4)船東或傭船人行使運送契約所賦予之權利

在運送契約中運送人為保留其航行的彈性,避免變成偏航或變更航程,故於運送契約中載入自由航行條款(Liberty Clauses),主要是強調運送人可以採用任何運送或儲存方式,自由裁量選擇任何航路、停經任何港口、選擇任何地點裝卸貨物等,故當運送人行使運送契約下所賦予的自由權利而致之危險變更者,也因為非被保險人可以控制,故保險契約並不因此而失其效力。

第二節　運送契約終止條款

海上貨物保險是附隨於海上運送契約而產生的另一獨立契約,兩種契約間雖因其不同的契約約定各自獨立,然當運送契約終止時,表示原定的航程已然中斷,連帶影響貨物保險航程於抵達保險契約所載的最後目的地前中斷。實務上,發生運送契約終止的情況可能發生海難、也可能為貨物退運,造成原運送契約中斷,此時,此時因保險契約所承保的航程危險已經改變,故保險契約的效力亦將會發生變化。ICC,2009 第 9 條即為規定此種情況的條款,本條於 ICC,2009 三套條款的規定都相同。列如表 11-6。

表 11-6　ICC,2009 運送契約終止

條款	內容
ICC,2009 第 9 條	Termination of Contract of Carriage 9. If owing to circumstances beyond the control of the Assured either the contract of carriage is terminated at a port or place other than the destination named therein or the transit is otherwise terminated before unloading of the subject-matter insured as provided for in Clause 8 above, then this insurance shall also terminate unless prompt notice is given to the Insurers and continuation of cover is requested when this insurance shall remain in force, subject to an additional premium if required by the Insurers, either 9.1 until the subject-matter insured is sold and delivered at such port or place, or, unless otherwise specially agreed, until the expiry of 60 days after arrival of the subject-matter insured at such port or place, whichever shall first occur, or 9.2 if the subject-matter insured is forwarded within the said period of 60 days（or any agreed extension thereof）to the destination named in the contract of insurance or to any other destination, until terminated in accordance with the provisions of Clause 8 above.
	運送契約終止 若被保險人無法控制之情況下，運送契約在保單載明目的港以外之港口或地點終止時，或航程因故未能如前述第8條所規定之保險標的物卸載前終止時，本保險契約之效力亦同時終止。除非被保險人於獲悉後立即通知保險人及要求繼續保險，則在同意保險人要求應加付保險費後，本保險仍繼續有效，以迄下述情況之一時終止。 9.1 除有其他特別約定外，在保險標的到達該港口或地點屆滿六十天時間之期限，或保險人必須在該地將保險標的出售並送達；兩者以先發生者為準。 9.2 若保險標的在上述六十天之期限內（或同意延長的期間），將保險標的轉運至原預定目的地，或其他變更後之目的地時，則保險契約的效力將依上述第8條之規定而終止。

資料來源：作者整理

　　運送契約終止條款所規範的情況為貨物未運達最終卸貨港「前」之情況，而第8條則是規範貨物運達最終卸貨港「後」的狀況。本條重點為在被保險人無法控制情況下，而運送契約在其保險單所載明之目的港以外的港口或地點終止，或者貨物因其他原因運送被終止而未能依原正常運送過程將貨物送達原預定目的地，此時保險契約之效力

即應隨之終止。除非被保險人獲悉後立即通知保險人，並要求繼續延長保險契約的效力，同時若保險人考量危險後，要求加收保險費，則被保險人若同意繳付必要的加收保險費，則保險契約仍將繼續有效。

雖於本條第一項規定可知被保險人可因履行上述的條件而使保險單效力不中斷，但保險單效力並不是限期延長，因此，在9.1及9.2兩款內容規定險契約終止的情形。依第9.1款規定，保險已經繼續有效後，被保險人仍必須在該保險標的抵達港口後六十天的期限內將貨物在避難港出售並送達到新貨主處，則保險契約的效力終止；換言之，若超過六十天被保險人仍未將貨物出售，則保險契約的效力亦將終止，並以兩者先發生者先終止。

依第9.2款規定，若被保險人選擇將保險標的運往原目的地或其他變更後的目的地，除非有同意延長日數，否則必須在六十天的期限內，將保險標的開始運送。故若保險標的停留在港避難港超過六十天，保險契約亦告終止。而當開始發航向原目的地或變更之目的地時，則保險契約再依第8條所規定終止之情形發生時終止。

國際物流過程經常是採複合運送（multimodal transport，又稱多式聯運）方式，在全程運輸與倉儲過程中，極有可能因意外事故發生而中斷運送，若因此而使保險契約終止，將對貨主產生危險管理缺口，雖然可經由通知保險人並加繳應付的保險費後，讓保險契約繼續有效，然畢竟海運實務上，發生運送契約終止的情況，不外乎發生海難事故，內陸運輸則可能為車禍，雖謂航程危險已經變更，但並非被保險人（貨主）可以控制的危險，故條款中允許被保險人知道運送航程已經終止後，應立即通知保險人再評估危險後使保險契約有效，至為公允。

ICC,2009第9條相較於第1982年版並未有大幅修定，僅接續ICC,2009第8條精神，將原條款第一項「約定交貨前」一句由"before delivery of goods"修訂為"before unloading of the subject-matter insured"，如前條所述，此項修訂係為了避免"delivery"一詞於實務解釋上之困難及混淆，並擴大保險人的保險期間為保險標的物於避難港卸貨完成之前。此外，ICC,2009第9條其餘之修正為將9.2款中之"herein"修訂為"in the contract of insurance"；以及將條款中"goods"一詞皆修訂為"subject-matter insured"。可見條款內文句簡化，將使保險契約的雙方當事人於閱讀條款時，能更清楚了解其規範的內容與其責任歸屬，對保險契約實質權利及義務內容並沒有影響。

第三節　變更航程

　　航程保險單維持保險效力的關鍵乃在於是否保持在「正常運輸航程」，若未能維持在原投保時所保險的航程，就危險評估角度而言，即謂是危險變更。發生危險變更有時候是外在因素造成，有時亦可能是由被保險人本身造成。不論如何，被保險人都應於知悉危險變更後通知保險人，若危險增加後保險人得提議另定保險費，被保險人若對另定保險費不同意者，契約即為終止。反之，若危險減少，被保險人得請求保險人重新核定保費，方為公平，此即我國保險法第59條及60條所規定之精神。ICC,2009第10條為被保險人自願變更保險航程之保險效力與理賠規定，三套條款亦為相同之規定。條款內容列如表11-7。

表 11-7　ICC,2009 第 10 條變更航程

條款	內容
Change of Voyage	10.1 Where, after attachment of this insurance, the destination is changed by the Assured, this must be notified promptly to Insurers for rates and terms to be agreed. Should a loss occur prior to such agreement being obtained cover may be provided but only if cover would have been available at a reasonable commercial market rate on reasonable market terms. 10.2 Where the subject-matter insured commences the transit contemplated by this insurance（in accordance with Clause 8.1）, but, without the knowledge of the Assured or their employees the ship sails for another destination, this insurance will nevertheless be deemed to have attached at commencement of such transit.
	10.1 本保險生效後，被保險人變更其目的地者，必須立即通知保險人洽訂費率與條件；若在雙方合議達成之前發生損失，僅限於在如合理商業市場上，所允許之保險條件及費率下獲得賠償。 10.2 當保險標的依本保險開始運送時（依據第 8.1 款規定），但被保險人或其受僱人並不知該船將駛往其他目的地時，本保險仍視為自保險標的起運時起，保險效力即已開始。

資料來源：作者整理

　　依 MIA,1906 第 45 條之規定，當航程開始後，船舶之目的地自保險單所載明之目的地，自願性（voluntarily）任意變更。即若保險契約上所記載的航程為「從高雄港至鹿特丹」（from Kaohsiung to Rotterdam），當船舶於高雄港發航後，若改以除鹿特丹港以外的港口為目的港，則被保險航程之目的地已經變更，此稱為「變更航程」。概念如圖 11-1。

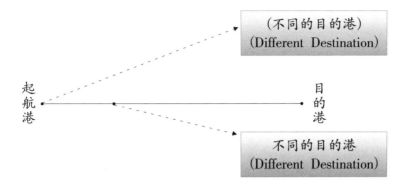

（不同的目的港）
(Different Destination)

起航港　　　　　　　　　　　　　目的港

不同的目的港
(Different Destination)

圖 11-1　雙更航程概念圖

資料來源：作者自繪

　　若有自願性變更航程情況，MIA,1906 第 45 條規定，除保險契約另有規定外，保險人自顯示改變決定之時起，即解除責任（Unless the policy otherwise provides, where there is a change of voyage the insurer is discharged from liability as from the time of change, that is to say, as from the time when the determination to change it is manifested）。條文規定為「解除責任（discharged liability）」，而非解除契約或終止契約，乃在避免是否退還保險費的問題產生；由此字義亦表示於此情況之下保險契約仍存在，僅往後不生效力，亦便於另訂條款與加費繼續承保，否則若其法律效果為契約消滅，即不得再加保[3]。

　　本條款規定保險單效力開始後，被保險人決意變更目的地，則若被保險人能立即通知保險公司要求繼續延長保險單效力，並加繳保險人所要求增收的保險費，則保險仍將繼續有效。於上條件的限制之下，保險人得使保險契約效力暫時承保（Held covered）。然，若被保險人不履行以上條件，則保險單效力仍自保險人改變目的地時終止。

---

[3] 莊雲雁（2007），《海上貨物保險之研究》，長榮大學航運管理研究所碩士論文，頁 24。

惟 ICC,2009 刪除 ICC,1982 條款中之"Held covered"字句，因"Held covered"一詞籠統不明，一般大眾對於此專有名詞甚難了解，於閱讀本條時常無法理解其規範內容而產生糾紛，ICC,2009 改以更簡明的文句敘述與解釋其暫保的意義，使簽訂保險契約之當事人更能清楚了解其條款規定。

第 10.1 條再新增若在新保險條件洽定之前發生貨損，則依當前實務上客觀合理的費率與承保條件（reasonable commercial market rate on reasonable market terms）而決定理賠責任。 此外，ICC,2009 新增10.2 款規定，當保險標的物開始運送之時，被保險人或其受僱人並不知其變更航程的事宜，則保險效力仍視爲有效，以平衡當事雙方權益，此修訂結果對於被保險人應較爲有利。

ICC,2009 相較於 ICC,1982 新增之條款部分，可讓被保險人求償時有一新的彈性條件，即雖然被保險人已經通知變更航程，但在新的保險條件及費率尚未確定時，若發生保險事故，保險人仍然須依當前實務上客觀合理費率與承保條件處理理賠。故在 ICC,2009 規定下，加強核保人員專業素養是當務之急，尤其應對航運實務及各區域海運地理熟悉，方能對航程變更之前後做出危險正確的危險評估。而一旦新的保險條件尚未協議之前發生保險事故，除核保人員須客觀評估費率與承保條件，理賠人員亦同時審核理賠文件處理賠款事宜，對保險公司而言，收取保險費與保險理賠間之對價關係將可能極爲懸殊，故此新條款規定，可能將是核保與理賠實務運作的挑戰。

至於 ICC,2009 新增第 10.2 款規定，當保險標的物依保險契約開始運送時，若被保險人或其員工並不知該船將駛往其他目的地時，本保險仍視爲自保險標的物開始運送時即已生效。一旦發生保險事故時，要如何判斷被保險人或其受僱人於開始運送前是否知情將變更航程，實務上應該有一定的困難；換言之，若事故發生於爲了裝載的第一次移動開始，若保險人無法舉證該運送將變更原來目的地，則保險人仍應負保險賠償之責。

12

第十二章 •••••••••

ICC,2009 之理賠事項

第一節　保險利益

　　ICC,2009 條款結構中自第 11 條至第 14 條屬於有關保險事故後的理賠規定，ICC,2009(A)、(B) 及 (C) 三組條款內容均相同。第 11 條為貨物保險利益條款，內容如表 12-1。

表 12-1　ICC,2009 第 11 條

條款	內容
ICC,2009 第 11 條 保險利益	11.1 In order to recover under this insurance the Assured must have an insurable interest in the subject-matter insured at the time of the loss. 11.2 Subject to Clause 11.1 above, the Assured shall be entitled to recover for insured loss occurring during the period covered by this insurance, notwithstanding that the loss occurred before the contract of insurance was concluded, unless the Assured were aware of the loss and the Insurers were not.
	11.1 被保險人欲獲得本保險之賠償，需於損害發生時對保險標的具有保險利益。 11.2 依據上述第 11.1 條款規定，除非被保險人已知該損失已經發生而保險人不知者，縱使損失是發生於保險契約簽訂之前，被保險人仍有權要求保險期間內所發生承保範圍內之損失賠償。

資料來源：作者整理

　　所謂貨物保險利益指貨物所有權人對該貨物的關係，基於此種關係，當於意外事故發生時，將受到或財務上之不利益或者減損，此種關係於保險契約中即稱爲保險利益。保險人處理賠案首要考量的三件要素爲是否爲保險事故、是否發生於保險期間，以及求償人是否具有保險利益，足見保險利益在保險契約中的重要性。保險契約一定要具有保險利益的目的除了可避免道德危險以及賭博行爲外，保險利益於補償性的保險契約中，可做爲決定保險人賠償責任的限額。

　　依本條第 11.1 規定，被保險人應於事故發生時具有保險利益方可向保險人求償，此款可謂完全繼受 MIA,1906 第 6 條第 1 項前段之規定，其內容爲 "The assured must be interested in the subject-matter insured at the time of the loss though he need not be interested when the insurance is effected." 實務上，貨物所有人對貨物基於所有權的關係，因貨物安全運抵目的地而不喪失其經濟上的利害關係；反之，將因貨物之滅失、毀滅或被留置而喪失，或減少其經濟上的利害關係；因此，貨物所有權人於事故發生時必須具有保險利益，並且遭受損害，方得享有保險給付請求權。可知被保險人於保險事故發生時，對保險標的物則必須要有利益關係，但於保險契約訂立時，並不需具有保險利益。此一規定主要是因海上貿易而產生，如於保險期間內保險標的可能會有出售或移轉的情形，或可能被保險人於保險契約締訂時可能尚未持有保險利益，嗣後於損害發生前取得保險利益，如 FOB 貿易條件之買方爲被保險人，於投保時可能貨物尚未裝船，故並未具有保險利益，但此保險契約仍然有效，只要意外事故發生時，買方（被保險人）已經有保險利益，保險人則應該要負賠償責任；又如 CIF 爲貿易條件出口之買方，當保險單轉讓及貨物裝船後，也具有保險利益。故貨物買受人或保單受讓人，雖訂約時尚未有保險利益，但在損害發生時，保險給付請求權人（實際受有損害的人）應確認具有保險利益。

　　又如實務上大型進出口貿易公司爲節省保險投保時效，與保險公司訂立預約保險契約（open policy），即把各種承保條件一次談妥如條款、保險投保乘數、貨物種類、費率、地區、申報方式、理賠約定以及承保限額等事項，並約定一年爲合約期間的保險契約，然後由被保險人再按月彙報進出口貨物資料給保險公司計算保費。所以，預約保險於訂約時絕大部分情況貨物根本尚未起運，尤其就進口而言，絕對無法稱已具有保險利益，但也不會因此而使預約保險單失效。換言之，被保險人於保險契約訂立時，對保險標的是否具有保險利益並不重要，惟保險契約需基於保險利益而存在，故在損害發生時請求權人需具有保險利益，才得請求依保險契約損害賠償。

　　第 11.2 款與 MIA,1906 第 6 條第 1 項後段但書之規定雖文句上不同，但精神意義卻是相同，其條款之內容爲 "Provided that where the subject–matter is insured "lost or not lost", the assured may recover although he may not have acquired his interest until after the loss, unless at the time of effecting the contract of insurance the assured as aware of the loss, and the insurer was not." 由條文規定可知，如保險標的係以 "lost or not lost" 爲條件保險時，被保險人在不知損失已發生情況下，雖於損失發生後才取得保險利益，其保險契約仍然有效，可自保險人處獲得理賠。在早期，海上事故發生後，因資訊傳達落後，貨主並無法即時得知貨損情況與原因，可能對被保險的貨物（保險標的）仍不斷地轉手，以致常有保險事故已發生，但因交易當事人在不知情下仍受讓貨物情況，此時的保險利益之取得係於保險事故發生後，爲避免不知情的善意受讓人蒙受損害，故有此但書規定。因此，海上貨物保險之保險利益存在時點，並無硬性規定要求被保險人在保險契約生效開始至保險契約終止的這段期間內，對保險標的物必須有繼續性的保險利益關係，即使訂約時無保險利益存在，只要於保險事故發生時具有保險利益，即可請求保險理賠。

　　如同 MIA,1906 的 "lost or not lost" 概念也見於我國保險法第 51 條，條文爲：「保險契約訂立時，保險標的之危險已發生或已消滅者，其契約無效。但為當事人雙方所不知者，不在此限。訂約時，僅要保人知危險已發生者，保險人不受契約的拘束。訂約時，僅保險人知危險已消滅者，要保人不受契約之拘束。」第51條所規定之兩個重點為保險標的之危險已發生，和保險標的之危險已消滅。所謂「保險標的危險已發生」指保險事故或損失已經發生了，如火災或碰撞已經發生；而「保險標的之危險已消滅」指損失發生的機率為零，也就是不可能再發生了，這個在實務上很難想像有什麼危險是絕對不可能發生，且就保險學理角度，這也不符合危險是「損失的不確定」的定義。不論如何，這兩種情況之保險契約的效力都是自始無效。至於若有當事人一方已知者，則另一方不受契約的拘束。所謂「不受拘束」指的是當事人的一方可以主張保險契約對他方不發生效力，但該相對人則沒有權利主張契約不生效力。

以海上貨物保險角度而言，如 FOB 進口商於投保時並不知貨物已在國外運輸途中或倉儲期間，甚至裝櫃時已經遭受損害，則保險人仍應對此損害負賠償責任；除非貨主已知貨物已遭受損害，而仍向保險人訂立保險契約，則依保險法規定，保險契約自始無效。

第二節　轉運費用

海上運送難免發生意外事故，若因保險事故發生後承運船舶無法繼續航行，為使貨物可以順利抵達原目的地，勢必要安排轉運，若運送人願意安排轉運則相關轉運費用由運送人吸收，但若該海上意外非運送人應負責之事故，可能該轉運費用仍必須由貨主自行負擔，因此 ICC,2009 第 12 條規定，當保險事故發生時，保險人願意賠償被保險人相關的轉運費用。轉運費用條款於 ICC,2009 (A)、(B) 及 (C) 三組條款內容均相同。條款內容如 12-2。

表 12-2　ICC,2009 第 12 條

條款	內容
ICC,2009 第 12 條 轉運費用	Where, as a result of the operation of a risk covered by this insurance, the insured transit is terminated at a port or place other than that to which the subject-matter insured is covered under this insurance, the Insurers will reimburse the Assured for any extra charges properly and reasonably incurred in unloading storing and forwarding the subject-matter insured to the destination to which it is insured. This Clause 12, which does not apply to general average or salvage charges, shall be subject to the exclusions contained in Clauses 4, 5, 6 and 7 above, and shall not include charges arising from the fault negligence insolvency or financial default of the Assured or their employees.
	當本保險所承保的危險事故發生後，保險航程在非屬本保險契約載明的港口或地點終止時，保險人將補償被保險人因保險標的卸載、儲存及轉運至目的地之適當且合理發生的額外費用。 本第 12 條不適用於共同海損或救助費用，並應受前述第 4、5、6 及 7 條除外條款規定的限制，且不包括被保險人或其受僱人之過失疏忽破產或財務糾紛所引起的費用。

資料來源：作者整理

　　本條為貨物運輸保險之專有條款，在船舶保險中並不適用，因為只有貨物才會因運送的船舶在航程中發生問題，而需要轉運的現象，而船舶在發生問題之後，除了修護以後自行駛離避難港口外，便是要中止航程（abandon voyage）不再繼續運送。若船舶開航後遭遇到危險事故迫使航程終止，船舶並駛至正常航程以外的港口進行避難，則保險人將補償被保險人相關合理且適當的額外費用，如在避難港的卸貨及儲存費用，轉運至保險單原先所承保的地點而發生的合理轉運費用。由條款觀之，所謂「轉運費用」其範圍不僅僅在於「運費」而已，尚包括保險標的在避難港自遇難船舶上卸下的費用，在避難港暫存的費用以及再轉運的費用三項，其中轉運的運費中就航運實務而言，當也已包括了在避難港的重新裝船費用了。

另，本條的轉運費用意義，是不與共同海損（General Average）和救助費用（Salvage Charges）一併計算，前述兩者費用的產生，有各自所需的要件，不能混爲計算。換言之，如果事故發生後，若未宣布共同海損，其轉運費用當然就不是共同海損費用；相同的邏輯下，當救助費用產生，也不能計算於轉運費用之中。

轉運費用的性質，原本極爲類似損害防阻費用，因爲保險事故發生，使得運送航程在目的地「以外」的地點終止，此時貨物若不加以適當的處理，則在卸貨之後受風吹雨打，日曬雨淋，甚至被竊等，都會使得貨物發生損失，爲了防止這種現象，便應鼓勵被保險人儘快將貨物轉運至原目的地，所發生的合理費用也應該合理補償，自是符合損害防阻費用的原則。1982 年以前以損害防阻費用名義給付的這種費用，至 1982 年以後便更名爲轉運費用，若符合轉運費用定義的相關費用，被保險人即可直接依本條文獲得賠理賠[1]。

轉運費用雖然具有減少損害或避免全損的涵義，但本條也特別明訂轉運費用，並非共同海損費用或者救助費用，因不論是共同海損或者是救助費用都有其成立的要件，各自獨立認定，有關共同海損及救助費用意義，請參考本書第九章第二節。但是若發生海難後，船東一旦宣布共同海損，若轉運費用之發生符合共同海損費用之要件，則將併入共同海損費用之計算，由全體利害關係人一起分擔，保險人未來也就待理算完成後，直接賠付被保險人應分攤的共同海損分擔，此時也就不會再以轉運費用賠償了。

本條另有一點須特別注意，即條款明文規定保險人除同意賠付於保險事故發生後之轉運費用，但也進一步限制若是因第 4 條、第 5 條、第 6 條及第 7 條等除外事項所引起之轉運費用，保險人也不負賠償之責，尤其若是由被保險人或其受僱人因過失、破產或財務問題所

---

[1] 徐當仁、曾文瑞（2000），《初學者海上保險基礎理論與實務》，第四章，頁 21–22。

產生的轉運費用，自然更不在本條的支付範圍之內。故在ICC,2009
(A)條款中因為是採概括式承保，故只要不是除外事項所造成的轉運
費用，保險人都會賠償，而ICC,2009(B)及(C)條款為採列舉式之承
保範圍，故保險人賠償轉運費用的條件除了必須是承保危險之事故
外，也不能是除外事項所引之事故，如船舶碰撞雖然是列舉的危險事
故，但若是因為戰爭所引起的船舶碰撞，則之後的轉運費用保險人仍
然不負賠償之責，因為船舶碰撞是由戰爭所引起。故採列舉式之承保
方式下，保險人所同意賠償之轉運費用，除了須是承保危險所引起，
也必須同時考量該危險事故是否為除外事項所造成，兩者要件為嚴格
的交集認定，以決定保險人的賠償責任。

第三節　推定全損

　　在損害填補原則之下被保險人若不能證明保險標的已發生全部損
失，不得請求保險人以全損理賠；根據 MIA,1906 第 56 條之規定，海
上保險之損失若不是全部損失，則必為部分損失（A loss may be
either total or partial. Any loss other than a total loss, as hereinafter
defined, is a partial loss.）。惟於海上保險實務上，有時保險標的雖非
全損，卻與全損無異，海上保險之保險標的具有高度的流動性及國際
性，往往在事故發生時損失評估鑑定不易，究是以全損或部分損失索
賠，當損失鑑定程序曠日廢時，為使航貿業者能儘速獲得賠償，乃將
部分損失以一特殊認定方式承認其為全損，也就是所謂的推定全損
（Constructive Total Loss）。在 ICC,2009 第 13 條對於推定全損的理
賠有詳細規定。本條款於 ICC,2009(A)、(B)及(C)三組條款內容均相
同詳如表 12–3。

表 12-3　ICC,2009 第 13 條

條款	內容
ICC,2009 第 13 條 推定全損	No claim for Constructive Total Loss shall be recoverable hereunder unless the subject-matter insured is reasonably abandoned either on account of its actual total loss appearing to be unavoidable or because the cost of recovering, reconditioning and forwarding the subject-matter insured to the destination to which it is insured would exceed its value on arrival.
	除非保險標的已經合理委付，或因實際全損已無法避免，或將回復、整理及轉運至保險契約載明目的地的費用合計，超過到達目的地之價值者，否則不得以推定全損請求賠償。

資料來源：作者整理

一、實際全損之意義

依 MIA,1906 第 56 條第 1 項規定，海上保險的損失分類採二分法，即不是全部損失就是部份損失，再依第 2 項規定，全部損失又再二分為實際全損（Actual Total Loss）以及推定全損（A total loss may be either an actual total loss, or a constructive total loss.）。其邏輯概念如圖 12-1 所示。

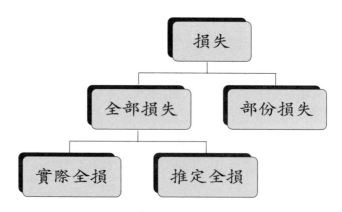

圖 12-1　英國海上保險法損失分類
資料來源：作者自繪

MIA,1906 第 57 條對實際全損所下之定義是：「凡保險標的毀損或損壞至不復為原保險標的或保險標的之物權喪失而不能再歸復為被保險人者，即為實際全損。」（Where the subject-matter insured is destroyed, or so damaged as to cease to be a thing of the kind insured, or where the assured is irretrievably deprived thereof, there is an actual total loss.）

由上述條文可知，實際全損 MIA,1906 之規定下，有下列三種狀況：

1.保險標的物完全毀損（Where the subject-matter insured is destroyed）。指保險標的因保險事故之發生造成保險標的的完全毀損、滅失，無法再回復原狀者，如沉沒、火災焚毀。

2.保險標的喪失原保險標的之屬性（Where the subject matter ceases to be a thing of the kind insured）。指保險標的從商業觀點而言，已喪失原有屬性（loss of specie）及商業價值，如遭濕損的紙卷、變質的液態化學品，其雖未完全毀損，但原有屬性已不復存在也無法再做為商業銷售，則亦為實際全損。

3.被保險人喪失對保險標的之所有權（Where the assured is irretrievably deprived of the subject matter）。被保險人對其所有權保險利益已確定不能回復，如貨物失竊。

另一個視為實際全損之概念見於 MIA,1906 第 58 條，其規定：「凡航行中船舶失蹤經過相當合理期間，仍未有消息時可視為實際全損。」（Where the ship concerned in the adventure is missing, and after the lapse of a reasonable time no news of her has been received, an actual total loss may be presumed.）

此項規定指船舶自最後得知其訊息至現在，已經過一段合理期間（missing after the lapse of a reasonable time），因 1906 年以前通訊不發達，船舶結構也不如現在的船舶，若有一段時間都沒有消息，即有可能已經沉沒，為避免無法處理全損賠案，則將此情況視為實際全損。而又何謂「合理期間」？則係一個案問題。依 MIA 第 88 條則明白指出合理期間為一事實上的個案認定問題（the question what is reasonable is a question of fact）。亦即必須依每一個不同案例實際狀況做判定，流露出相當濃厚英美法的特色。

二、推定全損之意義

"Constructive Total Loss" 於國內大都譯為「推定全損」，但也有部分學者認為應譯為「擬制全損」。推定者，係對於某種事實之存在或不存在，因無明顯之證據，而參考周圍情事或已知的事理，藉以推論未知事實。但此種推定，原則上為謀處理上之便利而設，倘若能證明其所推定並非真實，自可舉反證加以推翻。所謂擬制者，係對於某種事實之存在或不存在，基於公益上需要，依據法律政策而為的法律效果的擬定。換言之，擬制者就是以法律承認，虛擬狀態可以發生真實效果的特別規定，通常在法律條文中有「視為」之字樣者，即屬於擬制規定。擬制是「法律效果的賦予」，只有構成要件是否合致判斷的問題，不可舉反證推翻，與「推定」不同，推定的效力輕弱而不確定，若有反證出現，即得推翻之，而擬制的法律效果強而有確定[2]。

筆者以為既然 MIA,1906 第 57 條已經規定實際全損之定義，若不能符合該定義之損失可能為部分損失，但也可能是如依 MIA, 1906 第 60 條第 1 項所規定之 "constructive total loss"。被保險人於事故發生後欲以全損或部分損失請求賠償，為被保險人的權利，如 MIA, 1906 第 62 條第 1 項之規定，若被保險人未發出委付通知給保險人，則以部分損失處理；反之，保險人是否接受被保險人的委付，保險人也有決定權，此確認或協議過程純由當事人舉證以決定是否為全損，

---

[2] 汪紹銘，民法上之推定與擬制之探討，《法學評論》，第 52 卷第 10 期，民國 75 年 10 月，頁 12–13。

故雖被保險人主張全損之賠償，但保險人若有反證，自也可以推翻該全損求償之論點，或由法院依法及事實證據裁決是否為全損。雖然，一旦法院裁判或保險人承認後，表示即發生全損之效果，且被保險人不得再撤銷其請求全損之意思，如 MIA,1906 第 62 條第 6 項及海商法第 148 條均有明文，但此乃成立全損後之效果，與是否得以成立全損的推定不同。綜上所述，"constructive total loss" 之翻譯就其是否得以成立全損的過程觀之，以及以「推定全損」為中文翻譯已是我國海上保險業長久的習慣，故宜應譯為「推定全損」方可貼近其法律規定概念及符合實務運作共識。

推定全損之學說起源於海上保險，亦也應只適用於海上保險，MIA,1906 第 60 條第 1 項對於推定全損之定義為：「除了保險單上有任何明示之規定，若保險標的因實際全損已無法避免而合理委付者，或如不支付超過其修復後價值之費用，將無法避免實際全損者，即為推定全損。」（Subject to any express provision in the policy, there is a constructive total loss where the subject-matter insured is reasonably abandoned on account of its actual total loss appearing to the unavoidable, or because it could not be preserved from actual total loss without an expenditure which would exceed its value when the expenditure had been incurred.）

第 2 項再進一步規定在下列情況下可成立推定全損：

1.被保險人因保險危險事故發生，導致喪失其對於船舶或貨物之所有權，且(a)似乎無收回其船舶或貨物之可能或(b)收回其船舶或貨物之費用將超過收回後的價值。（Where the assured is deprived of the possession of his ship or goods by a peril insured against, and (a) it is unlikely that he can recover the ship or goods, as the case may be, or (b) the cost of recovering the ship or goods, as the case my be, would exceed their when recovered.）

2.船舶因保險事故發生而遭受損害，其修理費用將超過修復後的價值。（In the case of damage to a ship, where she is so damaged by a peril insured against that the cost of repairing the damage would exceed the value of the ship when repaired.）

本款更進一步規定修理費用估計是以若有可自其他利益關係人處收回的共同海損分攤不需自修理費用中扣除，但將來必須分攤的共同海損分攤及救助費用應併入修理費用估計（In estimating the cost of repairs, no deduction is to be made in respect of general average contributions to those repairs payable by other interests, but account is to be taken of the expense of future salvage operations and of any future general average contributions to which the ship would be liable if repaired）。這樣的規定無非是爲使估計之回復原狀的費用相對增加，可以更容易達到全損被推定成立的門檻，符合推定全損的商業考量及經濟效率的立法精神。但此修理費用估算只應用來判斷是否可成立推定全損之依據，切不可做爲當推定全損無法成立，不同當事人間應賠償金額的最後決定。

3.貨物遭受損害，其修理費用及轉運至目的地費用將超過該貨物抵達目的地之價值。（In the case of damage to goods, where the cost of repairing the damage and forwarding the goods to their destination would exceed their value on arrival.）

由 MIA,1906 第 60 條之規定歸納可知成立推定全損之情形有二：

1.意外事故發生後，實際全損已無法避免。例如貨物置於貨櫃集散站準備運送出口，遭颱風侵襲造成櫃場積水嚴重貨櫃幾乎滅頂或飄流，短時間內大雨仍無法停止，故全損勢所難免。

2.恢復保險標的之費用將超過標的物回復後的價值。這一點大都爲實務上主要考量的判斷標準，也完全自商業及經濟考量被保險人是否得以全損索賠。保險事故發生後，若估計回復原狀之費用（或稱修理費用）船舶修理費用超過船舶經修理後的價值，如估計之修理費美金 3,000 萬，但修復後的價值僅剩美金 2,800 萬，就社會資源及經濟價值而言，已經不具再修復的價值，故 MIA,1906 在此情況下推定其全損成立；而貨物之全損推定則是以估計的修理費用加上轉運費用合計的金額，是否超過貨物修復後到達目的地的價值做為評估依據。

綜上可知，MIA,1906 於在成立推定全損的門檻方面，是以「估計之船舶修理費用」必須超出「估計修復後之價值」；而貨物則是必須超出「修復後貨物抵達目的地的價值」，亦即估計的回復費用若高於回復後的價值或至目的地的價值，則認為在商業經濟觀點已無再修復必要，徒增社會有效資源的浪費，故直接逕以全損索賠。惟求償過程中若保險人不同意被保險人的估價，都可以舉出反證推翻此估價推定，最後是否得以成立推定全損則視保險人是否同意，或交由法院裁判而決定。MIA,1906 舶船推定全損概念如圖 12.-2，貨物推定全損概念如圖 12-3。

圖 12-2　MIA, 1906 船舶推定全損概念圖
資料來源：作者自繪

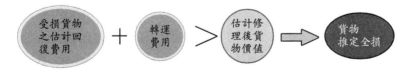

圖 12-3　MIA, 1906 貨物推定全損概念圖
資料來源：作者自繪

ICC,2009 第 13 條中對於推定全損之規定，原則上可謂完全繼受 MIA,1906 第 60 條第 2 項第 3 款而來。在條款中僅將推定全損成立標準語句改爲貨物的恢復（recovering）、整修（reconditioning）與轉運（forwarding）的費用合計，超過貨物到達目的地的價值則可構成推定全損。但概念上 MIA,1906 的「修理（repair）」，其實與 ICC,2009 的「恢復（recovering）」及「整修（reconditioning）」並無不同，故實質內容並無改變。

三、委付（abandon）之意義

當被保險人認爲其保險標的所受到的損害已經嚴重到達到推定全損的條件時，就可向保險人進行委付。委付是指保險事故發生後，被保險人移轉保險標的物之一切權利於保險人，而請求支付該保險標的物全部保險金額之行爲。換言之，被保險人爲成立推定全損必須險向保險人做一明確的意思表示，在實務上稱爲委付通知（notice of abandonment）。不論實際全損或推定全損，被保險人最終目的是希望能獲得全部的保險金額賠款，然而僅有在推定全損情況下才做委付通知。MIA,1906 第 57 條第 2 項規定若符合實際全損條件，被保險人並不需發委付通知（In the case of an actual total loss no notice of abandonment need be given.）。反之，若欲以推定全損向保險人求償則須發出委付通知，否則將被認爲僅以部分損失索賠，此爲 MIA, 1906 第 62 條第 1 之明文規定：

"Subject to the provisions of this section, where the assured elects to abandon the subject–matter insured to the insurer, he must give notice of abandonment. If he fails to do so the loss can only be treated as a partial loss."

委付通知是一個請求推定全損意思表示，實務上並無限制其形式要件，被保險人可以書面或口頭表示，或部分書面部分口頭表示，或者任何足以表明委付之意思表示作委付通知，亦即只要清楚的不附任何條件表明委付之意思，均是委付通知。在委付通知的時效規定，被保險人必須在獲知損失發生之消息後，合理迅速地發出通知，但若對該損失消息有所質疑，被保險人可在一合理期間查詢後再決定是否發出委付通知。主要是希望被保險人在確定損失情況後立即做出決定，否則不論是權利義務的認定，或殘餘物利益處理均會比較困難，同時對保險人而言較不公平，有失法律衡平原則。

委付不可以有任何附帶條件（unconditionally），委付範圍必須是被保險人在保險標的上的全部保險利益，因為當決定委付即表示放棄保險標的所有權而準備以全損索賠，所以當然僅能以全部保險標的利益委付。在實務上有可能發生一張保險單上有多種可分割的保險標的，例如一個貨櫃內裝 50 個箱子，其中 10 個箱子發現符合推定全損的條件，則被保險人可以僅將這 10 個箱子進行委付，而不用全部 50 個箱子一起委付，這即所謂可分割的全損，在海上保險的理賠實務上是經常發生的。MIA,1906 第 76 條第 1 項後段也有提及這個觀念。委付通知是一種意思表示，所以被保險人對委付意思表示也有可能撤回，惟必須注意是只有在保險人尚未承諾同意前才可以撤回，換句話說，若委付通知已經被承諾有效後，就不可以再撤回了。此乃基於委付是被保險人的一個選擇權，在尚未決定或被承諾前，自可以選擇變更之；但是一旦保險人承認有效後，權利義務已確定移轉，若再輕易更改將使問題複雜化，且保險人無異也處於被動之不利地位，並不合理。

保險人接受委付或者法院判決有效後，保險人除必須給付全部保險金以外，尚有權取得（is entitled to take）保險標的物之殘餘利益，即其有選擇權決定是否接收殘餘物，而非強制性必須接收，因為極有可能保險人接收殘餘物之後將伴隨著龐大義務，如此對保險人而言，將處於不利地位，所以英國海上保險法認為保險人可以僅賠付全損而選擇不取得殘餘物，也不負擔基於該殘餘物的一切義務。此這個概念筆者認為於實際全損的情況，保險給付全部保險金之後之代位權取得，亦應該同樣適用。

實際全損與推定全損在取得保險標的所有權的時點並不相同，於推定全損情況下，保險標的物之殘餘利益移轉是在委付通知被接受時即發生，不須等到保險給付完成；而在實際全損之情況，則必須保險給付完成後，保險人取得代位權才發生保險標的物之殘餘利益移轉。當然，不論實際全損或推定全損，保險人履行其給付義務後，所代位取得對於有責第三人損害賠償請求權在兩者是一致的。

四、我國海商法的委付規定

我國海商法中並沒有實際全損及推定全損的規定，但於第 142 條則為定義委付之規定，並於第 143 條至第 145 條分別列舉船舶、貨物及運費的法定委付原因，將條文整理如表 12-4。

表 12-4　海商法中委付之意義及原因

委付之意義 （第 142 條）	海上保險之委付，指被保險人於發生第一百四十二條至第一百四十四條委付原因後，移轉保險標的物之一切權利於保險人，而請求支付該保險標的物全部保險金額之行為。
船舶委付之原因 （第 143 條）	被保險船舶有下列各款情形之一時，得委付之： 一、船舶被捕獲時。 二、船舶不能為修繕或修繕費用超過保險價額時。 三、船舶行蹤不明已逾二個月時。 四、船舶被扣押已逾二個月仍未放行時。 前項第四款所稱扣押不包含債權人聲請法院所為之查封、假扣押及假處分。
貨物委付之原因 （第 144 條）	被保險貨物有下列各款情形之一時，得委付之： 一、船舶因遭難，或其他事變不能航行已逾二個月而貨物尚未交付於受貨人、要保人或被保險人時。 二、裝運貨物之船舶，行蹤不明，已逾二個月時。 三、貨物因應由保險人員保險責任之損害，其回復原狀及繼續或轉運至目的地費用總額合併超過到達目的地價值時。
運費委付之原因 （第 145 條）	運費之委付得於船舶或貨物之委付時為之。

資料來源：作者整理自海商法

　　由上表規定可知，在我國海商法中將委付採列舉的方式，若符合法律規定則可以進行委付，但也就是因爲我國並沒有實際全損及推定全損之規定，故海商法中雖然法定委付原因之內容，就英國海上保險法而言，有些是屬於實質全損的情況，有的則是類似推定全損的情況，但在我國海商法規定中都須經過委付的程序方可求償全部保險金額，這是與英國海上保險法之規定極爲不同之處。雖然第142條並沒用使用「委付通知」的字樣，但依條文文字結構，理論上仍是要被保險人將委付的意思通知保險人，實務上也是如此進行。

　　另，海商法第146條規定委付應就保險標的物之全部爲之。但保險單上僅有其中一種標的物發生委付原因時，得就該一種標的物爲委付請求其保險金額。委付不得附有條件。此規定乃與英國海上保險法對於可分割全損之委付爲相同概念規定。當委付由保險人承認或法院判決有效後，我國海商法第147條規定保險標的物即「視爲」保險人所有。此項規定與英國海上保險之規定亦有明顯之不同；蓋在英國法中當推定全損成立後，保險人對於保險標的物之所有權乃是「有權取得」，故仍可以拋棄所有權的取得，但在海商法中已被「視爲」保險人所有，也就保險人一旦接受委付後不但取得殘餘物權，同時必須同時承擔因物權所伴隨著義務，如在港區內船舶擱淺後委付予保險人，當委付發生效力後保險人負有移除船舶的義務。

第四節　增值條款

　　在國際貿易的運輸的過程中，貨物價值基本上是以商業發票金額爲依據，爲求轉嫁運輸的風險，貨主可以原價加計10%做爲保險約定價額，並以此價額投保成爲保險金額。然國際貿易過程中或貨主爲賺取兩地市場間因供需關係所生的價差，亦可能仍在運送途中貨物已再轉手賣出，故貨物的價值也可能會隨著每次轉賣而增加。故就當時投保之原保險金額而言，幾經轉賣後極易形成不足額保險的情況，要增加保險金額的方法不外乎向保險人申請增加原保險單的保險金額，或再另外投保一張增值部分的保險。前者必須先向保險人申請並證明保險利益，若原保險人可能遠在他國，申請變更通知與變更後文件證明都必須寄送完成，有許多核保行政流程必須完成，可能緩不濟急。因此，英國協會貨物保險條款遂有「增值條款」（increased value clause）的產生，但本條在實務上並不多見。本條款在 ICC,2009 第 14 條之規定於三套條款都相同。條款規定如表 12-4。

表 12-4　ICC,2009 第 14 條

條款	內容
ICC,2009 第 14 條 增值條款	14.1　If any Increased Value insurance is effected by the Assured on the subject-matter insured under this insurance the agreed value of the subject-matter insured shall be deemed to be increased to the total amount insured under this insurance and all Increased Value insurances covering the loss, and liability under this insurance shall be in such proportion as the sum insured under this insurance bears to such total amount insured. In the event of claim the Assured shall provide the Insurers with evidence of the amounts insured under all other insurances. 14.2　Where this insurance is on Increased Value the following clause shall apply: The agreed value of the subject-matter insured shall be deemed to be equal to the total amount insured under the primary insurance and all Increased Value insurances covering the loss and effected on the subject-matter insured by the Assured, and liability under this insurance shall be in such proportion as the sum insured under this insurance bears to such total amount insured. In the event of claim the Assured shall provide the Insurers with evidence of the amounts insured under all other insurances.
	14.1　若被保險人對本保險之保險標的安排了增值保險，則該保險標的之約定價值將被視為增加至本保險與其他全部增值保險之保險金額之總和，而本保險之責任將按保險金額占全部保險金額之比例而定。 當被保險人求償時，必須提出所有其他已保險之保險金額之證明予保險人。 14.2　若本保險為增值保險則須適用下列條款： 保險標的之約定價值視為原保險與全部由被保險人安排投保相同損失之增值保險的保險金額總和，而本保險之責任將按其保險金額占全部保險金額之比例而定。 當被保險人索賠時，必須提出所有其他已保險之保險金額之證明給保險人。

資料來源：作者整理

　　依本條款意義，其所規定內容即為複保險概念，所謂複保險即被保險人與兩個或兩個以上之保險人針對同一保險標的、同一保險利

益、同一保險事故於同一保險期間內簽定二張以上的保險契約。在我國保險法中，將複保險分成善意以及惡意複保險，即意圖不當得利或未對複保險的情況通知各保險人者稱為惡意複保險，若發生惡意複保險時，根據保險法第 37 條之規定契約無效。但若為善意複保險，則各保險人僅就其所保金額負比例分擔之責。故原保險單（Primary Insurance）與「增加價值保險單」（Increased Value Insurance） 的被保險人一開始可能不是同一人，但原保險單一定會經過背書的手續移轉給「增加價值保險單」的被保險人，故就事實認定與請求權歸屬而言，兩張保險單的被保險人則是同一人，故依保險法規定必須要在投保增加價值保險時告知保險人此一情形，才不致於變成惡意複保險。

MIA,1906 第 32 條第 1 項規定複保險之定義： "Where two or more policies are effected by or on behalf of the assured on the same adventure and interest or any part thereof, and the sums insured exceed the indemnity allowed by this Act, the assured is said to be over-insured by double insurance." 可知當被保險人在同一航程中基於同一保險利益而向二個以上保險人訂立保險契約，且超額保險（over-insurance）時即稱為複保險。換言之，在英國法的概念中若兩張以上保險契約之總保險金額未超過保險標的之價值者，仍不構成複保險。故我國保險法中規定之複保險，則不論有無超額保險皆為複保險不同，且 MIA,1906 32 所規定者僅為超額保險需盡通知義務，而我國保險法中對於未構成超額保險也需盡通知的義務，否則契約無效，若就未超額保險之複保險而言，其已經變成危險分散投保之概念，只要沒有超額保險而就沒有不當得利問題，是否應通知有其他保險存在，仍有討論必要，更不應讓未通知變成契約無效的法定原因，對善意的被保險人似有不公。

發生複保險後被保險人求償時，於 MIA,1906 第 32 條第 2 項規定，可由被保險人先向任一保險人索賠全部的損失，而後再由該保險人向其他保險人求償，故概念上所有保險人間屬「連帶債務」的性質。至於保險人之間分攤的標準，則是以各保險單的「賠償金額」（the amount for which he is liable under his contract）爲基礎，負比例分攤之責，此概念在我國稱爲「獨立責任比例分攤法」，亦即先計算各保險人個別依其契約應賠償之金額，再按其對全保險人總賠償金額之比例負分攤賠償之責。

然依 ICC,2009 第 14 條之規定，若保險標的轉賣之後價值提高，被保險人或貨主對其貨物投保了增值保險，則原保險之約定價值與增值部分之約定價值加總即爲總保險金額。於保險事故發生後被保險人索賠時，則採用比例分擔原則計算各不同保險人應賠償金額，即「保險金額比例分攤制」的概念，以個別保險金額除以總保險金額爲其賠償之比例，爲其分攤基準。如原保險單保險金額爲美金 50,000 元，增值保險單之保險金額爲美金 30,000 元，若發生保險事故損失美金 20,000 元，則比例賠償計算如下：

原保險人　：20,000 X 50,000/（50,000 + 30,000）= 12,500
增值保險人：20,000 X 30,000/（50,000 + 30,000）= 7,500

最後，有關增值保險之保險利益方面，依我國保險法第 14 條規定：「要保人對於財產上之現有利益，或因財產上之現有利益而生之期待利益，有保險利益。」因現有利益而生的期待利益，謂保險契約成立時對被保險雖尚未存在，但本於現有之所有權，可以合理期待將來會產生的保險利益。如對於貨主於貨物到達時有合理估計的利潤，即可稱爲合理期待利益。

實務上，增值保險之被保險人於投保增值保險時，對於保險利益即屬於期待利益，原則上需與保險人協商貨物的期待利益做爲保險利益，此種保單則稱爲保單證明利益保險單（Policy proof of interest policy），簡稱 P.P.I 保單。被保險人應具有保險利益方可請求賠償，已為損害補償原則之鐵律。故當增值保險之被保險人於投保時僅以保險單證明保險利益，雖然在 MIA,1906 第 4 條第 2 項(b)款中規定，若保險單約定「除保險單本身以外不必進一步證明保險利益（Without further proof of interest than the policy itself），應視為無效之賭博性契約。但若事故發生後，被保險人可以證明其合理的預期利益，則性質上已非 P.P.I 保單，而是合法有效的保險利益，保險人依 ICC,2009 第 14 條規定仍應負賠償之責。

第 十三 章 ·········

保險權益

　　被保險人或基於有效保險契約之請求權人，因保險事故發生時具有保險利益，而向保險人請求損害賠償；然在貨物保險中，因貨物運送過程乃是由運送人或其履行輔助人監督與保管，故造成貨損原因可能是該運送人或其履行輔助人造成，此時保險人賠償予被保險人後將行使代位求償權向運送人或其履行輔助人追償，惟若在當時託運時於運送契約中訂定享有保險權益之條款，則將造成保險人於代位追權時無法順利索賠。

　　例如貨主（被保險人）進口貨物一批，保險金額為 800 萬元，在運送過程中因裝卸過程不當而導致貨物發生損壞，損失金額共計 100 萬元，此時被保險人依保險契約規定向保險人請求賠償後，保險人即依法取得保險代位權，進而轉向船公司求償 100 萬元。然若該保險請求權由被保險人貨主轉予運送人後，則變成由運送人賠付給貨主 100 萬元後，運送人可基於受讓後之請求權轉再向保險人求償。在此情況下，保險人因被保險人將請求權轉讓予他人，故無法進行保險代為向運送人追償 100 萬元，造成保險人不利。因此貨物保險人遂在保險條款中明訂運送人及其他關係人，不得享有保險契約的權益。本條款在 ICC,2009 第 15 條規定於三套條款都相同。條款規定如表 13–1。

表 13-1　ICC,2009 第 15 條

條款	內容
ICC,2009 第 15 條 Benefit of Insurance （保險權益）	This insurance 15.1 covers the Assured which included the person claiming indemnity either as the person by or on whose behalf the contract of insurance was effected or as an assignee, 15.2 shall not extend to or otherwise benefit the carrier or their bailee.
	本保險 15.1 承保之被保險人包括基於保險契約而求償之人、或代表有效保險契約而請求賠償之人，或是指受讓自保險契約之人。 15.2 不擴大承保或不擴及運送人或其他利害關係人之利益。

資料來源：作者整理

　　不論是我國海商法、1968 年海牙威士比規則規定，載貨證券內之任何條款、條件或約定，有免除或降低運送人依法應負有關於貨物之毀損滅失責任，或減輕義務者，一律無效，故若載貨證券或其他運送契約中若有約定保險契約利益歸屬於運送人之條款，如「保險權益條款」（Benefit of Insurance Clause），即規定若運送人應對貨物之毀損或滅失負責時，如果該批貨物已投保貨物保險時，運送人得要求享受該保險請求權。則該保險權益條款將被視為免除運送人責任之條款，應屬無效。

　　2009 年鹿特丹規則第 79 條第 1 項第 C 款直接規定，若依在運送契約中規定，將保險契約的權益轉讓給運送人或公約第 18 條所規定之其他履約關係人，則該條款無效。英文條文如下：

Article 79 General provisions

　　"Unless otherwise provided in the Convention, any term in a contract of carriage is void to the extent that it: (c)Assigns a benefit of insurance of the goods in favor of the carrier or a person referred to in Article 18."

　　然而，保險人也擔心若非適用海牙威士比規則強制責任期間，該保險權益由保險人享有之條款仍然有效，或該運送契約條款在不同國家若有不同解釋時，可能會對保險人不利，在不侵害被保險人之損害請求權原則下，爲避免上述情況發生使運送人仍能減輕或免除其責任者，保險人乃於貨物保險條款中訂立明確規定，即爲 ICC,2009 之保險權益條款。

　　其實在英國協會貨物保險條款中於 1963 年第 10 條、1982 年第 15 條中，即已經出現所謂「不受益條款」（Not to Inure Clause），2009 年新修訂條款只是將條款內容規定更爲詳盡。按條款文義解釋觀之，其運送人或其他利害關係人均不得享受其保險利益，即禁止保單之權益轉讓給運送人及其他利害關係人，以免發生影響保險人代位求償情況。ICC,1982 年第 15 條原文爲 "This insurance shall not insure to the benefit of the carrier or other bailee"，譯爲「本保險之權益不得轉讓予運送人或其他受託人」。其中 "inure" 之意爲 "pass into use"，即有逐漸受轉而擁有保險權益之意[1]。

　　同時在 ICC, 1982 第 16 條也呼應規定在任何情況下被保險人及其受僱人有義務採取適當地措施以防止或減輕損害，並確保所有對抗運送人及利害關係人及其他第三人之權利，得以完整掌握與行使，更可了解不僅不得將保險權益轉讓給運送人及其他利害關係人，更要求被保險人應盡保全對運送人及其他利害關係人求償權利的義務，以利後續保險人進行代位求償。

　　ICC,2009 與 1982 年版不同之處，除了刪除條文名稱，而直接歸類爲「保險權益」項目下外，主是爲了使保險條款內容更清楚，乃將條款修改爲 15.1 與 15.2 兩款，並將原條款之 "inure to…" 修訂成 "「extend to…"，讓 1982 年版條款中模稜兩可用語進而修改爲定

---

[1] Robert H. Brown, *Marie Insurance*, p.219. 轉註自林慧珊，《2009 年協會貨物保險條款增修內容之研究》，頁 147。

義更清楚之語法，以避免條款用語及解釋爭議。新增的第 15.1 款中之規定可知 ICC,2009 定義可請求保險理賠被保險人之義，並擴大被保險人之範圍爲代表有效保險契約而請求賠償之人，或是指受讓自保險契約之人。主要用意乃爲澄清對於本保險有賠償請求權之人除被保險人本人外，尚包括可以代表被保險人者，此外，亦將受讓人特別包括於被保險人之範圍。以國際貿易活動進出口商而言，若雙方所簽訂之買賣契約當中約定由賣方購買保險，賣方至押匯銀行進行押匯後並將保險單背書轉讓予買方，此時買方即成爲本款所謂之受讓人，再搭配國貿條規之危險負擔移轉的規定，無論貨物轉讓幾次，若受讓保險契約之人爲合法受讓人且具有保險利益時，依本款之規定即享保險請求權。

第 十四 章·········

被保險人之減少損失義務

第一節　損害防阻條款

　　保險人為避免意外事故發生時損失擴大及社會資源浪費，鼓勵被保險人應善盡減少損害義務，並承諾額外給付被保險人所合理產生的費用，即稱為損害防阻費用。損害防阻費用為海上保險中一項特殊的費用，英國海上保險法、我國海商法、我國保險法中均訂有損害防阻規定條款，就保險條款而言，ICC,2009 之第 16 條雖條款名稱是 Minimising losses（減少損害），然條款內容的實質規定即為損害害防阻費用條款。本條款在 ICC,2009 之 (A)、(B) 及 (C) 三套條款都相同。條款規定如表 14–1。

表 14-1　ICC,2009 第 16 條

條款	內容
ICC,2009 第 16 條 Minimising losses （減少損失）	It is the duty of the Assured and their employees and agents in respect of loss recoverable hereunder 16.1 to take such measures as may be reasonable for the purpose of averting or minimising such loss, and 16.2 to ensure that all rights against carriers, bailees or other third parties are properly preserved and exercised and the Insurers will, in addition to any loss recoverable hereunder, reimburse the Assured for any charges properly and reasonably incurred in pursuance of these duties.
	被保險人及其雇用人及代理人對本保險承保事故，有關索賠時，對於下列規定事項，為其應員之義務： 16.1 遇有損失發生時或發生後，應採取適當之措施以合理防止或減輕其損失，及 16.2 應確保對於一切對抗運送人，利害關係人或其他第三人權利之適當保留行使。被保險人因為履行上述之義務而適當及合理發生之費用，保險人得予補償之。

資料來源：作者整理

一、英國海上保險法之規定

　　就保險人而言，若完善的損害防阻措施被確實執行，當可大幅降低保險賠款。因此，於事故發生後，保險人希望被保險人能將損害降到最低，且為確保被保險人會盡力做好損害防阻措施，保險人承諾將補償被保險人因此所發生的費用，表示保險人正面積極鼓勵被保險人盡力做好損害防阻措施。MIA,1906 第 78 條損害防阻費用規定如下：

(1) Where the policy contains a suing and labouring clause, the engagement thereby entered into is deemed to be supplementary to the contract of insurance, and the assured may recover from the insurer any expenses properly incurred pursuant to the clause, notwithstanding that the insurer may have paid for a total loss, or

that the subject-matter may have been warranted free from particular average, either wholly or under a certain percentage.

(2)General average losses and contributions and salvage charges, as defined by this Act, are not recoverable under the suing and labouring clause.

(3)Expenses incurred for the purpose of averting or diminishing any loss not covered by the policy are not recoverable under the suing and labouring clause.

(4)It is the duty of the assured and his agents, in all cases, to take such measures as may be reasonable for the purpose of averting or minimising a loss.

　　由本條文之規定，將損害防阻行爲及其產生之費用主要性質歸納與分析如下：

　　1.依 MIA,1906 第 78-(1)條中可知，若保險單內有包括損害防阻條款，則此項規定視爲保險契約之附加（補充性）契約（is deemed to be supplementary to the contract of insurance），申言之，保險契約中的損害防阻條款費用具有獨立及附加之性質，而既爲該條款附加契約，自亦表示損害防阻條款爲附加在主契約之下的附約，主契約賠償之標的爲貨物之損失，而附約賠償之標的即爲損害防阻費用。故縱使保險人實際損害賠償金額與損害防阻費用的補償合計，雖然已經超過保險金額仍應如數賠償；或者保險人雖然已經賠付了全損的金額，仍應賠付損害防阻費用。換言之，被保險人於全部損失發生後所請求的全部保險金額並不包括損害防阻費用，損害防阻費用應另行計算。

　　若約定「單獨海損不賠」之保險契約下，保險事故發生時被保險人盡力避免損失之擴大，因此發生損害防阻費用，然若最後標的物並未發生全部損失，依保險契約對於此單獨海損無須理賠，惟保險人在此情況下，仍須賠償損害防阻費用。此項規定的主要原因乃是保險人希望於保險事故發生時，被保險人勿認為已經有保險之保障，而忽略採取對於可立即處置避免損失擴大的行動，如此不僅浪費社會資源亦勢將增加保險人的賠款金額，故為鼓勵被保險人執行此項損害防阻的行為，因而產生的合理必要費用，保險人承諾將予以補償。

一定百分比以下（under a certain percentage）之單獨海損不賠：在實務上如以散裝船運送如煤、礦砂、大宗穀物等貨物，其裝卸載方式與一般貨物不同，可能為輸送帶或抓斗、吸穀機等，故於裝卸過程中難免產生磅差，實務上則常將之視為正常耗損，保險人對此正常耗損並不負損害賠償之責。然保險理賠時為避免爭議，乃於保險單上約定在一定百分比下的單獨海損不賠，此百分比則以自負額的概念，由被保險人自行承擔損失。如於保險單中約定保險數量之 0.1% 以下之短少視為自負額，保險人不予賠償。上述單獨海損不賠或一定百分比以下的單獨海損不賠之保險契約，若合理發生損害防阻費用，保險人仍應賠付該費用予被保險人，以鼓勵其損害防阻之行為。

2. 凡依 MIA,1906 規定屬於共同海損損失（General Average losses）、共同海損分擔（General Average Contributions）及救助費用（Salvage Charges），均不能併入損害防阻條款中而將其認定為損害防阻費用而獲得賠償。損害防阻費用與共同海損損失、分攤及救助費用的概念雖均有防止損害擴大之義，但各有其成立要件與定義。救助費用係指與被救助者無契約關係之施救者，於救助有效果後，可依海事法之規定向被救助者要求相當報酬，此項報酬並不包括屬於被保險人或其代理人或受僱人為避免保險事故所提供施救性質的服務在內。共同海損損失乃係共同海損行為後所產生的額外犧牲與費用，共同海損分擔則為經過理算後之利害關係人應分擔共同海損，自與非共同海損行為所造成的損害防阻費用不同。另一原因為共同海損損失及救助費用均屬於部分損失（partial loss）範圍，即保險人之賠償與損失合計額必以保險金額為限；即無論共同海損損失或救助費用，倘單項或與標的物損害金額合併後之金額，若超過保險金額時，保險人的最高賠償責任，仍以保險金額爲限，但損害防阻費用因其爲附加契約之額外補償性質，故不受原保險金額之限制。

3.被保險人或其代理人應採取之合理措施以防止（averting）或減輕（diminishing）保險標的之損失，爲法律上的義務，並非契約上的義務。若由非被保險人或其代理人、受僱人以外的第三人所爲之避免減輕保險標的之行爲，可能將被認定係爲 MIA,1906 中所規定之基於海事法所產生的救助費用。其與損害防阻費用最大不同處乃在於行爲者角色，損害防阻措施之行爲者爲被保險人或其代理人，而救助措施的行爲人爲不包括被保險人或其代理人或受僱人。

4.保險人對於非承保事故所發生的損害防阻費用，並無賠償責任。此規定是以保險人立場而言，損害賠償責任僅限於所承保的危險，因此雖被保險人的損害防阻行爲是爲避免損失擴大，但因危險事故並非保險人之承保事故，保險人原並無損害賠償責任，故對於該損害防阻費用自亦無賠償責任。

5.關損害防阻費用的發生依 MIA,1906 概念必須是合理產生的（properly incurred）。亦即損害防阻措施並非不理性的行爲，因此所產生的費用當然也必須是一合理適當的費用，然而於何種情況下方得稱爲「合理的」損害防阻措施及費用，於 MIA,1906 第 78 條並無明文，但於同法第 88 條對於合理與否的規定乃指「事實認定的問題」（a question of fact），即必須個案判斷，並不適合以文字規定（Where by this Act any reference is made to reasonable time, reasonable premium, or reasonable diligence, the question what is reasonable is a question of fact）。惟就實務判斷而言，若被保險人在執行該損害防阻行爲，能秉持一如對待自己沒有保險的財物一般[1]，以「無保險原

---

[1] Robert H Brown: "he measure of his duty was the care a prudent uninsured owner would exercise in regard to his property", *The Cargo Insurance Contract and the Institute Cargo Clauses*, Section 8 ,p.3.

則」（doctrine of uninsured）認定，即假設被保險人若沒有保險契約的訂立，被保險人為使自己損失減至最輕，發生事故時必定選擇某種最合理的措施並耗用最合理的費用，以保全財物及減輕損害的發生，故在縱已投保之情況下，若亦能按同樣的方法，即應可認為是一謹慎與合理的措施。

6.若發生不足額保險的情形，依 MIA,1906 第 81 條之規定 "Where the assured is insured for an amount less than the insurable value or, in the case of a valued policy, for an amount less than the policy valuation, he is deemed to be his own insurer in respect of the uninsured balance." 也適用於損害防阻費用之賠償，即不足額保險時，損害防阻費用依保險金額與保險價額比例計算賠償。若在不足額保險（under-insurance）情況，MIA,1906 第 81 條關於比例負擔的原則，亦應適用於損害防阻費用賠償。亦即在不足額保險情況，損害防阻費用的賠償亦以保險金額與保險價額（或約定價額）的比例計算賠償。

基於以上，根據 MIA,1906 之規定，歸納關於損害防阻費用成立要件如下：

1.該費用之發生必須是承保的危險事故，即需為承保危險所生的損害防阻費用，保險人方有補償之責。

2.危險事故已經發生，即若承保危險尚未發生，則因被保險人的行為所產生之費用，應係損失預防措施所產生費用，並非為損害防阻費用。如颱風警報後，因擔心颱風來襲影響船舶之航行，預先將船舶駛入避難港而產生的停泊費，此並非真正颱風所造成之費用，不得列入損害防阻費用內。

3.需由被保險人或代理人或受僱人為履行該義務而發生的費用，此點主要是為與救助費用做一區別，損害防阻義務應由被保險人及其代理人或受僱人履行，若因他人所執行且為保全財產的自願性行為，MIA,1906 之規定乃屬救助行為，並不屬於損害防阻。

4.費用的發生需在航行中途且該損害防阻行為具急迫性。若費用的發生是在航程終了時，則並無立即海上危險，性質上已類似於清點、估計損失的公證費用，應稱為「單獨費用」。

5.非因共同危險下為保全財產所產生的費用，此要件係為區分因共同海損行為所發生的之費用。共同海損與損害防阻費用性質及成立要件皆不同，共同海損之目標為共同利益，損害防阻行為的目標僅單獨為減輕或防止船舶或者貨物之損失繼續擴大，因此所產生的費用將可於不同保險契約中獲償的損害防阻費用性質截然不同。

6.損害防阻費用之補償需受不足額保險之比例賠償限制。即保險理賠時，將依保險金額與保險價額之比例而決定之。

綜合上述有關損害防阻費用之賠償規定，保險人賠償損害防阻費用的可能情況如表 14-2。

表 14-2　損害防阻費用賠償情況表

	保險價額	保險金額	實際損失金額	損害防阻費用	保險人之總賠償
情況一	200 萬	200 萬	150 萬	20 萬	170 萬（150 萬 +20 萬）
情況二	200 萬	200 萬	190 萬	20 萬	210 萬（190 萬 +20 萬）
情況三	200 萬	200 萬	200 萬	20 萬	220 萬（200 萬 +20 萬）
情況四	200 萬	100 萬	100 萬	20 萬	60 萬（50 萬 +10 萬）

資料來源：作者整理

二、ICC,2009 第 16 條

於 ICC,2009 第 16 條規定 "It is the duty of the Assured and their employees and agents in respect of loss recoverable hereunder"

其中 "It is the duty of the Assured and their servants and agents" 即減輕損害行為人應當為被保險人（貨主）、其受僱人及代理人。當保險承保事故發生時，若欲由保險獲得賠償，則損害防阻措施就為被保險人、其受僱人及代理人之「義務」。而其所規範之義務有二；一為當損失發生時，貨主應當被要求去減輕損害；二為事故發生後，貨主應履行對運送之請求權來減輕損害，分別規範於第 16-(1)條與第 16-(2)條中。詳述如下：

1.ICC,2009 第 16-(1)條

ICC,2009 第 16-(1)條與 ICC,1982 之規定除了以 "employees" 代替 "servants" 外，其餘均相同。其是由 1963 年協會貨物保險條款第 9 條受託人條款（Bailee Clause）修訂而來，原條文為："It is the duty of the Assured and their Agents, in all cases, to take such measures as may be reasonable for the purpose of averting or minimizing a loss"。其中清楚規範了被保險人減輕損害的義務，且明文規定因此所發生的適當、合理費用，保險人願意補償。此條文乃完全繼受 MIA,1906 第 78-(4)條而來；惟 ICC,2009 與 MIA,1906 一樣，並未規定此費用的補償是否有一上限，即實務上依條款之義乃需個案討論其損害防阻費用之合理性，只要是合理保險人即需額外補償，雖極富彈性但卻也容易造成認定與金額的爭議。反觀 ITC,1983 第 13 條則有一補償限額條款將此費用限制以不超過保險金額為限，即損失金額加上損害防阻費用不超過兩倍的保險金額[2]。相類似規定於我國海商法第 130 條中亦可見，將損害防阻費用訂一賠償限額作法，筆者認為應係基於公平原則，即若損害防阻費用超過保險金額，則就保險契約而言，其不合理

---

[2] ITC,1983 第 13.6 條：The sum recoverable under this Clause 11 shall be in addition to the loss otherwise recoverable under this insurance but shall in no circumstances exceed the amount insured under this insurance in respect of the Vessel.

性則也相對增加。申言之，就保險契約之損害賠償而言，縱使發生全損，保險人也僅以保險金額爲賠償上限，若與損害防阻費用合計高出兩倍保險金額，亦應以兩倍保險金額爲賠償上限，保險人似也不應承負一無限制的損害防阻費用補償責任。

然若被保險人未履行該項義務，則保險人是否可以主張拒賠，此於 ICC,2009 與 MIA,1906 條文中均沒有任何規定，故保險理賠實務易生爭議。於 1993 年 Noble Resources Ltd. v. Greenwood（The Vasso）一案中，法官認爲若保險契約具有損害防阻條款，被保險人違反該義務與違反 MIA,1906 第 33 條所規定之「擔保（Warranty）」不同，損害防阻條款並非一明示擔保（express warranty），故保險人不能主張自被保險人違反時解除其責任，惟若被保險人未善盡損害防阻義務，保險人可以向被保險人要求賠償所受之損失。另 1921 年 British and Foreign Marine Insurance Co. v. Gaunt 一案中，法院認爲 MIA,1906 第 78-(4)條之規定，並非指被保險人若未善盡此一義務則無法請求保險理賠。換言之，損害防阻條款爲一附加契約，若被保險人違反此義務，保險人僅可拒絕若履行該行爲所可得減輕之損害，並不應影響原保險契約所應負責的賠償。

2.ICC,2009 第 16-(2)條

ICC,2009 第 16-(2)條，相較於英國海上保險法之規定內容，乃補充增列了保險人必須補償減免損害措施所產生的適當、合理費用規定，這是在 MIA,1906 及 ICC,1963 所沒有的，因此實務上在使用這個條文時，清楚地賦予被保險人減免損害的義務，且明訂因此所發生的適當、合理費用，保險人願意補償。損害防阻義務爲契約義務，雖然不具有強制性，但保險人還是鼓勵被保險人能盡力去搶救保險標的，避免或減輕損失擴大，造成社會資源浪費，方爲損害防阻費用之主要精神。

第 16-(2)條中規定另一項可能產生的損害防阻費用爲被保險人爲

確保一切權利能保全及執行，而對抗運送人及其他利害關係人而產生的費用。條款中所規定之"carriers, bailees or other third parties"指的當不只為運送人，還可能牽扯到履行輔助人[3]、獨立之契約人[4]其可能為貨櫃集散站、內陸拖車或拆、併櫃之人。而被保險人應適當確保與執行（properly preserved and exercised）對抗運送人、利害關係人或其他第三人的一切權利。例如依海商法第 56 條規定，若於提貨時能立即發現有毀損情形，則應立即以書面通知運送人或在收貨證件上做一詳細註記，或直接請運送人開立證明以保全證據；但實務上，運送人或其他關係人所開立的事故證明文件通常只會用很簡單的文字敘述，如「外箱破裂內品不詳」，一切仍需委請公證人實地查驗公證後方能確認損失。但若提貨時並無法自外表立即看出毀損情況，則必須於三天內以書面通知運送人該損失情況，否則依法運送人推定已完成交貨的義務。當然，如果貨物不是有破損的狀況，而是根本沒有運達的話，則被保險人（貨主）應該由運送人或貨櫃集散站處取得「短卸證明」（short landing certificate）。

---

[3] 運送履行輔助人係指債務人為履行債務，如同使喚自己手足般使用（使喚）之輔助人而言。輔助人就債務之履行並「無獨立」之地位，故債務人就專屬自己之給付亦可使用差遣之。但輔助人之故意、過失，債務人仍應負自己過失之責任。換言之，係指直接代債務人從事債務內容者，例如代運送人從事裝卸、倉儲之工人及運送人所僱用之船長、海員等，故包括代運送人履行運送債務之受僱人及代理人，均屬狹義之履行輔助人。曾國雄（2004），《海運貨損理賠關鍵詞釋義》，自版，頁 26。

[4] 獨立契約人係指代替債務人以「獨立」之地位履行之人而言。債務人雖特別被允許可使用該等輔助人，但就其選任監督若無過失，則不負責任。但在承攬之情況下，性質上並無非債務人必為履行不可之場合，若無特約之禁止，亦可使用次承攬人，當債務人有指揮之行為時應與上述狹義之運送履行輔助人相同，債務人應負全責。換言之，係指民法第二百二十四條規定之使用人而言，例如陸上裝卸工人，就裝卸業者而言為受僱人，然就運送人而言，則為使用人；因此受貨人就運送人所承運貨物之毀損滅失，對運送人請求損害賠償係依契約關係，對裝卸業者請求損害賠償則係依侵權行為之法律關係。獨立契約人又稱為廣義之運送履行輔助人。曾國雄（2004），《海運貨損理賠關鍵詞釋義》，自版，頁 26–27。

　　另外，如被保險人於保險人未賠償前先行委任律師來保全其權利，其中的律師費當可認爲第 16-(2)款中所述之損害防阻費用，因爲先行請律師爲被保險人爲了保全對運送人、利害關係人及其他第三人之請求權，而當保險人賠償後其代位權方可順利進行，此保全動作所產生的費用，保險人允諾額外賠償。反之，因保險人的代位權是由被保險人可得而行使的損害賠償權而來，故若被保險人未將此權利加以保全，即所謂代位之妨礙，保險人的代位權必將因此而受影響，甚至喪失代位權，所以保險人在條款中規定被保險人另一個義務即應善加保留此請求權，並不得擅自放棄而影響保險人的合法權益。此項補充增訂條款爲我國海商法第 130 條所無，值得我國參考。

　　蓋保險代位權應屬保險人於保險契約下之合理期待權益。因此，若被保險人若不能確保代位權之完整，將會影響到保險人的權利，甚至會使保險人的代位權喪失。所以在條款中規定被保險人應善加保留此請求權，不得擅自放棄而影響保險人的合理期待。

　　ICC,2009 第 16-(2)條基本上指的是保險人要求被保險人能保全代位權，而不希望有妨礙代位權情況出現，即對於有責任第三人的行使請求權是被保險人的一項義務，但此條款僅僅是就保險人之追償權利保全，與被保險人之損害防阻義務並無太多關係，勉強只能謂爲是幫保險人進行「代位權之損害防阻」。

　　英國協會貨物保險單之正面印有 "Important Clause"，即所謂「重要條款」，由於是以紅色文字印刷故亦稱爲紅色條款（Red Clause），此條款規定被保險人於損失發生時，關於權利保全的維護義務及應注的事項，否則將可能影響本保險上之權利（Failure to comply therewith may prejudice any claim under the policy），其爲：

"purpose of averting or minimising a loss and to ensure that all rights against Carriers, Bailees or other third parties are properly preserved and exercised. In particular, the Assured or their Agents are required:

1. To claim immediately on the Carriers, Port Authorities or other Bailees for any missing packages.

2. In no circumstances, except under written protest, to give clean receipts where goods are in doubtful condition.

3. When delivery is made by Container, to ensure that the Container and its seals are examined immediately by their responsible official.

If the Container is delivered damaged or with seals broken or missing or with seals other than as stated in the shipping documents, to clause the delivery receipt accordingly and retain all defective or irregular seals for subsequent identification.

4. To apply immediately for survey by Carriers' or other Bailees' Representatives if any loss or damage be apparent and claim on the Carriers or other Bailees for any actual loss or damage found at such survey.

5. To give notice in writing to the Carriers or other Bailees within 3 days of delivery if the loss or damage was not apparent at the time of taking delivery.

NOTE: The Consignees or their Agents are recommended to make themselves familiar with the Regulations of the Port Authorities at the Port of discharge.

6.No claim for loss by theft &/or pilferage shall be paid hereunder unless notice of survey has been given to this Company's agents, or Lloyd's agents or other duly constituted surveyor at destination within 10 days of the expiry of this insurance.

Any claim under this insurance, should be submitted without delay, accompanied by all correspondence with Carriers and other parties regarding their liability.

The following clause shall apply to interest insured on All Risks:

In the event of damage which may involve a claim under this Policy or Certificate, immediate notice of such damage should be given to and a Survey Report obtained from the Company's Office or Agents at port of discharge."

由此紅色條款規定可知於貨櫃運輸情況，應由海關檢視鉛封，若貨櫃有破損或鉛封破壞，或號碼與提單上記載不同時，應於受貨文件上註明。當貨物毀損時應立即向港務單位，或相關運送人提出求償；並於貨物有毀損疑慮時，不可簽署清潔收據（clean receipt）給運送人。若保險標的毀損情況無法確知時，應於提貨收據上確實註記。如果貨物損失明顯，應會同運送人或相關之受託人代表進行公證，確定損失與責任。若提貨時無法立即確定損失，應於提貨後三天內以書面通知運送人及相關應負責任之人。若貨物失竊未在十天內通知保險人或其代理人，進行公證，保險人將不負任何賠償責任。

因此，由紅色條款所載的規定事項可謂是與 ICC,2009 第 16-(2)條之保全代位義務相互呼應的條款。按此條款之規定在某些情況下，若被保險人違反此義務，保險人可以主張不負任何賠償責任，此條文載明於契約上可謂規定被保險人未善盡保全義務的一個相當嚴厲的條文。

三、我國海商法之規定

民國 88 年修正海商法中對於損害防阻費用規定乃於第 130 條，其條文如下：「保險事故發生時，要保人或被保險人應採取必要行為，以避免或減輕保險標的之損失，保險人對於要保人或被保險人未履行此項義務而擴大之損失，不負賠償責任。保險人對於要保人或被保險人，為履行前項義務所生的費用，負償還之責，其償還數額與賠償金額合計雖超過保險標的價值，仍應償還之。保險人對於前項費用的償還，以保險金額爲限。但保險金額不及保險標的物的價值時，則以保險金額對於保險標的之價值比例定之。」由海商法之規定可將損害防阻費用歸納如下：

1.依海商法規定，保險人對於減免損失費用之賠償責任爲一個法定賠償責任，並非如 MIA,1906 一樣爲契約責任，即依 MIA,1906 之規定，被保險人必須與保險人在保險單特別中訂有損害防阻條款，才可以向保險人索賠該費用，否則可能會僅被視爲一特別費用，其結果損失金額加上特別費用的賠償將不會超過保險金額。申言之，於適用我國海商法時，保險人對被保險人所爲損害防阻行爲所生之費用，均應負責賠償，而不論在保險契約中是否有特別約定。又賠償損害防阻費用之前提爲必要的損害防阻行爲，蓋若非避免或減輕保險標的損失之行爲所產生的費用，自不可認定爲損害防阻費用。

如台北地方法院 93 年度保險字第 194 號民事判決中法官認爲被保險人爲了將保險標的（牛油）取樣檢查，而產生的倉儲費用，不應列於損害防阻費用中，因抽取樣本而檢測之公證報告只爲證明貨物損害之證明文件，而無法減輕或避免損失擴大，即不得將公證費用併入損害防阻費用內計算。又於台北地方法院 94 年度保險字第 146 號民事判決指出公證費用之性質與保險法第 33 條之避免或減輕損害費用之規定不符，故不能列於損害防阻費用中求償。

2.海商法 88 年修正時增列若被保險人於保險事故發生時不爲該項義務時，對於因而造成的擴大損失，不負賠償責任規定。「損害防阻費用」條款雖然提供給被保險人相當的「誘因」，促使被保險人盡力搶救保險標的，但實務上此義務的履行保險人並無法確實監督。基於此，新海商法中增列保險人對於要保人或被保險人未履行此項義務而「擴大」的損失，保險人不負賠償責任。

此規定用意當爲對被保險人未履行損害防阻義務時的懲罰，然按其文義於理賠實務上恐有相當困難度，因損失發生時標的受損情況如何，除了被保險人自行清點或委託公證確定外，對於如何評估「因未履行損害防阻義務」而「擴大的損失」舉證上定會產生困擾，因畢竟被保險人未執行損害防阻行為，故究竟最後是否得以減輕損害？又可以減輕多少？也或許根本該損害防阻行為根本無法有效控制損失擴大等，均為一假設性的估計，使理賠損失確認時徒生爭議。因此，海商法此條文的規定充其量只是具有「宣示」作用而已。

3.依 MIA,1906 規定，損害防阻費用的償還是由於一獨立附加契約，故海上保險人除原保單保險金額以外，應承負的額外補償，且亦明文規定即使保險人賠付完全損後，仍有責任補償合理適當的損害防阻費用。由此可知，其重點觀念是在於損害防阻費用與損失金額合計雖超過「保險金額」時，保險人仍應賠付。關於這個觀念在保險法86 年修正時，已將原條文「保險標的之價值」修正為「保險金額」，蓋保險標的之價值與保險金額與保險理論中畢竟為不同的名詞，切不可混淆，但於海商法中並未將此做一變更，或可能是立法的疏漏。按海商法第 130 條中所謂的「保險標的之價值」與保險學所謂的「保險價額」是否為同一名詞似有進一步討論必要，因在保險名詞中保險價額（Insurable Value），指的是保險標的於投保時的可保價值，或可以說是投保時的公平市價；而約定價值（Insured Value，或稱 Agreed Value）則指在定值保單，雙方在無詐欺原則下，「約定之保險價值」；而保險金額（Sum Insured 或 Amount Insured）則為保險契約中保險人的最高賠償上限。因此，在財產保險中每一有形財產都會有一個「保險價額」，在定值保險中因價額已經約定，故以「約定價值」代替「保險價額」，然後在保險契約中載明投保「保險金額」；在實務上保險價額、約定價值、保險金額有時可能一樣，亦可能不一樣，但在保險學理論中此三個名詞為不同的概念，應加以區分。

依損害防阻費用的產生概念，在海商法第 130 條中所謂「保險標的之價值」，似應解釋為發生事故時保險標的之價值（不定值保險），或是保險標的之約定價值（定值保險），而非投保當時保險標的之保險價額（insurable value）。惟不論是事故時的保險標的價值或約定價值或保險價額，除在定值保險採足額保險（Full Insurance），否則均與保險金額不一樣，依損害防阻費用的立法意及特性，似應如保險法一樣，採「保險金額」替代「保險標的之價值」更爲適當。

4.明文規定損害防阻費用之償還，最多以保險金額爲限，即損失金額與損害防阻費用合計不超過兩倍的保險金額。主要是強調損害防阻費用的合理與適當性，即保險人承擔無限制的損害防阻費用，也並不公平。在 MIA,1906 中並無規定補償上限，此條文應是參仿 ITC, 1983 規定或 UNCTAD,1986 所通過公布的海上貨物標準條款而來。這個條文的適用，將來對於損害防阻費用的補償限制，則形成一法定上限，而非由於契約的約定。

5.不足額保險情況下的比例分擔原則於損害防阻費用亦有其適用。於 ITC,1995 第 13-(4)規定保險人應負責的損害防阻費用，爲保單所約定的保險金額與約定價額之比例，或保險金額與船舶完好價值（sound value）之比例（若船舶完好價值大於約定價額時）；而相類似規定在 MIA,1906 第 81 條我國保險法 77 條均可見，保險法第 77 條雖是規範火災保險，但這都是保險損害補償原則之通則，當然損害防阻費用亦不應例外。

6.我國海商法規定損害防阻義務之履行人爲要保人或被保險人，而不似英國法限制在被保險人及其代理人；於 ICC,1982 條文中再增列受僱人；蓋被保險人是保險事故發生時遭受損害享有賠償請求權之人，自應盡損害防阻義務；而代理人亦是代理本人（被保險人）履行損害防阻義務，至於要保人，若僅爲他人利益之情況下締約，如保險經紀人在英國法下並不是保險契約之當事人，且損失發生時要保人亦無法立即對於保險標的進行應有的損害防阻措施，在解釋與適用此條文時，當被保險人與要保人爲同一人時就不致有問題，但若不同一人則會發生要保人承負了過重的損害防阻義務。關於保險契約當事人的定位問題，國內已有學者做過深入精闢研究[5]，況且在我國海上貨物保險實務中，要保人通常即為被保險人，故海商法條文規定在我國實務上發生適用困難的可能性不大，故在此不擬再多做討論。

綜上條文的分析與相關裁判可知，損害防阻費用的發生需為「保險事故發生時」，被保險人所進行的避免或減輕保險標的之損失義務行為，而如純為檢驗損失之公證費用則不屬之。此為海商法修正時所增列的文字，以確定必須保險人所承保的危險事故發生，因履行該義務所產生的費用，才謂為損害防阻費用。關於此點之修正與 MIA, 1906 的規定是相同的，但在我國保險法第 33 條（減免損失費用之償還責任）卻無類似規定，該條文規定如下：「保險人對於要保人或被保險人，為避免或減輕損害之必要行為所生之費用，負償還之責。其償還數額與賠償金額合計雖超過保險金額，仍應償還。保險人對於前項費用之償還，以保險金額對於保險標的之價值，比例定之。」

於法條文義解釋上似乎不論是否是承保的危險事故發生，或是否僅限於危險事故發生時的避免減輕損害行為，即若被保險人運送前之損失預防措施，如花費相當的包裝費用，其目的亦是為避免或減輕損失，則該項費用是否得以補償，仍是存有疑問的。

綜合海商法第 130 條損害防阻費用賠償規定，保險人賠償損害防阻費用的可能情況如表 14–3。

---

[5] 黃正宗，《海運經營專題研討會論文》，1995；黃正宗，海上保險的基本性質與各當事人之基本定位，《船舶與海運》，633 期。

表 14-3　我國海商法損害防阻費用賠償情況表

	保險標的之價值	保險金額	實際損失金額	損害防阻費用	保險人之總賠償
情況一	200 萬	200 萬	150 萬	20 萬	170 萬（150 萬 +20 萬）
情況二	200 萬	200 萬	190 萬	20 萬	210 萬（190 萬 +20 萬）
情況三	200 萬	200 萬	200 萬	20 萬	220 萬（200 萬 +20 萬）
情況四	200 萬	100 萬	100 萬	20 萬	60 萬（50 萬 +10 萬）
情況五	200 萬	200 萬	180 萬	250 萬	380 萬（180 萬 +200 萬）
情況六	200 萬	100 萬	100 萬	220 萬	150 萬（50 萬 +100 萬）

資料來源：作者整理

第二節　損害防阻義務與委付

　　保險人鼓勵被保險人於事故發生時應盡力防阻損失擴大，並保全將來對有責任的第三人之求償權利，並同意因此所履行該義務所生之費用將額外補償。但不論是由保險人或被保險人執行該害防阻行為，其目的都是避免損失擴大，並不能與委付之通知或接受混為一談，此概念即規定於 ICC,2009 第 17 條，本條為宣示性的觀念溝通規定，在 ICC,2009 之(A)、(B)及(C)三套條款都相同。條款規定如表 14-4。

表 14-4 ICC,2009 第 17 條

條款	內容
ICC,2009 第 17 條 Waiver （放棄）	Measures taken by the Assured or the Insurers with the object of saving, protecting or recovering the subject-matter insured shall not be considered as a waiver or acceptance of abandonment or otherwise prejudice the rights of either party.
	被保險人或保險人對保險標的進行救助、保護或回復的措施時，不得被認為是被保險人放棄委付或保險人承諾委付，或其他影響至當事人雙方之權利。

資料來源：作者整理

　　就保險之賠償責任而言，因保險契約所約定承保之損失範圍不同而有所不同，例如保險契約僅承保全部損失（Total Loss Only）；或單獨海損不賠（Free From Particular Average）。在實務上保險人希望被保險人履行損害防阻義務，但若保險契約之賠償範圍是約定僅賠償因保險事故造成之全部損失，如果被保險人於事故發生時仍然盡力防阻損害擴大，則有可能將損失控制在部分損失；或者雖然保險契約不論全部損失或部分損失都承保，被保險人對保險標的之盡力保全行為，僅僅是履行損害防阻義務，切不可認為被保險人已經準備保留保險標的之所有權，而擬放棄委付保險標的之請求全損之權利。

　　蓋當被保標的物受損嚴重時，被保險人可能將之委付予保險人並要求按全損賠付後，而此委付通知可能尚在保險人考慮是否接受中，亦可能保險人會拒絕接受委付。表面上認為當被保險人委付後保險標的即為保險人所有，故保險標的之殘值高低，或可否再修復後使用，已經與被保險人無關，故當被保險人進行損害防阻之處置，可能會被誤認要保留保險標的之財產所有權，而準備放棄委付之權利。相對的，若由保險人輔助或協助被保險人進行損害防阻措施，也可能被誤認為保險人已經默許接受委付，而準備掌控保險標的之所有權。

　　為避免上述之誤解發生 ICC,2009 遂於第 17 條特別明訂無論如何

受損標的必須儘速防阻損害再繼續擴大，保險契約雙方當事人所進行的損害防阻處置，保險人不能認為此係被保險人已拋棄或已撤回其委付之表示；反之，如保險人對該標的進行回復或保全時，被保險人亦不能認為此係保險人已接受其委付之表示。換言之，委付之接受與否，應由推定全損之成立要件判斷，詳細規定與概念在 ICC,2009 第13 條中已經說明，在此不再贅述。所以委付之接受與拒絕，或者委付權利是否已經拋棄或準備通知委付，均與否與任何一方對於保險標的之保全、回復，以及任何損害防阻措施都沒有關係，或者影響到雙方當事人之任何權利。相類似之規定亦見於我國海商法第 147 條第 2項，其規定「委付未經承諾前，被保險人對於保險標的之一切權利不受影響。保險人或被保險人對於保險標的採取救助、保護或回復之各項措施，不視為已承諾或拋棄委付」。

第十五章 · · · · · · · · ·

避免遲延

　　保險事故發生後，保險人除希望並鼓勵被保險人履行損害防阻的義務外，同時也希望被保險人對於有關保險索賠或權益事項，均應合理的立即處理，避免遲延情況發生。ICC,2009 第 18 條在 1982 年版條款名稱即為「Reasonable Despatch Clause（合理迅速處置條款）」。本條款在 ICC,2009 第 18 條的規定於三套條款都相同。條款規定如表 15-1。

表 15-1　ICC,2009 第 18 條

條款	內容
ICC,2009 第 18 條 avoidance of delay （避免遲延）	It is condition of this insurance that the Assured shell act with reasonable dispatch in all circumstances within their control.
	被保險人於其可以控制之任何情況下，均應以合理迅速之方式處理，此係本保險契約之條件。

資料來源：作者整理

　　根據本條款規定，被保險人在其可控制情況下，於處理任何有關保險權益事項時，如貨損通知、損害防阻義務的履行或者保全代位權之證據取得等，都應該以合理迅速的方式處理。然條款中並未對何謂「合理迅速（reasonable dispatch）」說明其義，根據 MIA,1906 第 88 條規定，即為事實認定問題，不是一概而論。故如就貨損通知而言，

若被保險人於發現貨損當時非保險人上班時間，則被保險人若能於第一個上班日通知貨損則即可稱為合理的時間內通知了。我國海商法第149條規定：「要保人或被保險人，於知悉保險之危險發生後，應即通知保險人。」意即當被保人發現貨損時，應「立即」通知保險人，此概念與ICC,2009第18條所規定的「合理迅速」意義相同。

在MIA,1906中亦有相同的"reasonable dispatch"規定見於第48條Delay in voyage（航程遲延）的規定，其指出於航程保險的情形，航程均必須以合理速度進行，如無合法的理由其未如此，保險人自航程之遲延成為不合理時開始不負保險責任。（"In the case of a voyage policy, the adventure insured must be prosecuted throughout its course with reasonable dispatch, and, if without lawful excuse it is not so prosecuted, the insurer is discharged from liability as from the time when the delay became unreasonable."）

有關損失通知的規定，於保險法第58條中規定「要保人、被保險人或受益人，遇有保險人應負保險責任的事故發生，除本法另有規定，或契約另有訂定外，應於知悉後五日內通知保險人。」就法律適用而言，海商法海上保險章為海上保險特別法，故若為海上保險契約損害發生，被保險人向保險人通知貨損期間，係以英國海上保險法及我國海商法「合理迅速、立即」的規定知保險人，至於非海上保險事故發生，則被保險人通知貨損期間則適用保險法第58條之「五日內」規定。

另一個必須注意的期間為貨主向運送人索賠的時效，在海牙規則為自提貨時（或應提貨時）起算一年，我國海商法的規定則自貨物受領之日或自應受領之日起，一年內未起訴者，運送人或船舶所有人解除其責任，故就保險人立場為了保險賠付完之代位權可以順利行使，當然也會希望甚至要求被保險人（貨主）應該在期限內求償、起訴，否則依保險法第65條之規定，被保險人向保險人索賠的期限是兩年，亦可能發生貨主向運送人索賠的一年期限過後，但被保險人（貨主）向保險人索賠的權利卻仍未超過兩年，假設損害發生時也已經立即通知保險人，所有理賠文件於損失發生時都已依海商法第 151 條之規定於一個月之內交給保險人，則在此情況下，保險人仍要依保險契約賠償給被保險人，但已經無法向運送人進行代位求償了。若此情形的發生為被保險人之過失，則屬於妨礙代位概念，相關法律效果，請詳見第二篇第八章敘述。若此情況是保險人所造成，但筆者認為實務上發生一個賠償案件拖過一年的情形不多，有可能是金額過大尚在訴訟或協調處理中，或者是損失金額太小，雙方都疏忽忘記了賠案要處理，但不論如何既然問題發生在保險人，則無法進行代位也只好結案處理了。

綜上所述，被保險人發生保險事故後，就損失通知與索賠期限而言，海商法第 149 條視為「出險通知」，要求被保險人立即為之，但「損失清單」依海商法第 151 條規定，最遲要在「一個月」的時間內提出。整理如圖 15-1。

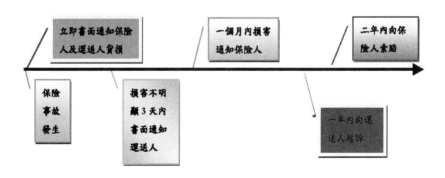

圖 15-1　損失通知及求償時效圖

資料來源：作者自繪

另，本條款具有契約條件（ Condition ）之概念，所謂 "Condition" 於英美法中是契約成立的基礎，係極為重要之條款，如其違反將構成契約的根本違反（ fundamental breach ），另一方得據以解除契約（avoid the contract）；此概念與我國民法第99條之附停止條件及附解除條件之「條件」明顯不同。民法第99條規定：「附停止條件之法律行為，於條件成就時，發生效力。附解除條件之法律行為，於條件成就時，失其效力。依當事人之特約，使條件成就之效果，不於條件成就之時發生者，依其特約。」

MIA,1906 中第36條及第42條亦分別有「中立（neutral）」以及「開航（commencement of risk）」默示條件（implied conditions）規定，其法律效力則亦認為是契約的基礎不得違反。

ICC,2009 第18條雖然是屬於英美法條件規定，但海上保險契約準據法也不一定是適用英國法；再者，我國為大陸法系國家，並未有如英美法契約條件（Condition）的概念，縱使被保險人未能合理迅速處理有關保險事務，實務上保險人很難主張免責，頂多發生妨礙代位的效果，故就我國海上貨物保險實務而言，本條款僅可謂為訓示的規定，對被保險人的權益影響甚少。

第 十 六 章 · · · · · · · · ·

法律與慣例

　　海上保險與國際貿易一樣都具有國際性，契約雙方當事人間易受不同國家不同法律及習慣影響。如出口商向甲國保險公司投保海上貨物運輸保險，船航經乙國時發生海難；貨物就地處理，進口商在丙國向原承保保險公司的代理人要求賠償，雖然進口商已取得經背書轉讓保險單，但因雙方當事人為不同國籍的法人，可能主張不同的準據法為其法律適用之依據，因而發生了涉外因素的法律衝突；因此，對於涉外因素的保險契約如何確認準據法，實一重要課題。為了解決此一問題以及統一保險契約的解釋，在 ICC,2009 第 19 條即規定了保險契約的準據法規定，第 19 條於 ICC,2009 之 (A)、(B) 及 (C) 三套條款都相同。條款規定如表 16-1。

表 16-1　ICC,2009 第 19 條

條款	內容
ICC,2009 第 19 條	This insurance is subject to English law and practice 本保險依據英國法律及慣例

資料來源：作者整理

　　海上保險本身即具有國際性分散危險的功能，因此常會有涉外因素；即當海上保險契約牽涉外國人或外國地時則具有涉外因素

（foreign elements），所以將會涉及雙方當事人所屬國法律；若發生糾紛時即所謂法律衝突（conflict of laws）時，則有賴國際私法來解決。所謂國際私法乃是對於涉外案件時，決定其應適用何國法院或法律管轄的法則。保險契約準據法的確認，可以三個順序來判定，第一是探求當事人明示意思表示；即可視契約中是否有明示的法律選擇條款（Choice of Law Clause），若有明示適用法律，則以該法為契約的準據法。第二為探求當事人的默示意思；即法律可從保險契約之管轄權條款或仲裁條款或尋求當事人之默示意思。第三為推定當事人意思，即法院以與保險契約最密切及最真實關連的法律為其準據法。

依我國民國 99 年 5 月 26 日最新修正的涉外民事法律適用法第 20 條規定：「法律行為發生債之關係者，其成立及效力，依當事人意思定其應適用之法律。當事人無明示之意思或其明示之意思依所定應適用之法律無效時，依關係最切之法律。法律行為所生之債務中有足為該法律行為之特徵者，負擔該債務之當事人行為時之住所地法，推定為關係最切之法律。」故依本條文解釋，決定涉外因素的保險契約準據法以尋求當事人的意思為優先；其次，再依關係最切之法律為準據法，而所謂關係最切之法律則指負擔債務的當事人行為時之住所地法律，如保險契約的損害賠償即為足為保險契約之特徵，故若契約中為能探知準據法之意思表示為何，則以保險人（負擔債務之當事人）簽約時之住所地法律為準據法。

然而 ICC,2009 第 19 條已有明示的準據法條款，規定有關本保險契約事項乃是適用英國法律及慣例，再依同法第 8 條規定：「依本法適用外國法時，如其適用之結果有背於中華民國公共秩序或善良風俗者，不適用之。」故在不違背我國公共秩序及善良風俗之下，依當事人意思主義，法院似應優先採英國法為契約之準據法。

涉外民事法律適用法僅在於具有涉外因素的保險契約，才予以適用，反之，若保險契約不具涉外因素，如臺灣的進口商以 FOB 為貿易條件進口，故進口商就在臺灣向保險人投保海上貨物保險，在此情況下，臺灣的進口商爲中華民國境內依公司法及相關法規成立之法人，而臺灣的保險公司亦爲依保險法及相關法律所成立之法人，當雙方當事人間若有保險契約之糾紛而訴諸法院裁判時，則法院爲保護臺灣的司法主權，自應以臺灣的法律爲契約的準據法。但是，就海上保險實務言之，目前乃是使用英國協會貨物保險條款爲保險契約，故有關條款內容的專有名詞如 "constructive total loss"、"deviation"、"change of voyage"、"warranty" 等等，在臺灣的法律並未規定，或有些規定與 MIA,1906 有所差異，如保險利益、共同海損、海難救助等，由於臺灣對海上保險的規定不足將無法完全配合國際實務，若發生糾紛而進行仲裁或訴訟時，將發生適用臺灣法律時的不適及困難，因而造成許多理賠糾紛。故不論是保險公司或法院，在此情況下都需再轉而參考 MIA,1906 之相關規定，方能確認保險責任。

除此以外，於下列情況下亦可能適用我國法律：

1.雖有涉外因素，但當事人雙方於理賠或訴訟時均未主張適用外國法律之情況下，法院可能適用我國法律爲準據法。

2.當事人之一雖主張適用外國法律爲保險契約的準據法，但是該規定若已然違背我國公共秩序或善良風俗，或任何法律之強制規定者，則仍應採我國法律爲準據法。

Institute Cargo Clauses, 2009 (A)

1/1/09

INSTITUTE CARGO CLAUSES (A)

RISKS COVERED

<u>Risks</u>

1. This insurance covers all risks of loss of or damage to the subject—matter insured except as excluded by the provisions of Clauses 4, 5, 6 and 7 below.

<u>General Average</u>

2. This insurance covers general average and salvage charges, adjusted or determined according to the contract of carriage and/or the governing law and practice, incurred to avoid or in connection with the avoidance of loss from any cause except those excluded in Clauses 4, 5, 6 and 7 below.

<u>"Both to Blame Collision Clause"</u>

3. This insurance indemnifies the Assured, in respect of any risk insured herein, against liability incurred under any Both to Blame Collision Clause in the contract of carriage. In the event of any claim by carriers under the said Clause, the Assured agree to notify the Insurers who shall have the right, at their own cost and expense, to defend the

Assured against such claim.

EXCLUSIONS

4. In no case shall this insurance cover

4.1 loss damage or expense attributable to wilful misconduct of the Assured

4.2 ordinary leakage, ordinary loss in weight or volume, or ordinary wear and tear of the subject–matter insured

4.3 loss damage or expense caused by insufficiency or unsuitability of packing or preparation of the subject–matter insured to withstand the ordinary incidents of the insured transit where such packing or preparation is carried out by the Assured or their employees or prior to the attachment of this insurance (for the purpose of these Clauses "packing" shall be deemed to include stowage in a container and "employees" shall not include independent contractors)

4.4 loss damage or expense caused by inherent vice or nature of the subject–matter insured

4.5 loss damage or expense caused by delay, even though the delay be caused by a risk insured against (except expenses payable under Clause 2 above)

4.6 loss damage or expense caused by insolvency or financial default of the owners managers charterers or operators of the vessel where, at the time of loading of the subject–matter insured on board the vessel, the Assured are aware, or in the ordinary course of business should be aware, that such insolvency or financial default could prevent the normal prosecution of the voyage This exclusion shall not apply where the contract of insurance has been assigned to the party claiming hereunder who has bought or agreed to buy the subject–matter insured in good faith under a binding contract

4.7 loss damage or expense directly or indirectly caused by or arising from the use of any weapon or device employing atomic or nuclear fission and/or fusion or other like reaction or radioactive force or matter.

5. 5.1 In no case shall this insurance cover loss damage or expense arising from

5.1.1 unseaworthiness of vessel or craft or unfitness of vessel or craft for the safe carriage of the subject–matter insured, where the Assured are privy to such unseaworthiness or unfitness, at the time the subject–matter insured is loaded therein

5.1.2 unfitness of container or conveyance for the safe carriage of the subject–matter insured, where loading therein or thereon is carried out prior to attachment of this insurance or by the Assured or their employees and they are privy to such unfitness at the time of loading.

5.2 Exclusion 5.1.1 above shall not apply where the contract of insurance has been assigned to the party claiming hereunder who has bought or agreed to buy the subject–matter insured in good faith under a binding contract.

5.3 The Insurers waive any breach of the implied warranties of seaworthiness of the ship and fitness of the ship to carry the subject–matter insured to destination.

6. In no case shall this insurance cover loss damage or expense caused by

6.1 war civil war revolution rebellion insurrection, or civil strife arising therefrom, or any hostile act by or against a belligerent power

6.2 capture seizure arrest restraint or detainment (piracy excepted), and the consequences thereof or any attempt thereat

6.3 derelict mines torpedoes bombs or other derelict weapons of war.

7. In no case shall this insurance cover loss damage or expense

7.1 caused by strikers, locked–out workmen, or persons taking part in labour disturbances, riots or civil commotions

7.2 resulting from strikes, lock-outs, labour disturbances, riots or civil commotions

7.3 caused by any act of terrorism being an act of any person acting on behalf of, or in connection with, any organisation which carries out activities directed towards the overthrowing or influencing, by force or violence, of any government whether or not legally constituted

7.4 caused by any person acting from a political, ideological or religious motive.

DURATION

Transit Clause

8. 8.1 Subject to Clause 11 below, this insurance attaches from the time the subject-matter insured is first moved in the warehouse or at the place of storage (at the place named in the contract of insurance) for the purpose of the immediate loading into or onto the carrying vehicle or other conveyance for the commencement of transit, continues during the ordinary course of transit and terminates either

8.1.1 on completion of unloading from the carrying vehicle or other conveyance in or at the final warehouse or place of storage at the destination named in the contract of insurance,

8.1.2 on completion of unloading from the carrying vehicle or other conveyance in or at any other warehouse or place of storage, whether prior to or at the destination named in the contract of insurance, which the Assured or their employees elect to use either for storage other than in the ordinary course of transit or for allocation or distribution, or

8.1.3 when the Assured or their employees elect to use any carrying vehicle or other conveyance or any container for storage other than in the ordinary course of transit or

8.1.4 on the expiry of 60 days after completion of discharge overside of the subject—matter insured from the oversea vessel at the final port of discharge, whichever shall first occur.

8.2 If, after discharge overside from the oversea vessel at the final port of discharge, but prior to termination of this insurance, the subject—matter insured is to be forwarded to a destination other than that to which it is insured, this insurance, whilst remaining subject to termination as provided in Clauses

8.1.1 to 8.1.4, shall not extend beyond the time the subject—matter insured is first moved for the purpose of the commencement of transit to such other destination.

8.3 This insurance shall remain in force (subject to termination as provided for in Clauses 8.1.1 to 8.1.4 above and to the provisions of Clause 9 below) during delay beyond the control of the Assured, any deviation, forced discharge, reshipment or transhipment and during any variation of the adventure arising from the exercise of a liberty granted to carriers under the contract of carriage.

Termination of Contract of Carriage

9. If owing to circumstances beyond the control of the Assured either the contract of carriage is terminated at a port or place other than the destination named therein or the transit is otherwise terminated before unloading of the subject—matter insured as provided for in Clause 8 above, then this insurance shall also terminate unless prompt notice is given to the Insurers and continuation of cover is requested when this insurance shall remain in force, subject to an additional premium if required by the Insurers, either

9.1 until the subject—matter insured is sold and delivered at such port or place, or, unless otherwise specially agreed, until the expiry of 60 days after arrival of the subject—matter insured at such port or place, whichever shall first occur, or

9.2 if the subject—matter insured is forwarded within the said period of

60 days (or any agreed extension thereof) to the destination named in the contract of insurance or to any other destination, until terminated in accordance with the provisions of Clause 8 above.

Change of Voyage

10. 10.1 Where, after attachment of this insurance, the destination is changed by the Assured, this must be notified promptly to Insurers for rates and terms to be agreed. Should a loss occur prior to such agreement being obtained cover may be provided but only if cover would have been available at a reasonable commercial market rate on reasonable market terms.

10.2 Where the subject–matter insured commences the transit contemplated by this insurance (in accordance with Clause 8.1), but, without the knowledge of the Assured or their employees the ship sails for another destination, this insurance will nevertheless be deemed to have attached at commencement of such transit.

CLAIMS

Insurable Interest

11. 11.1 In order to recover under this insurance the Assured must have an insurable interest in the subject–matter insured at the time of the loss.

11.2 Subject to Clause 11.1 above, the Assured shall be entitled to recover for insured loss occurring during the period covered by this insurance, notwithstanding that the loss occurred before the contract of insurance was concluded, unless the Assured were aware of the loss and the Insurers were not.

Forwarding Charges

12. Where, as a result of the operation of a risk covered by this

insurance, the insured transit is terminated at a port or place other than that to which the subject–matter insured is covered under this insurance, the Insurers will reimburse the Assured for any extra charges properly and reasonably incurred in unloading storing and forwarding the subject–matter insured to the destination to which it is insured.

This Clause 12, which does not apply to general average or salvage charges, shall be subject to the exclusions contained in Clauses 4, 5, 6 and 7 above, and shall not include charges arising from the fault negligence insolvency or financial default of the Assured or their employees.

Constructive Total Loss

13. No claim for Constructive Total Loss shall be recoverable hereunder unless the subject–matter insured is reasonably abandoned either on account of its actual total loss appearing to be unavoidable or because the cost of recovering, reconditioning and forwarding the subject–matter insured to the destination to which it is insured would exceed its value on arrival.

Increased Value

14. 14.1 If any Increased Value insurance is effected by the Assured on the subject–matter insured under this insurance the agreed value of the subject–matter insured shall be deemed to be increased to the total amount insured under this insurance and all Increased Value insurances covering the loss, and liability under this insurance shall be in such proportion as the sum insured under this insurance bears to such total amount insured.

In the event of claim the Assured shall provide the Insurers with evidence of the amounts insured under all other insurances.

14.2 Where this insurance is on Increased Value the following clause shall apply: The agreed value of the subject—matter insured shall be deemed to be equal to the total amount insured under the primary insurance and all Increased Value insurances covering the loss and effected on the subject—matter insured by the Assured, and liability under this insurance shall be in such proportion as the sum insured under this insurance bears to such total amount insured.

In the event of claim the Assured shall provide the Insurers with evidence of the amounts insured under all other insurances.

BENEFIT OF INSURANCE

15. This insurance

    15.1 covers the Assured which includes the person claiming indemnity either as the person by or on whose behalf the contract of insurance was effected or as an assignee,

    15.2 shall not extend to or otherwise benefit the carrier or other bailee.

MINIMISING LOSSES

Duty of Assured

16. It is the duty of the Assured and their employees and agents in respect of loss recoverable hereunder

    16.1 to take such measures as may be reasonable for the purpose of averting or minimising such loss,and

    16.2 to ensure that all rights against carriers, bailees or other third parties are properly preserved and
    exercised and the Insurers will, in addition to any loss recoverable hereunder, reimburse the Assured for any charges properly and reasonably incurred in pursuance of these duties.

Waiver

17. Measures taken by the Assured or the Insurers with the object of saving, protecting or recovering the subject–matter insured shall not be considered as a waiver or acceptance of abandonment or otherwise prejudice the rights of either party.

AVOIDANCE OF DELAY

18. It is a condition of this insurance that the Assured shall act with reasonable despatch in all circumstances within their control.

LAW AND PRACTICE

19. This insurance is subject to English law and practice.

NOTE:–Where a continuation of cover is requested under Clause 9, or a change of destination is notified under Clause 10, there is an obligation to give prompt notice to the Insurers and the right to such cover is dependent upon compliance with this obligation.

@ Copyright: 11/08 –Lloyd´s Market Association (LMA) and International Underwriting Association of London (IUA).

CL382

01/01/2009

附 錄 二

Institute Cargo Clauses, 2009 (B)

1/1/09

INSTITUTE CARGO CLAUSES (B)

RISKS COVERED

<u>Risks</u>

1. This insurance covers, except as excluded by the provisions of Clauses 4, 5, 6 and 7 below,

   1.1 loss of or damage to the subject–matter insured reasonably attributable to

      1.1.1 fire or explosion

      1.1.2 vessel or craft being stranded grounded sunk or capsized

      1.1.3 overturning or derailment of land conveyance

      1.1.4 collision or contact of vessel craft or conveyance with any external object other than water

      1.1.5 discharge of cargo at a port of distress

      1.1.6 earthquake volcanic eruption or lightning,

   1.2 loss of or damage to the subject–matter insured caused by

      1.2.1 general average sacrifice

      1.2.2 jettison or washing overboard

      1.2.3 entry of sea lake or river water into vessel craft hold conveyance container or place of storage,

1.3 total loss of any package lost overboard or dropped whilst loading on to, or unloading from, vessel or craft.

<u>General Average</u>

2. This insurance covers general average and salvage charges, adjusted or determined according to the contract of carriage and/or the governing law and practice, incurred to avoid or in connection with the avoidance of loss from any cause except those excluded in Clauses 4, 5, 6 and 7 below.

<u>"Both to Blame Collision Clause"</u>

3. This insurance indemnifies the Assured, in respect of any risk insured herein, against liability incurred under any Both to Blame Collision Clause in the contract of carriage. In the event of any claim by carriers under the said Clause, the Assured agree to notify the Insurers who shall have the right, at their own cost and expense, to defend the Assured against such claim.

EXCLUSIONS

4. In no case shall this insurance cover

   4.1 loss damage or expense attributable to wilful misconduct of the Assured

   4.2 ordinary leakage, ordinary loss in weight or volume, or ordinary wear and tear of the subject—matter insured

   4.3 loss damage or expense caused by insufficiency or unsuitability of packing or preparation of the subject—matter insured to withstand the ordinary incidents of the insured transit where such packing or preparation is carried out by the Assured or their employees or prior to the attachment of this insurance (for the purpose of these Clauses "packing" shall be deemed to include stowage in a container and "employees" shall not include independent contractors)

4.4 loss damage or expense caused by inherent vice or nature of the subject-matter insured

4.5 loss damage or expense caused by delay, even though the delay be caused by a risk insured against (except expenses payable under Clause 2 above)

4.6 loss damage or expense caused by insolvency or financial default of the owners managers charterers or operators of the vessel where, at the time of loading of the subject-matter insured on board the vessel, the Assured are aware, or in the ordinary course of business should be aware, that such insolvency or financial default could prevent the normal prosecution of the voyage This exclusion shall not apply where the contract of insurance has been assigned to the party claiming hereunder who has bought or agreed to buy the subject-matter insured in good faith under a binding contract

4.7 deliberate damage to or deliberate destruction of the subject-matter insured or any part thereof by the wrongful act of any person or persons

4.8 loss damage or expense directly or indirectly caused by or arising from the use of any weapon or device employing atomic or nuclear fission and/or fusion or other like reaction or radioactive force or matter.

5. 5.1 In no case shall this insurance cover loss damage or expense arising from

5.1.1 unseaworthiness of vessel or craft or unfitness of vessel or craft for the safe carriage of the subject-matter insured, where the Assured are privy to such unseaworthiness or unfitness, at the time the subject-matter insured is loaded therein

5.1.2 unfitness of container or conveyance for the safe carriage of the subject-matter insured, where loading therein or thereon is carried out prior to attachment of this insurance or by the Assured or their employees and they are privy to such unfitness at the time of loading.

5.2 Exclusion 5.1.1 above shall not apply where the contract of insurance has been assigned to the party claiming hereunder who has bought or agreed to buy the subject–matter insured in good faith under a binding contract.

5.3 The Insurers waive any breach of the implied warranties of seaworthiness of the ship and fitness of the ship to carry the subject–matter insured to destination.

6. In no case shall this insurance cover loss damage or expense caused by

6.1 war civil war revolution rebellion insurrection, or civil strife arising therefrom, or any hostile act by or against a belligerent power

6.2 capture seizure arrest restraint or detainment, and the consequences thereof or any attempt thereat

6.3 derelict mines torpedoes bombs or other derelict weapons of war.

7. In no case shall this insurance cover loss damage or expense

7.1 caused by strikers, locked–out workmen, or persons taking part in labour disturbances, riots or civil commotions

7.2 resulting from strikes, lock–outs, labour disturbances, riots or civil commotions

7.3 caused by any act of terrorism being an act of any person acting on behalf of, or in connection with, any organisation which carries out activities directed towards the overthrowing or influencing, by force or violence, of any government whether or not legally constituted

7.4 caused by any person acting from a political, ideological or religious motive.

DURATION

<u>Transit Clause</u>

8. 8.1 Subject to Clause 11 below, this insurance attaches from the time

the subject—matter insured is first moved in the warehouse or at the place of storage (at the place named in the contract of insurance) for the purpose of the immediate loading into or onto the carrying vehicle or other conveyance for the commencement of transit, continues during the ordinary course of transit and terminates either

8.1.1 on completion of unloading from the carrying vehicle or other conveyance in or at the final warehouse or place of storage at the destination named in the contract of insurance,

8.1.2 on completion of unloading from the carrying vehicle or other conveyance in or at any other warehouse or place of storage, whether prior to or at the destination named in the contract of insurance, which the Assured or their employees elect to use either for storage other than in the ordinary course of transit or for allocation or distribution, or

8.1.3 when the Assured or their employees elect to use any carrying vehicle or other conveyance or any container for storage other than in the ordinary course of transit or

8.1.4 on the expiry of 60 days after completion of discharge overside of the subject—matter insured from the oversea vessel at the final port of discharge, whichever shall first occur.

8.2 If, after discharge overside from the oversea vessel at the final port of discharge, but prior to termination of this insurance, the subject—matter insured is to be forwarded to a destination other than that to which it is insured, this insurance, whilst remaining subject to termination as provided in Clauses 8.1.1 to 8.1.4, shall not extend beyond the time the subject—matter insured is first moved for the purpose of the commencement of transit to such other destination.

8.3 This insurance shall remain in force (subject to termination as provided for in Clauses 8.1.1 to 8.1.4 above and to the provisions of

Clause 9 below) during delay beyond the control of the Assured, any deviation, forced discharge, reshipment or transhipment and during any variation of the adventure arising from the exercise of a liberty granted to carriers under the contract of carriage.

<u>Termination of Contract of Carriage</u>

9. If owing to circumstances beyond the control of the Assured either the contract of carriage is terminated at a port or place other than the destination named therein or the transit is otherwise terminated before unloading of the subject-matter insured as provided for in Clause 8 above, then this insurance shall also terminate unless prompt notice is given to the Insurers and continuation of cover is requested when this insurance shall remain in force, subject to an additional premium if required by the Insurers, either

9.1 until the subject-matter insured is sold and delivered at such port or place, or, unless otherwise specially agreed, until the expiry of 60 days after arrival of the subject-matter insured at such port or place, whichever shall first occur, or

9.2 if the subject-matter insured is forwarded within the said period of 60 days (or any agreed extension thereof) to the destination named in the contract of insurance or to any other destination, until terminated in accordance with the provisions of Clause 8 above.

<u>Change of Voyage</u>

10. 10.1 Where, after attachment of this insurance, the destination is changed by the Assured, this must be notified promptly to Insurers for rates and terms to be agreed. Should a loss occur prior to such agreement being obtained cover may be provided but only if cover would have been available at a reasonable commercial market rate on reasonable market terms.

10.2 Where the subject-matter insured commences the transit

contemplated by this insurance (in accordance with Clause 8.1), but, without the knowledge of the Assured or their employees the ship sails for another destination, this insurance will nevertheless be deemed to have attached at commencement of such transit.

CLAIMS

Insurable Interest

11. 11.1 In order to recover under this insurance the Assured must have an insurable interest in the subject– matter insured at the time of the loss.

    11.2 Subject to Clause 11.1 above, the Assured shall be entitled to recover for insured loss occurring during the period covered by this insurance, notwithstanding that the loss occurred before the contract of insurance was concluded, unless the Assured were aware of the loss and the Insurers were not.

Forwarding Charges

12. Where, as a result of the operation of a risk covered by this insurance, the insured transit is terminated at a port or place other than that to which the subject–matter insured is covered under this insurance, the Insurers will reimburse the Assured for any extra charges properly and reasonably incurred in unloading storing and forwarding the subject–matter insured to the destination to which it is insured.

    This Clause 12, which does not apply to general average or salvage charges, shall be subject to the exclusions contained in Clauses 4, 5, 6 and 7 above, and shall not include charges arising from the fault negligence insolvency or financial default of the Assured or their employees.

Constructive Total Loss

13. No claim for Constructive Total Loss shall be recoverable hereunder unless the subject−matter insured is reasonably abandoned either on account of its actual total loss appearing to be unavoidable or because the cost of recovering, reconditioning and forwarding the subject−matter insured to the destination to which it is insured would exceed its value on arrival.

Increased Value

14. 14.1 If any Increased Value insurance is effected by the Assured on the subject−matter insured under this insurance the agreed value of the subject−matter insured shall be deemed to be increased to the total amount insured under this insurance and all Increased Value insurances covering the loss, and liability under this insurance shall be in such proportion as the sum insured under this insurance bears to such total amount insured.

In the event of claim the Assured shall provide the Insurers with evidence of the amounts insured under all other insurances.

14.2 Where this insurance is on Increased Value the following clause shall apply: The agreed value of the subject−matter insured shall be deemed to be equal to the total amount insured under the primary insurance and all Increased Value insurances covering the loss and effected on the subject−matter insured by the Assured, and liability under this insurance shall be in such proportion as the sum insured under this insurance bears to such total amount insured.

In the event of claim the Assured shall provide the Insurers with evidence of the amounts insured under all other insurances.

BENEFIT OF INSURANCE

15. This insurance

    15.1 covers the Assured which includes the person claiming indemnity either as the person by or on whose behalf the contract of insurance was effected or as an assignee,

    15.2 shall not extend to or otherwise benefit the carrier or other bailee.

MINIMISING LOSSES

<u>Duty of Assured</u>

16. It is the duty of the Assured and their employees and agents in respect of loss recoverable hereunder

    16.1 to take such measures as may be reasonable for the purpose of averting or minimising such loss, and

    16.2 to ensure that all rights against carriers, bailees or other third parties are properly preserved and

        exercised and the Insurers will, in addition to any loss recoverable hereunder, reimburse the Assured for any charges properly and reasonably incurred in pursuance of these duties.

<u>Waiver</u>

17. Measures taken by the Assured or the Insurers with the object of saving, protecting or recovering the subject–matter insured shall not be considered as a waiver or acceptance of abandonment or otherwise prejudice the rights of either party.

AVOIDANCE OF DELAY

18. It is a condition of this insurance that the Assured shall act with reasonable despatch in all circumstances within their control.

LAW AND PRACTICE

19. This insurance is subject to English law and practice.

NOTE:–Where a continuation of cover is requested under Clause 9, or a change of destination is notified under Clause 10, there is an obligation to give prompt notice to the Insurers and the right to such cover is dependent upon compliance with this obligation.

@ *Copyright: 11/08 –Lloyd′s Market Association (LMA) and International Underwriting Association of London (IUA).*

CL383

01/01/2009

附 錄 三 • • • • • • • • • •

Institute Cargo Clauses, 2009 (C)

1/1/09

INSTITUTE CARGO CLAUSES (C)

RISKS COVERED

<u>Risks</u>

1. This insurance covers, except as excluded by the provisions of Clauses 4, 5, 6 and 7 below,

   1.1 loss of or damage to the subject–matter insured reasonably attributable to

   1.1.1 fire or explosion

   1.1.2 vessel or craft being stranded grounded sunk or capsized

   1.1.3 overturning or derailment of land conveyance

   1.1.4 collision or contact of vessel craft or conveyance with any external object other than water

   1.1.5 discharge of cargo at a port of distress,

   1.2 loss of or damage to the subject–matter insured caused by

   1.2.1 general average sacrifice

   1.2.2 jettison.

<u>General Average</u>

2. This insurance covers general average and salvage charges, adjusted or

determined according to the contract of carriage and/or the governing law and practice, incurred to avoid or in connection with the avoidance of loss from any cause except those excluded in Clauses 4, 5, 6 and 7 below.

"Both to Blame Collision Clause"

3. This insurance indemnifies the Assured, in respect of any risk insured herein, against liability incurred under any Both to Blame Collision Clause in the contract of carriage. In the event of any claim by carriers under the said Clause, the Assured agree to notify the Insurers who shall have the right, at their own cost and expense, to defend the Assured against such claim.

EXCLUSIONS

4. In no case shall this insurance cover
   4.1 loss damage or expense attributable to wilful misconduct of the Assured
   4.2 ordinary leakage, ordinary loss in weight or volume, or ordinary wear and tear of the subject-matter insured
   4.3 loss damage or expense caused by insufficiency or unsuitability of packing or preparation of the subject-matter insured to withstand the ordinary incidents of the insured transit where such packing or preparation is carried out by the Assured or their employees or prior to the attachment of this insurance (for the purpose of these Clauses "packing" shall be deemed to include stowage in a container and "employees" shall not include independent contractors)
   4.4 loss damage or expense caused by inherent vice or nature of the subject-matter insured
   4.5 loss damage or expense caused by delay, even though the delay be caused by a risk insured against (except expenses payable under

Clause 2 above)

4.6 loss damage or expense caused by insolvency or financial default of the owners managers charterers or operators of the vessel where, at the time of loading of the subject–matter insured on board the vessel, the Assured are aware, or in the ordinary course of business should be aware, that such insolvency or financial default could prevent the normal prosecution of the voyage This exclusion shall not apply where the contract of insurance has been assigned to the party claiming hereunder who has bought or agreed to buy the subject–matter insured in good faith under a binding contract

4.7 deliberate damage to or deliberate destruction of the subject–matter insured or any part thereof by the wrongful act of any person or persons

4.8 loss damage or expense directly or indirectly caused by or arising from the use of any weapon or device employing atomic or nuclear fission and/or fusion or other like reaction or radioactive force or matter.

5. 5.1 In no case shall this insurance cover loss damage or expense arising from

5.1.1 unseaworthiness of vessel or craft or unfitness of vessel or craft for the safe carriage of the subject–matter insured, where the Assured are privy to such unseaworthiness or unfitness, at the time the subject–matter insured is loaded therein

5.1.2 unfitness of container or conveyance for the safe carriage of the subject–matter insured, where loading therein or thereon is carried out prior to attachment of this insurance or   by the Assured or their employees and they are privy to such unfitness at the time of loading.

5.2 Exclusion 5.1.1 above shall not apply where the contract of insurance has been assigned to the party claiming hereunder who has bought or agreed to buy the subject—matter insured in good faith under a binding contract.

5.3 The Insurers waive any breach of the implied warranties of seaworthiness of the ship and fitness of the ship to carry the subject—matter insured to destination.

6. In no case shall this insurance cover loss damage or expense caused by

6.1 war civil war revolution rebellion insurrection, or civil strife arising therefrom, or any hostile act by or against a belligerent power

6.2 capture seizure arrest restraint or detainment, and the consequences thereof or any attempt thereat

6.3 derelict mines torpedoes bombs or other derelict weapons of war.

7. In no case shall this insurance cover loss damage or expense

7.1 caused by strikers, locked—out workmen, or persons taking part in labour disturbances, riots or civil commotions

7.2 resulting from strikes, lock—outs, labour disturbances, riots or civil commotions

7.3 caused by any act of terrorism being an act of any person acting on behalf of, or in connection with, any organisation which carries out activities directed towards the overthrowing or influencing, by force or violence, of any government whether or not legally constituted

7.4 caused by any person acting from a political, ideological or religious motive.

DURATION

Transit Clause

8. 8.1 Subject to Clause 11 below, this insurance attaches from the time the subject—matter insured is first moved in the warehouse or at the place of storage (at the place named in the contract of insurance) for the purpose of the immediate loading into or onto the carrying

vehicle or other conveyance for the commencement of transit, continues during the ordinary course of transit and terminates either

8.1.1 on completion of unloading from the carrying vehicle or other conveyance in or at the final warehouse or place of storage at the destination named in the contract of insurance,

8.1.2 on completion of unloading from the carrying vehicle or other conveyance in or at any other warehouse or place of storage, whether prior to or at the destination named in the contract of insurance, which the Assured or their employees elect to use either for storage other than in the ordinary course of transit or for allocation or distribution, or

8.1.3 when the Assured or their employees elect to use any carrying vehicle or other conveyance or any container for storage other than in the ordinary course of transit or

8.1.4 on the expiry of 60 days after completion of discharge overside of the subject−matter insured from the oversea vessel at the final port of discharge, whichever shall first occur.

8.2 If, after discharge overside from the oversea vessel at the final port of discharge, but prior to termination of this insurance, the subject−matter insured is to be forwarded to a destination other than that to which it is insured, this insurance, whilst remaining subject to termination as provided in Clauses

8.1.1 to 8.1.4, shall not extend beyond the time the subject−matter insured is first moved for the purpose of the commencement of transit to such other destination.

8.3 This insurance shall remain in force (subject to termination as provided for in Clauses 8.1.1 to 8.1.4 above and to the provisions of Clause 9 below) during delay beyond the control of the Assured, any deviation, forced discharge, reshipment or transhipment and during any variation of the adventure arising from the exercise of a liberty granted to carriers under the contract of carriage.

Termination of Contract of Carriage

9. If owing to circumstances beyond the control of the Assured either the contract of carriage is terminated at a port or place other than the destination named therein or the transit is otherwise terminated before unloading of the subject—matter insured as provided for in Clause 8 above, then this insurance shall also terminate unless prompt notice is given to the Insurers and continuation of cover is requested when this insurance shall remain in force, subject to an additional premium if required by the Insurers, either

9.1 until the subject—matter insured is sold and delivered at such port or place, or, unless otherwise specially agreed, until the expiry of 60 days after arrival of the subject—matter insured at such port or place, whichever shall first occur, or

9.2 if the subject—matter insured is forwarded within the said period of 60 days (or any agreed extension thereof) to the destination named in the contract of insurance or to any other destination, until terminated in accordance with the provisions of Clause 8 above.

Change of Voyage

10. 10.1 Where, after attachment of this insurance, the destination is changed by the Assured, this must be notified promptly to Insurers for rates and terms to be agreed. Should a loss occur prior to such agreement being obtained cover may be provided but only if cover would have been available at a reasonable commercial market rate on reasonable market terms.

10.2 Where the subject—matter insured commences the transit contemplated by this insurance (in accordance with Clause 8.1), but, without the knowledge of the Assured or their employees the ship sails for another destination, this insurance will nevertheless be deemed to have attached at commencement of such transit.

CLAIMS

<u>Insurable Interest</u>

11. 11.1 In order to recover under this insurance the Assured must have an insurable interest in the subject– matter insured at the time of the loss.

    11.2 Subject to Clause 11.1 above, the Assured shall be entitled to recover for insured loss occurring during the period covered by this insurance, notwithstanding that the loss occurred before the contract of insurance was concluded, unless the Assured were aware of the loss and the Insurers were not.

<u>Forwarding Charges</u>

12. Where, as a result of the operation of a risk covered by this insurance, the insured transit is terminated at a port or place other than that to which the subject–matter insured is covered under this insurance, the Insurers will reimburse the Assured for any extra charges properly and reasonably incurred in unloading storing and forwarding the subject–matter insured to the destination to which it is insured.

    This Clause 12, which does not apply to general average or salvage charges, shall be subject to the exclusions contained in Clauses 4, 5, 6 and 7 above, and shall not include charges arising from the fault negligence insolvency or financial default of the Assured or their employees.

<u>Constructive Total Loss</u>

13. No claim for Constructive Total Loss shall be recoverable hereunder unless the subject–matter insured is reasonably abandoned either on

account of its actual total loss appearing to be unavoidable or because the cost of recovering, reconditioning and forwarding the subject—matter insured to the destination to which it is insured would exceed its value on arrival.

Increased Value

14. 14.1 If any Increased Value insurance is effected by the Assured on the subject—matter insured under this insurance the agreed value of the subject—matter insured shall be deemed to be increased to the total amount insured under this insurance and all Increased Value insurances covering the loss, and liability under this insurance shall be in such proportion as the sum insured under this insurance bears to such total amount insured.

In the event of claim the Assured shall provide the Insurers with evidence of the amounts insured under all other insurances.

14.2 Where this insurance is on Increased Value the following clause shall apply: The agreed value of the subject—matter insured shall be deemed to be equal to the total amount insured under the primary insurance and all Increased Value insurances covering the loss and effected on the subject—matter insured by the Assured, and liability under this insurance shall be in such proportion as the sum insured under this insurance bears to such total amount insured.

In the event of claim the Assured shall provide the Insurers with evidence of the amounts insured under all other insurances.

BENEFIT OF INSURANCE

15. This insurance

15.1 covers the Assured which includes the person claiming indemnity either as the person by or on whose behalf the contract of insurance was effected or as an assignee,

15.2 shall not extend to or otherwise benefit the carrier or other bailee.

MINIMISING LOSSES

<u>Duty of Assured</u>

16. It is the duty of the Assured and their employees and agents in respect of loss recoverable hereunder
    16.1 to take such measures as may be reasonable for the purpose of averting or minimising such loss, and
    16.2 to ensure that all rights against carriers, bailees or other third parties are properly preserved and
    exercised and the Insurers will, in addition to any loss recoverable hereunder, reimburse the Assured for any charges properly and reasonably incurred in pursuance of these duties.

<u>Waiver</u>

17. Measures taken by the Assured or the Insurers with the object of saving, protecting or recovering the subject–matter insured shall not be considered as a waiver or acceptance of abandonment or otherwise prejudice the rights of either party.

AVOIDANCE OF DELAY

18. It is a condition of this insurance that the Assured shall act with reasonable despatch in all circumstances within their control.

LAW AND PRACTICE

19. This insurance is subject to English law and practice.

NOTE:–*Where a continuation of cover is requested under Clause 9, or a change of destination is notified under Clause 10, there is an obligation to give prompt notice to the Insurers and the right to such cover is dependent upon compliance with this obligation.*

CL384

01/01/2009

Marine Insurance Act 1906

Marine Insurance

1. MARINE INSURANCE DEFINED

A contract of marine insurance is a contract whereby the insurer undertakes to indemnify the assured, in manner and to the extent thereby by agreed, against marine losses, that is to say, the losses incident to marine adventure.

2. MIXED SEA AND LAND RISKS

1. A contract of marine insurance may, by its express terms, or by usage of trade, be extended so as to protect the assured against losses on inland waters or on any land risk which may be incidental to any sea voyage.

2. Where a ship in course of building, or the launch of a ship, or any adventure analogous to a marine adventure, is covered by a policy in the form of a marine policy, the provisions of this Act, in so far as applicable, shall apply thereto; but, except as by this section provided, nothing in this Act shall alter or affect any rule of law applicable to any contract of insurance other than a contract of marine insurance as by this Act defined.

3. MARINE ADVENTURE AND MARITIME PERILS DEFINED

1. Subject to the provisions of this Act, every lawful marine adventure

may be the subject of a contract of marine insurance.

2. In particular there is a marine adventure where—

a. Any ship, goods or other moveables are exposed to maritime perils. Such property is in this Act referred to as "insurable property";

b. The earning or acquisition of any freight, passage money, commission, profit, or other pecuniary benefit, or the security for any advances, loan, or disbursements, is endangered by the exposure of insurable property to maritime perils;

c. Any liability to a third party may be incurred by the owner of, or other person interested in or responsible for, insurable property, by reason of maritime perils.

"Maritime perils" means the perils consequent on, or incidental to, the navigation of the sea, that is to say, perils of the sea, fire, war perils, pirates, rovers, thieves, captures, seizures, restraints, and detainments of princes and peoples, jettisons, barratry, and any other perils, either of the like kind or which may be designated by the policy.

Insurable Interest

4. AVOIDANCE OF WAGERING OR GAMING CONTRACTS

1. Every contract of marine insurance by way of gaming or wagering is void.

2. A contract of marine insurance is deemed to be a gaming or wagering contract—

a. Where the assured has not an insurable interest as defined by this Act, and the contract is entered into with no expectation of acquiring such an interest; or

b. Where the policy is made "interest or no interest", or "without further proof of interest than the policy itself", or "without benefit of salvage to the insurer", or subject to any other like term

Provided that, where there is no possibility of salvage, a policy may be effected without benefit of salvage to the insurer.

5. INSURABLE INTEREST DEFINED

1. Subject to the provisions of this Act, every person has an insurable interest who is interested in a marine adventure.

2. In particular a person is interested in a marine adventure where he stands in any legal or equitable relation to the adventure or to any insurable property at risk therein, in consequence of which he may benefit by the safety or due arrival of insurable property, or may be prejudiced by its loss, or damage thereto, or by the detention thereof, or may incur liability in respect thereof.

6. WHEN INTEREST MUST ATTACH

1. The assured must be interested in the subject−matter insured at the time of the loss though he need not be interested when the insurance is effected:

Provided that where the subject−matter is insured "lost or not lost", the assured may recover although he may not have acquired his interest until after the loss, unless at the time of effecting the contract of insurance the assured was aware of the loss, and the insurer was not.

2. Where the assured has no interest at the time of the loss, he cannot acquire interest by any act or election after he is aware of the loss.

7. DEFEASIBLE OR CONTINGENT INTEREST

1. A defeasible interest is insurable, as also is a contingent interest.

2. In particular, where the buyer of goods has insured them, he has an insurable interest, notwithstanding that he might, at his election, have rejected the goods, or have treated them as at the seller's risk, by reason of the latter's delay in making delivery or otherwise.

8. PARTIAL INTEREST

A partial interest of any nature is insurable.

9. RE-INSURANCE

1. The insurer under a contract of marine insurance has an insurable interest in his risk, and may re-insure in respect of it.
2. Unless the policy otherwise provides, the original assured has no right or interest in respect of such re-insurance.

10. BOTTOMRY

The lender of money on bottomry or respondentia has an insurable interest in respect of the loan.

11. MASTER'S AND SEAMEN'S WAGES

The master or any member of the crew of a ship has an insurable interest in respect of his wages.

12. ADVANCE FREIGHT

In the case of advance freight, the person advancing the freight has an insurable interest, in so far as such freight is not repayable in case of loss.

13. CHARGES OF INSURANCE

The assured has an insurable interest in the charges of any

insurance which he may effect.

14. QUANTUM OF INTEREST

1. Where the subject–matter insured is mortgaged, the mortgagor has an insurable interest in the full value thereof, and the mortgagee has an insurable interest in respect of any sum due or to become due under the mortgage.

2. A mortgagee, consignee, or other person having an interest in the subject–matter insured may insure on behalf and for the benefit of other persons interested as well as for his own benefit.

3. The owner of insurable property has an insurable interest in respect of the full value thereof, notwithstanding that some third person may have agreed, or be liable, to indemnify him in case of loss.

15. ASSIGNMENT OF INTEREST

Where the assured assigns or otherwise parts with his interest in the subject–matter insured, he does not thereby transfer to the assignee his rights under the contract of insurance, unless there be an express or implied agreement with the assignee to that effect. But the provisions of this section do not affect a transmission of interest by operation of law.

Insurable Value

16. MEASURE OF INSURABLE VALUE

Subject to any express provision or valuation in the policy, the insurable value of the subject–matter insured must be ascertained as follows—

1. In insurance on ship, the insurable value is the value, at the

commencement of the risk, of the ship, including her outfit, provisions and stores for the officers and crew, money advanced for seamen's wages, and other disbursements (if any) incurred to make the ship fit for the voyage or adventure contemplated by the policy, plus the charges of insurance upon the whole;

The insurable value, in the case of a steamship, includes also the machinery, boilers, and coals and engine stores if owned by the assured, and, in the case of a ship engaged in a special trade, the ordinary fittings requisite for that trade;

2. In insurance on freight, whether paid in advance or otherwise, the insurance value is the gross amount of the freight at the risk of the assured, plus the charges of insurance;

3. In insurance on goods or merchandise, the insurable value is the prime cost of the property insured, plus the expenses of and incidental to shipping and the charges of insurance upon the whole;

4. In insurance on any other subject-matter, the insurable value is the amount at the risk of the assured when the policy attaches, plus the charges of insurance.

Disclosure And Representations

17. INSURANCE IS UBERRIMAE FIDEI

A contract of marine insurance is a contract based upon the utmost good faith, and, if the utmost good faith be not observed by either party, the contract may be avoided by the other party.

18. DISCLOSURE BY ASSURED

1. Subject to the provisions of this section, the assured must disclose

to the insurer, before the contract is concluded, every material circumstance which is known to the assured, and the assured is deemed to know every circumstance which, in the ordinary course of business, ought to be known by him. If the assured fails to make such disclosure, the insurer may avoid the contract.

2. Every circumstance is material which would influence the judgment of a prudent insurer in fixing the premium, or determining whether he will take the risk.

3. In the absence of inquiry the following circumstances need not be disclosed, namely:—

   a. Any circumstance which diminishes the risk;

   b. Any circumstance which is known or presumed to be known to the insurer. The insurer is presumed to know matters of common notoriety or knowledge, and matters which an insurer in the ordinary course of his business, as such, ought to know;

   c. Any circumstance as to which information is waived by the insurer;

   d. Any circumstance which it is superfluous to disclose by reason of any express or implied warranty.

4. Whether any particular circumstance, which is not disclosed, be material or not is, in each case, a question of fact.

5. The term "circumstance" includes any communication made to, or information received by, the assured.

19. DISCLOSURE BY AGENT EFFECTING INSURANCE

Subject to the provisions of the preceding section as to circumstances which need not be disclosed, where an insurance is effected for the assured by an agent, the agent must disclose to the insurer—

   a. Every material circumstance which is known to himself, and an agent to insure is deemed to know every circumstance which in the ordinary course of business ought to be known by, or to have been communicated to, him; and

b. Every material circumstance which the assured is bound to disclose, unless it come to his knowledge too late to communicate it to the agent.

20. REPRESENTATIONS PENDING NEGOTIATION OF CONTRACT

1. Every material representation made by the assured or his agent to the insurer during the negotiations for the contract, and before the contract is concluded, must be true. If it be untrue the insurer may avoid the contract.

2. A representation is material which would influence the judgment of a prudent insurer in fixing the premium, or determining whether he will take the risk.

3. A representation may be either a representation as to a matter of fact, or as to a matter of expectation or belief.

4. A representation as to matter of fact is true, if it be substantially correct, that is to say, if the difference between what is represented and what is actually correct would not be considered material by a prudent insurer.

5. A representation as to a matter of expectation or belief is true if it be made in good faith.

6. A representation may be withdrawn or corrected before the contract is concluded.

7. Whether a particular representation be material or not is, in each ease, a question of fact.

21. WHEN CONTRACT IS DEEMED TO BE CONCLUDED

A contract of marine insurance is deemed to be concluded when the proposal of the assured is accepted by the insurer, whether the policy be then issued or not; and, for the purpose of showing when the proposal was accepted, reference may be made to the slip or covering note or other customary memorandum of the contract, [although it be stamped].

NOTE:

[Words in italics] deleted by the Finance Act 1959, s 37(5), Sch 8, Pt II.

22. CONTRACT MUST BE ENBODIED IN POLICY

Subject to the provisions of any statute, a contract of marine insurance is inadmissible in evidence unless it is embodied in a marine policy in accordance with this Act. The policy may be executed and issued either at the time when the contract is concluded, or afterwards.

23. WHAT POLICY MUST SPECIFY

A Marine policy must specify—

1. The name of the assured, or of some person who effects the insurance on his behalf:
2. The subject–matter insured and the risk insured against;
3. The voyage, or period of time, or both , as the case may be, cover3ed by the insurance;
4. The sum or sums insured;
5. The name or names of the insurers.

NOTE:

Sub–ss (2) – (5): repealed by the Finance Act 1959, ss 30(5), (7), 37 (5), Sch 8, Pt II.

24. SIGNATURE OF INSURER

1. A marine policy must be signed by or on behalf of the insurer, provided that in the case of a corporation the corporate seal may be sufficient, but nothing in this section shall be construed as

requiring the subscription of a corporation to be under seal.

2. Where a policy is subscribed by or on behalf of two or more insurers, each subscription, unless the contrary be expressed, constitutes a distinct contract with the assured.

25. VOYAGE AND TIME POLICIES

1. Where the contract is to insure the subject-matter "at and from", or from one place to another or others, the policy is called a "voyage policy", and where the contract is to insure the subject-matter for a definite period of time the policy is called a "time policy". A contract for both voyage and time may be included in the same policy.

2. Subject to the provisions of s 11 of the Finance Act, 1901, a time policy which is made for any time exceeding 12 months is invalid.

NOTE:

Sub-s (2): repealed by the Finance Act 1959, ss 30(5), (7), 37(5), Sch 8, Pt II.

26. DESIGNATION OF SUBJECT-MATTER

1. The subject-matter insured must be designated in a marine policy with reasonable certainty.

2. The nature and extent of the interest of the assured in the subject-matter insured need not be specified in the policy.

3. Where the policy designates the subject-matter insured in general terms, it shall be construed to apply to the interest intended by the assured to be covered.

4. In the application of this section regard shall be had to any usage regulating the designation of the subject-matter insured.

27. VALUED POLICY

1. A policy may be either valued or unvalued.

2. A valued policy is a policy which specifies the agreed value of the subject—matter insured.

3. Subject to the provisions of this Act, and in the absence of fraud, the value fixed by the policy is, as between the insurer and assured, conclusive of the insurable value of the subject intended to be insured, whether the loss be total or partial.

4. Unless the policy otherwise provides, the value fixed by the policy is not conclusive for the purpose of determining whether there has been a constructive total loss.

28. UNVALUED POLICY

An unvalued policy is a policy which does not specify the value of the subject—matter insured, but, subject to the limit of the sum insured, leaves the insurable value to be subsequently ascertained, in the manner hereinbefore specified.

29. FLOATING POLICY BY SHIP OR SHIPS

1. A floating policy is a policy which describes the insurance in general terms, and leaves the name of the ship or ships and other particulars to be defined by subsequent declaration.

2. The subsequent declaration or declarations may be made by indorsement on the policy, or in other customary manner.

3. Unless the policy otherwise provides, the declarations must be made in the order of dispatch or shipment. They must, in the case of goods, comprise all consignments within the terms of the policy, and the value of the goods or other property must be honestly stated, but an omission or erroneous declaration may be rectified even after loss or arrival, provided the omission or declaration was made in good faith.

4. Unless the policy otherwise provides, where a declaration of value

is not made until after notice of loss or arrival, the policy must be treated as an unvalued policy as regards the subject—matter of that declaration.

30. CONSTRUCTION OF TERMS IN POLICY

1. A policy may be in the form in the First Schedule of this Act.
2. Subject to the provisions of this Act, and unless the context of the policy otherwise requires, the terms and expressions mentioned in the First Schedule to this Act shall be construed as having the scope and meaning in that schedule assigned to them.

31. PREMIUM TO BE ARRANGED

1. Where an insurance is effected at a premium to be arranged, and no arrangement is made, a reasonable premium is payable.
2. Where an insurance is effected on the terms that an additional premium is to be arranged in a given event, and that event happens but no arrangement is made, then a reasonable additional premium is payable.

Double Insurance

32. DOUBLE INSURANCE

1. Where two or more policies are effected by or on behalf of the assured on the same adventure and interest or any part thereof, and the sums insured exceed the indemnity allowed by this Act, the assured is said to be over—insured by double insurance.
2. Where the assured is over—insured by double insurance—
   a. The assured, unless the policy otherwise provides, may claim payment from the insurers in such order as he may think fit,

provided that he is not entitled to receive any sum in excess of the indemnity allowed by this Act;

b. Where the policy under which the assured claims is a valued policy, the assured must give credit as against the valuation for any sum received by him under any other policy without regard to the actual value of the subject–matter insured;

c. Where the policy under which the assured claims is an unvalued policy he must give credit, as against the full insurable value, for any sum received by him under any other policy;

d. Where the assured receives any sum in excess of the indemnity allowed by this Act, he is deemed to hold such sum in trust for the insurers, according to their right of contribution among themselves.

Warranties, Etc.

33. NATURE OF WARRANTY

1. A warranty, in the following sections relating to warranties, means a promissory warranty, that is to say, a warranty by which the assured undertakes that some particular thing shall or shall not be done, or that some condition shall be fulfilled, or whereby he affirms or negatives the existence of a particular state of facts.

2. A warranty may be express or implied.

3. A warranty, as above defined, is a condition which must be exactly complied with, whether it be material to the risk or not. If it be not so complied with, then, subject to any express provision in the policy, the insurer is discharged from liability as from the date of the breach of warranty, but without prejudice to any liability

incurred by him before that date.

34. WHEN BREACH OF WARRANTY EXCUSED

1. Non–compliance with a warranty is excused when, by reason of a change of circumstances, the warranty ceases to be applicable to the circumstances of the contract, or when compliance with the warranty is rendered unlawful by any subsequent law.

2. Where a warranty is broken, the assured cannot avail himself of the defence that the breach has been remedied, and the warranty complied with, before loss.

3. A breach of warranty may be waived by the insurer.

35. EXPRESS WARRANTIES

1. An express warranty may be in any form of words from which the intention to warrant is to be inferred.

2. An express warranty must be included in, or written upon, the policy, or must be contained in some document incorporated by reference into the policy.

3. An express warranty does not exclude an implied warranty, unless it be inconsistent therewith.

36. WARRANTY OF NEUTRALITY

1. Where insurable property, whether ship or goods, is expressly warranted neutral, there is an implied condition that the property shall have a neutral character at the commencement of the risk, and that, so far as the assured can control the matter, its neutral character shall be preserved during the risk.

2. Where a ship is expressly warranted "neutral" there is also an implied condition that, so far as the assured can control the matter, she shall be properly documented, that is to say, that she shall

carry the necessary papers to establish her neutrality, and that she shall not falsify or suppress her papers, or use simulated papers. If any loss occurs through breach of this condition, the insurer may avoid the contract.

37. NO IMPLIED WARRANTY OF NATIONALITY

There is no implied warranty as to the nationality of a ship, or that her nationality shall not be changed during the risk.

38. WARRANTY OF GOOD SAFETY

Where the subject-matter insured is warranted "well" or "in good safety" on a particular day, it is sufficient if it be safe at any time during that day.

39. WARRANTY OF SEAWORTHINESS OF SHIP

1. In a voyage policy there is an implied warranty that at the commencement of the voyage the ship shall be seaworthy for the purpose of the particular adventure insured.

2. Where the policy attaches while the ship is in port, there is also an implied warranty that she shall, at the commencement of the risk, be reasonably fit to encounter the ordinary perils of the port.

3. Where the policy relates to a voyage which is performed in different stages, during which the ship requires different kinds of or further preparation or equipment, there is an implied warranty that at the commencement of each stage the ship is seaworthy in respect of such preparation or equipment for the purposes of that stage.

4. A ship is deemed to be seaworthy when she is reasonably fit in all respects to encounter the ordinary perils of the seas of the adventure insured.

5. In a time policy there is no implied warranty that the ship shall be seaworthy at any stage of the adventure, but where, with the privity of the assured, the ship is sent to sea in an unseaworthy state, the insurer is not liable for any loss attributable to unseaworthiness.

40. NO IMPLIED WARRANTY THAT GOODS ARE SEAWORTHY

1. In a policy on goods or other moveables there is no implied warranty that the goods or moveables are seaworthy.

2. In a voyage policy on goods or other moveables there is an implied warranty that at the commencement of the voyage the ship is not only seaworthy as a ship, but also that she is reasonably fit to carry the goods or other moveables to the destination contemplated by the policy.

41. WARRANTY OF LEGALITY

There is an implied warranty that the adventure insured is a lawful one, and that, so far as the assured can control the matter, the adventure shall be carried out in a lawful manner.

The Voyage

42. IMPLIED CONDITION AS TO COMMENCEMENT OF RISK

1. Where the subject-matter is insured by a voyage policy "at and from" or "from" a particular place, it is not necessary that the ship should be at that place when the contract is concluded, but there is an implied condition that the adventure shall be commenced within a reasonable time, and that if the adventure be not so commenced the insurer may avoid the contract.

2. The implied condition may be negatived by showing that the delay was caused by circumstances known to the insurer before the contract was concluded, or by showing that he waived the condition.

43. ALTERATION OF PORT OF DEPARTURE

Where the place of departure is specified by the policy, and the ship instead of sailing from that place sails from any other place, the risk does not attach.

44. SAILING FOR DIFFERENT DESTINATION

Where the destination is specified in the policy, and the ship, instead of sailing for that destination, sails for any other destination, the risk does not attach.

45. CHANGE OF VOYAGE

1. Where, after the commencement of the risk, the destination of the ship is voluntarily changed from the destination contemplated by the policy, there is said to be a change of voyage.
2. Unless the policy otherwise provides, where there is a change of voyage, the insurer is discharged from liability as from the time of change, that is to say, as from the time when the determination to change it is manifested; and it is immaterial that the ship may not in fact have left the course of voyage contemplated by the policy when the loss occurs.

46. DEVIATION

1. Where a ship, without lawful excuse, deviates from the voyage contemplated by the policy, the insurer is discharged from liability as from the time of deviation, and it is immaterial that the ship

may have regained her route before any loss occurs.

2. There is a deviation from the voyage contemplated by the policy—

   a. Where the course of the voyage is specifically designated by the policy, and that course is departed from; or

   b. Where the course of the voyage is not specifically designated by the policy, but the usual and customary course is departed from.

3. The intention to deviate is immaterial; there must be a deviation in fact to discharge the insurer from his liability under the contract.

47. SEVERAL PORTS OF DISCHARGE

1. Where several ports of discharge are specified by the policy, the ship may proceed to all or any of them, but, in the absence of any usage or sufficient cause to the contrary, she must proceed to them, or such of them as she goes to, in the order designated by the policy. If she does not there is a deviation.

2. Where the policy is to "ports of discharge", within a given area, which are not named, the ship must, in the absence of any usage or sufficient cause to the contrary, proceed to them, or such of them as she goes to, in their geographical order. If she does not there is a deviation.

48. DELAY IN VOYAGE

In the case of a voyage policy, the adventure insured must be prosecuted throughout its course with reasonable dispatch, and, if without lawful excuse it is not so prosecuted, the insurer is discharged from liability as from the time when the delay became unreasonable.

49. EXCUSES FOR DEVIATION OR DELAY

1. Deviation or delay in prosecuting the voyage contemplated by the

policy is excused—

a. Where authorised by any special term in the policy; or

b. Where caused by circumstances beyond the control of the master and his employer; or

c. Where reasonably necessary in order to comply with an express or implied warranty; or

d. Where reasonably necessary for the safety of the ship or subject-matter insured; or

e. For the purpose of saving human life, or aiding a ship in distress where human life may be in danger; or

f. Where reasonably necessary for the purpose of obtaining medical or surgical aid for any person on board the ship; or

g. Where caused by the barratrous conduct of the master or crew, if barratry be one of the perils insured against.

2. When the cause excusing the deviation or delay ceases to operate, the ship must resume her course, and prosecute her voyage, with reasonable dispatch.

Assignment of Policy

50. WHEN AND HOW POLICY IS ASSIGNABLE

1. A marine policy is assignable unless it contains terms expressly prohibiting assignment. It may be assigned either before or after loss.

2. Where a marine policy has been assigned so as to pass the beneficial interest in such policy, the assignee of the policy is entitled to sue thereon in his own name; and the defendant is entitled to make any defence arising out of the contract which he would have been entitled to make if the action had been brought in the name of the person by or on behalf of whom the policy was effected.

3. A marine policy may be assigned by indorsement thereon or in other customary manner.

51. ASSURED WHO HAS NO INTEREST CANNOT ASSIGN

Where the assured has parted with or lost his interest in the subject–matter insured, and has not, before or at the time of so doing, expressly or impliedly agreed to assign the policy, any subsequent assignment of the policy is inoperative:

Provided that nothing in this section affects the assignment of a policy after loss.

The Premium

52. WHEN PREMIUM PAYABLE

Unless otherwise agreed, the duty of the assured or his agent to pay the premium, and the duty of the insurer to issue the policy to the assured or his agent, are concurrent conditions, and the insurer is not bound to issue the policy until payment or tender of the premium.

53. POLICY EFFECTED THROUGH BROKER

1. Unless otherwise agreed, where a marine policy is effected on behalf of the assured by a broker, the broker is directly responsible to the insurer for the premium, and the insurer is directly responsible to the assured for the amount which may be payable in respect of losses, or in respect of returnable premium.

2. Unless otherwise agreed, the broker has, as against the assured, a lien upon the policy for the amount of the premium and his charges in respect of effecting the policy; and, where he has dealt

with the person who employs him as a principal, he has also a lien on the policy in respect of any balance on any insurance account which may be due to him from such person, unless when the debt was incurred he had reason to believe that such person was only an agent.

54. EFFECT OF RECEIPT ON POLICY

Where a marine policy effected on behalf of the assured by a broker acknowledges the receipt of the premium, such acknowledgment is, in the absence of fraud, conclusive as between the insurer and the assured, but not as between the insurer and broker.

Loss and Abandonment

55. INCLUDED AND EXCLUDED LOSSES

1. Subject to the provisions of this Act, and unless the policy otherwise provides, the insurer is liable for any loss proximately caused by a peril insured against, but, subject as aforesaid, he is not liable for any loss which is not proximately caused by a peril insured against.

2. In particular—

   a. The insurer is not liable for any loss attributable to the wilful misconduct of the assured, but unless the policy otherwise provides, he is liable for any loss proximately caused by a peril insured against, even though the loss would not have happened but for the misconduct or negligence of the master or crew;

   b. Unless the policy otherwise provides, the insurer on ship or goods is not liable for any loss proximately caused by delay, although the delay be caused by a peril insured against;

c. Unless the policy otherwise provides, the insurer is not liable for ordinary wear and tear, ordinary leakage and breakage, inherent vice or nature of the subject—matter insured, or for any loss proximately caused by rats or vermin, or for any injury to machinery not proximately caused by maritime perils.

56. PARTIAL AND TOTAL LOSS

1. A loss may be either total or partial. Any loss other than a total loss, as hereinafter defined, is a partial loss.

2. A total loss may be either an actual total loss, or a constructive total loss.

3. Unless a different intention appears from the terms of the policy, an insurance against total loss includes a constructive, as well as an actual, total loss.

4. Where the assured brings an action for a total loss and the evidence proves only a partial loss, he may, unless the policy otherwise provides, recover for a partial loss.

5. Where goods reach their destination in specie, but by reason of obliteration of marks, or otherwise, they are incapable of identification, the loss, if any, is partial, and not total.

57. ACTUAL TOTAL LOSS

1. Where the subject—matter insured is destroyed, or so damaged as to cease to be a thing of the kind insured, or where the assured is irretrievably deprived thereof, there is an actual total loss.

2. In the case of an actual total loss no notice of abandonment need be given.

58. MISSING SHIP

Where the ship concerned in the adventure is missing, and after the lapse of a reasonable time no news of her has been received, an actual total loss may be presumed.

59. EFFECT OF TRANSSHIPMENT, ETC.

Where, by a peril insured against, the voyage is interrupted at an intermediate port or place, under such circumstances as, apart from any special stipulation in the contract of affreightment, to justify the master in landing and re–shipping the goods or other moveables or in transshipping them, and sending them on to their destination, the liability of the insurer continues, notwithstanding the landing or transshipment.

60. CONSTRUCTIVE TOTAL LOSS DEFINED

1. Subject to any express provision in the policy, there is a constructive total loss where the subject–matter insured is reasonably abandoned on account of its actual total loss appearing to be unavoidable, or because it could not be preserved from actual total loss without an expenditure which would exceed its value when the expenditure had been incurred.

2. In particular, there is a constructive total loss—
   i. Where the assured is deprived of the possession of his ship or goods by a peril insured against, and (a) it is unlikely that he can recover the ship or goods, as the case may be, or (b) the cost of recovering the ship or goods, as the case may be, would exceed their value when recovered; or
   ii. In the case of damage to a ship, where she is so damaged by a peril insured against that the cost of repairing the damage

would exceed the value of the ship when repaired.

In estimating the cost of repairs, no deduction is to be made in respect of general average contributions to those repairs payable by other interests, but account is to be taken of the expense of future salvage operations and of any future general average contributions to which the ship would be liable if repaired; or

iii. In the case of damage to goods, where the cost of repairing the damage and forwarding the goods to their destination would exceed their value on arrival.

61. EFFECT OF CONSTRUCTIVE TOTAL LOSS

Where there is a constructive total loss the assured may either treat the loss as a partial loss, or abandon the subject—matter insured to the insurer and treat the loss as if it were an actual total loss.

62. NOTICE OF ABANDONMENT

1. Subject to the provisions of this section, where the assured elects to abandon the subject—matter insured to the insurer, he must give notice of abandonment. If he fails to do so the loss can only be treated as a partial loss.

2. Notice of abandonment may be given in writing, or by word of mouth, or partly in writing and partly by word of mouth, and may be given in terms which indicate the intention of the assured to abandon his insured interest in the subject—matter insured unconditionally to the insurer.

3. Notice of abandonment must be given with reasonable diligence after the receipt of reliable information of the loss, but where the information is of a doubtful character the assured is entitled to a reasonable time to make inquiry.

4. Where notice of abandonment is properly given, the rights of the assured are not prejudiced by the fact that the insurer refuses to accept the abandonment.

5. The acceptance of an abandonment may be either express or implied from the conduct of the insurer. The mere silence of the insurer after notice is not an acceptance.

6. Where a notice of abandonment is accepted the abandonment is irrevocable. The acceptance of the notice conclusively admits liability for the loss and the sufficiency of the notice.

7. Notice of abandonment is unnecessary where, at the time when the assured receives information of the loss, there would be no possibility of benefit to the insurer if notice were given to him.

8. Notice of abandonment may be waived by the insurer.

9. Where an insurer has re-insured his risk, no notice of abandonment need be given by him.

63. EFFECT OF ABANDONMENT

1. Where there is a valid abandonment the insurer is entitled to take over the interest of the assured in whatever may remain of the subject-matter insured, and all proprietary rights incidental thereto.

2. Upon the abandonment of a ship, the insurer thereof is entitled to any freight in course of being earned, and which is earned by her subsequent to the casualty causing the loss, less the expenses of earning it incurred after the casualty; and, where the ship is carrying the owner's goods, the insurer is entitled to a reasonable remuneration for the carriage of them subsequent to the casualty causing the loss.

Partial Losses
(Including Salvage & General Average
& Particular Charges)

64. PARTICULAR AVERABE LOSS

1. A particular average loss is a partial loss of the subject—matter insured, caused by a peril insured against, and which is not a general average loss.

2. Expenses incurred by or on behalf of the assured for the safety or preservation of the subject—matter insured, other than general average and salvage charges, are called particular charges. Particular charges are not included in particular average.

65. SALVAGE CHARGES

1. Subject to any express provision in the policy, salvage charges incurred in preventing a loss by perils insured against may be recovered as a loss by those perils.

2. "Salvage charges" means the charges recoverable under maritime law by a salvor independently of contract. They do not include the expenses of services in the nature of salvage rendered by the assured or his agents, or any person employed for hire by them, for the purpose of averting a peril insured against. Such expenses, where properly incurred, may be recovered as particular charges or as a general average loss, according to the circumstal1ces under which they were incurred.

66. GENERAL AVERAGE LOSS

1. A general average loss is a loss caused by or directly consequential on a general average act. It includes a general

average expenditure as well as a general average sacrifice.

2. There is a general average act where any extraordinary sacrifice or expenditure is voluntarily and reasonably made or incurred in time of peril for the purpose of preserving the property imperilled in the common adventure.

3. Where there is a general average loss, the party on whom it falls is entitled, subject to the conditions imposed by maritime law, to a rateable contribution from the other parties interested, and such contribution is called a general average contribution.

4. Subject to any express provision in the policy, where the assured has incurred a general average expenditure, he may recover from the insurer in respect of the proportion of the loss which falls upon him; and, in the case of a general average sacrifice, he may recover from the insurer in respect of the whole loss without having enforced his right of contribution from the other parties liable to contribute.

5. Subject to any express provision in the policy, where the assured has paid, or is liable to pay, a general average contribution in respect of the subject insured, he may recover therefor from the insurer.

6. In the absence of express stipulation, the insurer is not liable for any general average loss or contribution where the loss was not incurred for the purpose of avoiding, or in connection with the avoidance of, a peril insured against.

7. Where ship, freight, and cargo, or any two of those interests, are owned by the same assured, the liability of the insurer in respect of general average losses or contributions is to be determined as if those subjects were owned by different persons.

Measure of Indemnity

67. EXTENT OF LIABILITY OF INSURER FOR LOSS

1. The sum which the assured can recover in respect of a loss on a policy by which he is insured, in the case of an unvalued policy to the full extent of the insurable value, or, in the case of a valued policy to the full extent of the value fixed by the policy, is called the measure of indemnity

2. Where there is a loss recoverable under the policy, the insurer, or each insurer if there be more than one, is liable for such proportion of the measure of indemnity as the amount of his subscription bears to the value fixed by the policy in the case of a valued policy, or to the insurable value in the case of an unvalued policy.

68. TOTAL LOSS

Subject to the provisions of this Act and to any express provision in the policy, where there is a total loss of the subject—matter insured,—

1. If the policy be a valued policy, the measure of indemnity is the sum fixed by the policy;

2. If the policy be an unvalued policy, the measure of indemnity is the insurable value of the subject—matter insured.

69. PARTIAL LOSS OF SHIP

Where a ship is damaged, but is not totally lost, the measure of indemnity, subject to any express provision in the policy, is as follows:—

1. Where the ship has been repaired, the assured is entitled to the reasonable cost of the repairs, less the customary deductions, but

not exceeding the sum insured in respect of any one casualty;

2. Where the ship has been only partially repaired, the assured is entitled to the reasonable cost of such repairs, computed as above, and also to be indemnified for the reasonable depreciation, if any, arising from the unrepaired damage, provided that the aggregate amount shall not exceed the cost of repairing the whole damage, computed as above;

3. Where the ship has not been repaired, and has not been sold in her damaged state during the risk, the assured is entitled to be indemnified for the reasonable depreciation arising from the unrepaired damage, but not exceeding the reasonable cost of repairing such damage, computed as above.

70. PARTIAL LOSS OF FREIGHT

Subject to any express provision in the policy, where there is a partial loss of freight, the measure of indemnity is such proportion of the sum fixed by the policy in the case of a valued policy, or of the insurable value in the case of an unvalued policy, as the proportion of freight lost by the assured bears to the whole freight at the risk of the assured under the policy.

71. PARTIAL LOSS OF GOODS, MERCHANDISE, ETC.

Where there is a partial loss of goods, merchandise, or other moveables, the measure of indemnity, subject to any express provision in the policy, is as follows:—

1. Where part of the goods, merchandise or other moveables insured by a valued policy is totally lost, the measure of indemnity is such proportion of the sum fixed by the policy as the insurable value of the part lost bears to the insurable value of the whole, ascertained as in the case of an unvalued policy;

2. Where part of the goods, merchandise, or other moveables insured by an unvalued policy is totally lost, the measure of indemnity is the insurable value of the part lost, ascertained as in case of total loss;

3. Where the whole or any part of the goods or merchandise insured has been delivered damaged at its destination, the measure of indemnity is such proportion of the sum fixed by the policy in the case of a valued policy, or of the insurable value in the case of an unvalued policy, as the difference between the gross sound and damaged values at the place of arrival bears to the gross sound value;

4. "Gross value" means the wholesale price or, if there be no such price, the estimated value, with, in either case, freight, landing charges, and duty paid beforehand; provided that, in the case of goods or merchandise customarily sold in bond, the bonded price is deemed to be the gross value. "Gross proceeds" means the actual price obtained at a sale where all charges on sale are paid by the sellers.

72. APPORTIONMENT OF VALUATION

1. Where different species of property are insured under a single valuation, the valuation must be apportioned over the different species in proportion to their respective insurable values, as in the case of an unvalued policy. The insured value of any part of a species is such proportion of the total insured value of the same as the insurable value of the part bears to the insurable value of the whole, ascertained in both cases as provided by this Act.

2. Where a valuation has to be apportioned, and particulars of the prime cost of each separate species, quality, or description of goods cannot be ascertained, the division of the valuation may be made

over the net arrived sound values of the different species, qualities, or descriptions of goods.

73. GENERAL AVERAGE CONTRIBUTIONS AND SALVAGE CHARGES

1. Subject to any express provision in the policy, where the assured has paid, or is liable for, any general average contribution, the measure of indemnity is the full amount of such contribution, if the subject—matter liable to contribution is insured for its full contributory value; but, if such subject—matter be not insured for its full contributory value, or if only part of it be insured, the indemnity payable by the insurer must be reduced in proportion to the under insurance, and where there has been a particular average loss which constitutes a deduction from the contributory value, and for which the insurer is liable, that amount must be deducted from the insured value in order to ascertain what the insurer is liable to contribute.

2. Where the insurer is liable for salvage charges the extent of his liability must be determined on the like principle.

74. LIABILITIES TO THIRD PARTIES

Where the assured has effected an insurance in express terms against any liability to a third party, the measure of indemnity, subject to any express provision in the policy, is the amount paid or payable by him to such third party in respect of such liability.

75. GENERAL PROVISIONS AS TO MEASURE OF INDEMNITY

1. Where there has been a loss in respect of any subject—matter not expressly provided for in the foregoing provisions of this Act, the measure of indemnity shall be ascertained, as nearly as may be, in accordance with those provisions, in so far as applicable to the

particular case.

2. Nothing in the provisions of this Act relating to the measure of indemnity shall affect the rules relating to double insurance, or prohibit the insurer from disproving interest wholly or in part, or from showing that at the time of the loss the whole or any part of the subject–matter insured was not at risk under the policy.

76. PARTICULAR AVERAGE WARRANTIES

1. Where the subject–matter insured is warranted free from particular average, the assured cannot recover for a loss of part, other than a loss incurred by a general average sacrifice, unless the contract contained in the policy be apportionable; but, if the contract be apportionable, the assured may recover for a total loss of any apportionable part.

2. Where the subject–matter insured is warranted free from particular average, either wholly or under a certain percentage, the insurer is nevertheless liable for salvage charges, and for particular charges and other expenses properly incurred pursuant to the provisions of the suing and labouring clause in order to avert a loss insured against.

3. Unless the policy otherwise provides, where the subject–matter insured is warranted free from particular average under a specified percentage, a general average loss cannot be added to a particular average loss to make up the specified percentage.

4. For the purpose of ascertaining whether the specified percentage has been reached, regard shall be had only to the actual loss suffered by the subject–matter insured. Particular charges and the expenses of and incidental to ascertaining and proving the loss must be excluded.

77. SUCCESSIVE LOSSES

1. Unless the policy otherwise provides, and subject to the provisions of this Act, the insurer is liable for successive losses, even though the total amount of such losses may exceed the sum insured.

2. Where, under the same policy, a partial loss, which has not been repaired or otherwise made good, is followed by a total loss, the assured can only recover in respect of the total loss:

   Provided that nothing in this section shall affect the liability of the insurer under the suing and labouring clause.

78. SUING & LABOURING CLAUSE

1. Where the policy contains a suing and labouring clause, the engagement thereby entered into is deemed to be supplementary to the contract of insurance, and the assured may recover from the insurer any expenses properly incurred pursuant to the clause, notwithstanding that the insurer may have paid for a total loss, or that the subject-matter may have been warranted free from particular average, either wholly or under a certain percentage.

2. General average losses and contributions and salvage charges, as defined by this Act, are not recoverable under the suing and labouring clause.

3. Expenses incurred for the purpose of averting or diminishing any loss not covered by the policy are not recoverable under the suing and labouring clause.

4. It is the duty of the assured and his agents, in all cases, to take such measures as may be reasonable for the purpose of averting or minimising a loss.

Rights of Insurer on Payment

79. RIGHT OF SUBROGATION

1. Where the insurer pays for a total loss, either of the whole, or in the case of goods of any apportionable part, of the subject–matter insured, he thereupon becomes entitled to take over the interest of the assured in whatever may remain of the subject–matter so paid for, and he is thereby subrogated to all the rights and remedies of the assured in and in respect of that subject–matter as from the time of the casualty causing the loss.

2. Subject to the foregoing provisions, where the insurer pays for a partial loss, he acquires no title to the subject–matter insured, or such part of it as may remain, but he is thereupon subrogated to all rights and remedies of the assured in and in respect of the subject–matter insured as from the time of the casualty causing the loss, in so far as the assured has been indemnified, according to this Act, by such payment for the loss.

80. RIGHT OF CONTRIBUTION

1. Where the assured is over–insured by double insurance, each insurer is bound, as between himself and the other insurers, to contribute rateably to the loss in proportion to the amount for which he is liable under his contract.

2. If any insurer pays more than his proportion of the loss, he is entitled to maintain an action for contribution against the other insurers, and is entitled to the like remedies as a surety who has paid more than his proportion of the debt.

81. EFFECT OF UNDER INSURANCE

Where the assured is insured for an amount less than the insurable value or, in the case of a valued policy, for an amount less than the policy valuation, he is deemed to be his own insurer in respect of the uninsured balance.

Return of Premium

82. ENFORCEMENT OF RETURN

Where the premium or a proportionate part thereof is, by this Act, declared to be returnable,—

   a. If already paid, it may be recovered by the assured from the insurer; and

   b. If unpaid, it may be retained by the assured or his agent.

83. RETURN BY AGREEMENT

Where the policy contains a stipulation for the return of the premium, or a proportionate part thereof, on the happening of a certain event, and that event happens, the premium, or, as the case may be, the proportionate part thereof, is thereupon returnable to the assured.

84. RETURN FOR FAILURE OF CONSIDERATION

   1. Where the consideration for the payment of the premium totally fails, and there has been no fraud or illegality on the part of the assured or his agents, the premium is thereupon returnable to the assured.

   2. Where the consideration for the payment of the premium is

apportionable and there is a total failure of any apportionable part of the consideration, a proportionate part of the premium is, under the like conditions, thereupon returnable to the assured.

3. In particular—

a. Where the policy is void, or is avoided by the insurer as from the commencement of the risk, the premium is returnable, provided that there has been no fraud or illegality on the part of the assured; but if the risk is not apportionable, and has once attached, the premiun1 is not returnable;

b. Where the subject—matter insured, or part thereof, has never been imperilled, the premium, or, as the case may be, a proportionate part thereof, is returnable:

Provided that where the subject—matter has been insured "lost or not lost" and has arrived in safety at the time when the contract is concluded, the premium is not returnable unless, at such time, the insurer knew of the safe arrival.

c. Where the assured has no insurable interest throughout the currency of the risk, the premium is returnable, provided that this rule does not apply to a policy effected by way of gaming or wagering;

d. Where the assured has a defeasible interest which is terminated during the currency of the risk, the premium is not returnable;

e. Where the assured has over—insured under an unvalued policy, a proportionate part of the premium is returnable;

f. Subject to the foregoing provisions, where the assured has over—insured by double insurance, a proportionate part of the several premiums is returnable:

Provided that, if the policies are effected at different times, and any earlier policy has at any time borne the entire risk, or if a clainm has been paid on the policy in respect of the full sum insured thereby, no premium is returnable in respect of that policy, and when the double insurance is effected knowingly by the assured no premium is returnable.

Mutual Insurance

85. MODIFICATION OF ACT IN CASE OF MUTUAL INSURANCE

1. Where two or more persons mutually agree to insure each other against marine losses there is said to be a mutual insurance.
2. The provisions of this Act relating to the premium do not apply to mutual insurance, but a guarantee, or such other arrangement as may be agreed upon, may be substituted for the premium.
3. The provisions of this Act, in so far as they may be modified by the agreement of the parties, may in the case of mutual insurance be modified by the terms of the policies issued by the association, or by the rules and regulations of the association.
4. Subject to the exceptions mentioned in this section, the provisions of this Act apply to a mutual insurance.

Supplemental

86. RATIFICATION BY ASSURED

Where a contract of marine insurance is in good faith effected by one person on behalf of another, the person on whose behalf it is effected may ratify the contract even after he is aware of a loss.

87. IMPLIED OBLIGATIONS VARIED BY AGREEMENT OR USAGE

1. Where any right, duty, or liability would arise under a contract of

marine insurance by implication of law, it may be negatived or varied by express agreement, or by usage, if the usage be such as to bind both parties to the contract.

2. The provisions of this section extend to any right, duty, or liability declared by this Act which may be lawfully modified by agreement.

88. REASONABLE TIME, ETC., A QUESTION OF FACT

Where by this Act any reference is made to reasonable time, reasonable premium, or reasonable diligence, the question what is reasonable is a question of fact.

89. SLIP AS EVIDENCE

Where there is a duly stamped policy, reference may be made, as heretofore, to the slip or covering note, in any legal proceeding.

90. INTERPRETATION OF TERMS

In this Act, unless the context or subject–matter otherwise requires,—

"**Action**" includes counter–claim and set off:

"**Freight**" includes the profit derivable by a shipowner from the employment of his ship to carry his own goods or moveables, as well as freight payable by a third party, but does not include passage money:

"**Moveables**" means any moveable tangible property, other than the ship, and includes money, valuable securities, and other documents:

"**Policy**" means a marine policy.

91. Savings

1. Nothing in this Act, or in any repeal effected thereby, shall affect—

   a. The provisions of the Stamp Act 1891, or any enactment for the time being in force relating to the revenue:

b. The provisions of the Companies Act 1862, or any enactment amending or substituted for the same;

c. The provisions of any statute not expressly repealed by this Act.

2. The rules of the common law including the law merchant, save in so far as they are inconsistent with the express provisions of this Act, shall continue to apply to contracts of marine insurance.

92. REPEALS

The enactments mentioned in the Second Schedule to this Act are hereby repealed to the extent specificed in that schedule.

NOTE:

Repealed by the Statute Law Revision Act 1927.

93. COMMENCEMENT

This Act shall come into operation on the first day of January, 1907.

NOTE:

Repealed by the Statute Law Revision Act 1927.

94. SHORT TITLE

This Act may be cited as the Marine Insurance Act 1906.

SCHEDULES
FIRST SCHEDULE (s 30)
Form of policy

BE IT KNOWN THAT ⋯ as well in ⋯ own name as for and in the name and names of all and every other person or persons to whom the same doth, may, or shall appertain, in part or in all doth make assurance and cause ⋯ and them, and every one of them, to be insured lost or not lost, at and from ⋯

Upon any kind of goods and merchandise, and also upon the body, tackle, apparel, ordnance, munition, artillery, boat, and other furniture, of and in the good ship or vessel called the ⋯ whereof is master under God, for this present voyage, ⋯ or whosoever else shall to for master in the said ship, or by whatsoever other name or names the said ship, or the master thereof, is or shall be named or called; beginning the adventure upon the said goods and merchandises from the loading thereof aboard the said ship.

upon the said ship, etc.

and so shall continue and endure, during her abode there,. upon the said ship, etc.

And further, until the said ship, with all her ordnance, tackle, apparel; etc., and goods and merchandises whatsoever shall be arrived at ⋯

upon the said ship, etc., until she hath moored at anchor twenty–four hours in good safety; and upon the goods and merchandises, until the same be there discharged and safely landed. And it shall be lawful for the said ship, etc., in this voyage to proceed and sail to and touch and stay at any ports or places whatsoever.

附錄五 ●●●●●●●●

保險法（摘錄）

第一章　總則

第一節　定義及分類

第 1 條　本法所稱保險，謂當事人約定，一方交付保險費於他方，他方對於因不可預料，或不可抗力之事故所致之損害，負擔賠償財物之行為。

根據前項所訂之契約，稱為保險契約。

第 2 條　本法所稱保險人，指經營保險事業之各種組織，在保險契約成立時，有保險費之請求權；在承保危險事故發生時，依其承保之責任，負擔賠償之義務。

第 3 條　本法所稱要保人，指對保險標的具有保險利益，向保險人申請訂立保險契約，並負有交付保險費義務之人。

第 4 條　本法所稱被保險人，指於保險事故發生時，遭受損害，享有賠償請求權之人；要保人亦得為被保險人。

第 5 條　本法所稱受益人，指被保險人或要保人約定享有賠償請求權之人，要保人或被保險人均得為受益人。

第 6 條　本法所稱保險業，指依本法組織登記，以經營保險為業之機構。

本法所稱外國保險業，指依外國法律組織登記，並經主管機關許可，在中華民國境內經營保險為業之機構。

第 7 條　本法所稱保險業負責人，指依公司法或合作社法應負責之人。

第 8 條　本法所稱保險代理人，指根據代理契約或授權書，向保險人收取費用，並代理經營業務之人。

第 8-1 條　本法所稱保險業務員，指為保險業、保險經紀人公司、保險代理人公司，從事保險招攬之人。

第 9 條　本法所稱保險經紀人，指基於被保險人之利益，洽訂保險契約或提供相關服務，而收取佣金或報酬之人。

第 10 條　本法所稱公證人，指向保險人或被保險人收取費用，為其辦理保險標的之查勘、鑑定及估價與賠款之理算、洽商，而予證明之人。

第 11 條　本法所定各種準備金，包括責任準備金、未滿期保費準備金、特別準備金、賠款準備金及其他經主管機關規定之準備金。

第 12 條　本法所稱主管機關為行政院金融監督管理委員會。但保險合作社除其經營之業務，以行政院金融監督管理委員會為主管機關外，其社務以合作社之主管機關為主管機關。

第 13 條　保險分為財產保險及人身保險。

財產保險，包括火災保險、海上保險、陸空保險、責任保險、保證保險及經主管機關核准之其他保險。

人身保險，包括人壽保險、健康保險、傷害保險及年金保險。

第二節　保險利益

第 14 條　要保人對於財產上之現有利益，或因財產上之現有利益而生之期待利益，有保險利益。

第 15 條　運送人或保管人對於所運送或保管之貨物，以其所負之責任為限，有保險利益。

第 16 條　要保人對於左列各人之生命或身體，有保險利益。

一、本人或其家屬。

二、生活費或教育費所仰給之人。

三、債務人。

四、為本人管理財產或利益之人。

第 17 條　要保人或被保險人，對於保險標的物無保險利益者，保險契約失其效力。

第 18 條　被保險人死亡或保險標的物所有權移轉時，保險契約除另有訂定外，仍為繼承人或受讓人之利益而存在。

第 19 條　合夥人或共有人聯合為被保險人時，其中一人或數人讓與保險利益於他人者，保險契約不因之而失效。

第 20 條　凡基於有效契約而生之利益，亦得為保險利益。

第三節　保險費

第 21 條　保險費分一次交付，及分期交付兩種。保險契約規定一次交付，或分期交付之第一期保險費，應於契約生效前交付之，但保險契約簽訂時，保險費未能確定者，不在此限。

第 22 條　保險費應由要保人依契約規定交付。信託業依信託契約有交付保險費義務者，保險費應由信託業代為交付之。

要保人為他人利益訂立之保險契約，保險人對於要保人所得為之抗辯，亦得以之對抗受益人。

第 23 條　以同一保險利益，同一保險事故，善意訂立數個保險契約，其保險金額之總額超過保險標的之價值者，在危險發生前，要保人得依超過部分，要求比例返還保險費。

保險契約因第三十七條之情事而無效時，保險人於不知情之時期內，仍取得保險費。

第 24 條　保險契約因第五十一條第二項之情事，而保險人不受拘束時，保險人得請求償還費用。其已收受之保險費，無須返還。

保險契約因第五十一條第三項之情事而要保人不受拘束時，保險人不得請求保險費及償還費用。其已收受者，應返還之。

保險契約因第六十條或第八十一條之情事而終止，或部分終止時，除保險費非以時間為計算基礎者外，終止後之保險費已交付者，應返還之。

第 25 條　保險契約因第六十四條第二項之情事而解除時，保險人無須返還其已收受之保險費。

第 26 條　保險費依保險契約所載增加危險之特別情形計算者，其情形在契約存續期內消滅時，要保人得按訂約時保險費率，自其情形消滅時起算，請求比例減少保險費。

前項減少保險費不同意時，要保人得終止契約。其終止後之保險費已交付者，應返還之。

第 27 條　保險人破產時，保險契約於破產宣告之日終止，其終止後之保險費，已交付者，保險人應返還之。

第 28 條　要保人破產時，保險契約仍為破產債權人之利益而存在，但破產管理人或保險人得於破產宣告三個月內終止契約。其終止後之保險費已交付者，應返還之。

第四節　保險人之責任

第 29 條　保險人對於由不可預料或不可抗力之事故所致之損害，負賠償責任。但保險契約內有明文限制者，不在此限。

保險人對於由要保人或被保險人之過失所致之損害，負賠償責任。但出於要保人或被保險人之故意者，不在此限。

第 30 條　保險人對於因履行道德上之義務所致之損害，應負賠償責任。

第 31 條　保險人對於因要保人，或被保險人之受僱人，或其所有之物或動物所致之損害，應負賠償責任。

第 32 條　保險人對於因戰爭所致之損害，除契約有相反之訂定外，應負賠償責任。

第 33 條　保險人對於要保人或被保險人，為避免或減輕損害之必要行為所生之費用，負償還之責。其償還數額與賠償金額，合計雖超過保險金額，仍應償還。

保險人對於前項費用之償還，以保險金額對於保險標的之價值比例定之。

第 34 條　保險人應於要保人或被保險人交齊證明文件後，於約定期限內給付賠償金額。無約定期限者，應於接到通知後十五日內給付之。

保險人因可歸責於自己之事由致未在前項規定期限內為給付者，應給付遲延利息年利一分。

第五節　複保險

第 35 條　複保險，謂要保人對於同一保險利益，同一保險事故，與數保險人分別訂立數個保險之契約行為。

第 36 條　複保險，除另有約定外，要保人應將他保險人之名稱及保險金額通知各保險人。

第 37 條　要保人故意不為前條之通知，或意圖不當得利而為複保險者，其契約無效。

第 38 條　善意之複保險，其保險金額之總額超過保險標的之價值者，除另有約定外，各保險人對於保險標的之全部價值，僅就其所保金額負比例分擔之責。但賠償總額，不得超過保險標的之價值。

第六節　再保險

第 39 條　再保險，謂保險人以其所承保之危險，轉向他保險人為保險之契約行為。

第 40 條　原保險契約之被保險人，對於再保險人無賠償請求權。但原保險契約及再保險契約另有約定者，不在此限。

第 41 條　再保險人不得向原保險契約之要保人請求交付保險。

第 42 條　原保險人不得以再保險人不履行再保險金額給付之義務為理由，拒絕或延遲履行其對於被保險人之義務。

第二章　保險契約

第一節　通則

第 43 條　保險契約，應以保險單或暫保單為之。

第 44 條　保險契約，由保險人於同意要保人聲請後簽訂。
　　　　　利害關係人，均得向保險人請求保險契約之謄本。

第 45 條　要保人得不經委任，為他人之利益訂立保險契約。受益人有疑義時，推定要保人為自己之利益而訂立。

第 46 條　保險契約由代理人訂立者，應載明代訂之意旨。

第 47 條　保險契約由合夥人或共有人中之一人或數人訂立，而其利益及於全體合夥人或共有人者，應載明為全體合夥人或共有人訂立之意旨。

第 48 條　保險人得約定保險標的物之一部份，應由要保人自行負擔由危險而生之損失。

有前項約定時，要保人不得將未經保險之部份，另向他保險人訂立保險契約。

第 49 條　保險契約除人身保險外，得為指示式或無記名式。

保險人對於要保人所得為之抗辯，亦得以之對抗保險契約之受讓人。

第 50 條　保險契約分不定值保險契約，及定值保險契約。

不定值保險契約，為契約上載明保險標的之價值，須至危險發生後估計而訂之保險契約。

定值保險契約，為契約上載明保險標的一定價值之保險契約。

第 51 條　保險契約訂立時，保險標的之危險已發生或已消滅者，其契約無效。但為當事人雙方所不知者，不在此限。

訂約時，僅要保人知危險已發生者，保險人不受契約之拘束。

訂約時，僅保險人知危險已消滅者，要保人不受契約之拘束。

第 52 條　為他人利益訂立之保險契約，於訂約時，該他人未確定者，由要保人或保險契約所載可得確定之受益人，享受其利益。

第 53 條　被保險人因保險人應負保險責任之損失發生，而對於第三人有損失賠償請求權者，保險人得於給付賠償金額後，代位行使被保險人對於第三人之請求權；但其所請求之數額，以不逾賠償金額為限。

前項第三人為被保險人之家屬或受僱人時，保險人無代位請求權。但損失係由其故意所致者，不在此限。

第 54 條　本法之強制規定，不得以契約變更之。但有利於被保險人者，不在此限。

保險契約之解釋，應探求契約當事人之真意，不得拘泥於所用之文字；如有疑義時，以作有利於被保險人之解釋為原則。

第 54-1 條　保險契約中有左列情事之一，依訂約時情形顯失公平者，該部分之約定無效：

一、免除或減輕保險人依本法應負之義務者。

二、使要保人、受益人或被保險人拋棄或限制其依本法所享之權利者。

三、加重要保人或被保險人之義務者。

四、其他於要保人、受益人或被保險人有重大不利益者。

第二節　基本條款

第 55 條　保險契約，除本法另有規定外，應記載左列各款事項：

一、當事人之姓名及住所。

二、保險之標的物。

三、保險事故之種類。

四、保險責任開始之日時及保險期間。

五、保險金額。

六、保險費。

七、無效及失權之原因。

八、訂約之年月日。

第 56 條　變更保險契約或恢復停止效力之保險契約時，保險人於接到通知後十日內不為拒絕者，視為承諾。但本法就人身保險有特別規定者，從其規定。

第 57 條　當事人之一方對於他方應通知之事項而怠於通知者，除不可抗力之事故外，不問是否故意，他方得據為解除保險契約之原因。

第 58 條　要保人、被保險人或受益人，遇有保險人應負保險責任之事故發生，除本法另有規定，或契約另有訂定外，應於知悉後五日內通知保險人。

第 59 條　要保人對於保險契約內所載增加危險之情形應通知者，應於知悉後通知保險人。

危險增加，由於要保人或被保險人之行為所致，其危險達於應增加保險費或終止契約之程度者，要保人或被保險人應先通知保險人。

危險增加，不由於要保人或被保險人之行為所致者，要保人或被保險人應於知悉後十日內通知保險人。

危險減少時，被保險人得請求保險人重新核定保費。

第 60 條　保險遇有前條情形，得終止契約，或提議另定保險費。要保人對於另定保險費不同意者，其契約即為終止。但因前條第二項情形終止契約時，保險人如有損失，並得請求賠償。

保險人知危險增加後，仍繼續收受保險費，或於危險發生後給付賠償金額，或其他維持契約之表示者，喪失前項之權利。

第 61 條　危險增加如有左列情形之一時，不適用第五十九條之規定：

一、損害之發生不影響保險人之負擔者。

二、為防護保險人之利益者。

三、為履行道德上之義務者。

第 62 條　當事人之一方對於左列各款，不負通知之義務：

一、為他方所知者。

二、依通常注意為他方所應知，或無法諉為不知者。

三、一方對於他方經聲明不必通知者。

第 63 條　要保人或被保險人不於第五十八條，第五十九條第三項所規定之限期內為通知者，對於保險人因此所受之損失，應負賠償責任。

第 64 條　訂立契約時，要保人對於保險人之書面詢問，應據實說明。

要保人故意隱匿，或因過失遺漏，或為不實之說明，足以變更或減少保險人對於危險之估計者，保險人得解除契約；其危險發生後亦同。但要保人證明危險之發生未基於其說明或未說明之事實時，不在此限。

前項解除契約權，自保險人知有解除之原因後，經過一個月不行使而消滅；或契約訂立後經過二年，即有可以解除之原因，亦不得解除契約。

第 65 條　由保險契約所生之權利，自得為請求之日起，經過二年不行使而消滅。有左列各款情形之一者，其期限之起算，依各該款之規定：

一、要保人或被保險人對於危險之說明，有隱匿、遺漏或不實者，自保險人知情之日起算。

一、危險發生後，利害關係人能證明其非因疏忽而不知情者，自其知情之日起算。

三、要保人或被保險人對於保險人之請求，係由於第三人之請求而生者，自要保人或被保險人受請求之日起算。

第三節　特約條款

第 66 條　特約條款，為當事人於保險契約基本條款外，承認履行特種義務之條款。

第 67 條　與保險契約有關之一切事項，不問過去現在或將來，均得以特約條款定之。

第 68 條　保險契約當事人之一方違背特約條款時，他方得解除契約；其危險發生後亦同。

第六十四條第三項之規定，於前項情形準用之。

第 69 條　關於未來事項之特約條款，於未屆履行期前危險已發生，或其履行為不可能，或在訂約地為不合法而未履行者，保險契約不因之而失效。

第三章　財產保險

第一節　火災保險

第 70 條　火災保險人，對於由火災所致保險標的物之毀損或滅失，除契約另有訂定外，員賠償之責。

因救護保險標的物，致保險標的物發生損失者，視同所保危險所生之損失。

第 71 條　就集合之物而總括為保險者，被保險人家屬、受僱人或同居人之物，亦得為保險標的，載明於保險契約，在危險發生時，就其損失享受賠償。

前項保險契約，視同並為第三人利益而訂立。

第 72 條　保險金額為保險人在保險期內，所員責任之最高額度。保險人應於承保前，查明保險標的物之市價，不得超額承保。

第 73 條　保險標的，得由要保人，依主管機關核定之費率及條款，作定值或不定值約定之要保。

保險標的，以約定價值為保險金額者，發生全部損失或部份損失時，均按約定價值為標準計算賠償。

保險標的未經約定價值者，發生損失時，按保險事故發生時實際價值為標準，計算賠償，其賠償金額，不得超過保險金額。

第 74 條　第七十三條所稱全部損失，係指保險標的全部滅失或毀損，達於不能修復或其修復之費用，超過保險標的恢復原狀所需者。

第 75 條　保險標的物不能以市價估計者，得由當事人約定其價值。賠償時從其約定。

第 76 條　保險金額超過保險標的價值之契約，係由當事人一方之詐欺而訂立者，他方得解除契約。如有損失，並得請求賠償。無詐欺情事者，除定值保險外，其契約僅於保險標的價值之限度內為有效。

前無詐欺情事之保險契約，經當事人一方將超過價值之事實通知他方後，保險金額及保險費，均應按照保險標的之價值比例減少。

第 77 條　保險金額不及保險標的物之價值者，除契約另有訂定外，保險人之負擔，以保險金額對於保險標的物之價值比例定之。

第 78 條　損失之估計，因可歸責於保險人之事由而遲延者，應自被保險人交出損失清單一個月後加給利息。損失清單交出二個月後損失尚未完全估定者，被保險人得請求先行交付其所應得之最低賠償金額。

第 79 條　保險人或被保險人為證明及估計損失所支出之必要費用，除契約另有訂定外，由保險人負擔之。

前保險金額不及保險標的物之價值時，保險人對於前項費用，依第七十七條規定比例負擔之。

第 80 條　損失未估定前，要保人或被保險人除為公共利益或避免擴大損失外，非經保險人同意，對於保險標的物不得加以變更。

第 81 條　保險標的物非因保險契約所載之保險事故而完全滅失時，保險契約即為終止。

第 82 條　保險標的物受部份之損失者，保險人與要保人均有終止契約之權。終止後，已交付未損失部份之保險費應返還之。

前項終止契約權，於賠償金額給付後，經過一個月不行使而消滅。

保險人終止契約時，應於十五日前通知要保人。

要保人與保險人均不終止契約時，除契約另有訂定外，保險人對於以後保險事故所致之損失，其責任以賠償保險金額之餘額為限。

第 82-1 條　第七十三條至第八十一條之規定，於海上保險、陸空保
　　　　　　險、責任保險、保證保險及其他財產保險準用之。
　　　　　　第一百二十三條及第一百二十四條之規定，於超過一年之
　　　　　　財產保險準用之。

第二節　海上保險

第 83 條　海上保險人對於保險標的物，除契約另有規定外，因海上
　　　　　一切事變及災害所生之毀損、滅失及費用，負賠償之責。
第 84 條　關於海上保險，適用海商法海上保險章之規定。

第三節　陸空保險

第 85 條　陸上、內河及航空保險人，對於保險標的物，除契約另有
　　　　　訂定外，因陸上、內河及航空一切事變及災害所致之毀
　　　　　損、滅失及費用，負賠償之責。
第 86 條　關於貨物之保險，除契約另有訂定外，自交運之時以迄於
　　　　　其目的地收貨之時為其期間。
第 87 條　保險契約，除記載第五十五條規定事項外，並應載明左列
　　　　　事項：
　　　　　一、運送路線及方法。
　　　　　二、運送人姓名及商號名稱。
　　　　　三、交運及取貨地點。
　　　　　四、運送有期限者，其期限。
第 88 條　因運送上之必要，暫時停止或變更運送路線或方法時，保
　　　　　險契約除另有訂定外，仍繼續有效。
第 89 條　航行內河船舶運費及裝載貨物之保險，除本節另有規定

外，準用海上保險有關條文之規定。

第四節　責任保險

第 90 條　責任保險人於被保險人對於第三人，依法應負賠償責任，而受賠償之請求時，負賠償之責。

第 91 條　被保險人因受第三人之請求而為抗辯，所支出之訴訟上或訴訟外之必要費用，除契約另有訂定外，由保險人負擔之。

被保險人得請求保險人墊給前項費用。

第 92 條　保險契約係為被保險人所營事業之損失賠償責任而訂立者，被保險人之代理人、管理人或監督人所負之損失賠償責任，亦享受保險之利益，其契約視同並為第三人之利益而訂立。

第 93 條　保險人得約定被保險人對於第三人就其責任所為之承認、和解或賠償，未經其參與者，不受拘束。但經要保人或被保險人通知保險人參與而無正當理由拒絕或藉故遲延者，不在此限。

第 94 條　保險人於第三人由被保險人應負責任事故所致之損失，未受賠償以前，不得以賠償金額之全部或一部給付被保險人。

被保險人對第三人應負損失賠償責任確定時，第三人得在保險金額範圍內，依其應得之比例，直接向保險人請求給付賠償金額。

第 95 條　保險人得經被保險人通知，直接對第三人為賠償金額之給付。

第四節之一　保證保險

第 95-1 條　保證保險人於被保險人因其受僱人之不誠實行為或其債務人之不履行債務所致損失，負賠償之責。

第 95-2 條　以受僱人之不誠實行為為保險事故之保證保險契約，除記載第五十五條規定事項外，並應載明左列事項：

一、被保險人之姓名及住所。

二、受僱人之姓名、職稱或其他得以認定為受僱人之方式。

第 95-3 條　以債務人之不履行債務為保險事故之保證保險契約，除記載第五十五條規定事項外，並應載明左列事項：

一、被保險人之姓名及住所。

二、債務人之姓名或其他得以認定為債務人之方式。

第五節　其他財產保險

第 96 條　其他財產保險為不屬於火災保險、海上保險、陸空保險、責任保險及保證保險之範圍，而以財物或無形利益為保險標的之各種保險。

第 97 條　保險人有隨時查勘保險標的物之權，如發現全部或一部份處於不正常狀態，經建議要保人或被保險人修復後，再行使用。如要保人或被保險人不接受建議時，得以書面通知終止保險契約或其有關部份。

第 98 條　要保人或被保險人，對於保險標的物未盡約定保護責任所致之損失，保險人不負賠償之責。

危險事故發生後，經鑑定係因要保人或被保險人未盡合理方法保護標的物，因而增加之損失，保險人不負賠償之責。

第 99 條　　保險標的物受部份之損失，經賠償或回復原狀後，保險契約繼續有效。但與原保險情況有異時，得增減其保險費。

第 100 條　　（刪除）

附 錄 六 ·········

海商法

第一章　通則

第 1 條　　本法稱船舶者，謂在海上航行，或在與海相通之水面或水
　　　　　　中航行之船舶。

第 2 條　　本法稱船長者，謂受船舶所有人僱用主管船舶一切事務之
　　　　　　人員；稱海員者，謂受船舶所有人僱用由船長指揮服務於
　　　　　　船舶上所有人員。

第 3 條　　下列船舶除因碰撞外，不適用本法之規定：

　　　　　　一、船舶法所稱之小船。

　　　　　　二、軍事建制之艦艇。

　　　　　　三、專用於公務之船舶。

　　　　　　四、第一條規定以外之其他船舶。

第 4 條　　船舶保全程序之強制執行，於船舶發航準備完成時起，以
　　　　　　迄航行至次一停泊港時止，不得為之。但為使航行可能所
　　　　　　生之債務，或因船舶碰撞所生之損害，不在此限。

　　　　　　國境內航行船舶之保全程序，得以揭示方法為之。

第 5 條　　海商事件，依本法之規定，本法無規定者，適用其他法律
　　　　　　之規定。

第二章 船舶

第一節 船舶所有權

第 6 條　船舶除本法有特別規定外，適用民法關於動產之規定。

第 7 條　除給養品外，凡於航行上及營業上必需之一切設備及屬具，皆視為船舶之一部。

第 8 條　船舶所有權或應有部分之讓與，非作成書面並依下列之規定，不生效力：

一、在中華民國，應申請讓與地或船舶所在地航政主管機關蓋印證明。

二、在外國，應申請中華民國駐外使領館、代表處或其他外交部授權機構蓋印證明。

第 9 條　船舶所有權之移轉，非經登記，不得對抗第三人。

第 10 條　船舶建造中，承攬人破產而破產管理人不為完成建造者，船舶定造人，得將船舶及業經交付或預定之材料，照估價扣除已付定金給償收取之，並得自行出資在原處完成建造，但使用船廠應給與報償。

第 11 條　共有船舶之處分及其他與共有人共同利益有關之事項，應以共有人過半數並其應有部分之價值合計半數之同意為之。

第 12 條　船舶共有人有出賣其應有部分時，其他共有人，得以同一價格儘先承買。

因船舶共有權一部分之出賣，致該船舶喪失中華民國國籍時，應得共有人全體之同意。

第 13 條　船舶共有人，以其應有部分供抵押時，應得其他共有人過半數之同意。

第 14 條　船舶共有人，對於利用船舶所生之債務，就其應有部分，員比例分擔之責。

共有人對於發生債務之管理行為，曾經拒絕同意者，關於此項債務，得委棄其應有部分於他共有人而免其責任。

第 15 條　船舶共有人為船長而被辭退或解任時，得退出共有關係，並請求返還其應有部分之資金。

前項資金數額，依當事人之協議定之，協議不成時，由法院裁判之。

第一項所規定退出共有關係之權，自被辭退之日起算，經一個月不行使而消滅。

第 16 條　共有關係，不因共有人中一人之死亡、破產或受監護宣告而終止。

第 17 條　船舶共有人，應選任共有船舶經理人，經營其業務，共有船舶經理人之選任，應以共有人過半數，並其應有部分之價值合計過半數之同意為之。

第 18 條　共有船舶經理人關於船舶之營運，在訴訟上或訴訟外代表共有人。

第 19 條　共有船舶經理人，非經共有人依第十一條規定之書面委任，不得出賣或抵押其船舶。

船舶共有人，對於共有船舶經理人權限所加之限制，不得對抗善意第三人。

第 20 條　共有船舶經理人，於每次航行完成後，應將其經過情形，報告於共有人，共有人亦得隨時檢查其營業情形，並查閱帳簿。

第 21 條　船舶所有人對下列事項所員之責任，以本次航行之船舶價值、運費及其他附屬費為限：

一、在船上、操作船舶或救助工作直接所致人身傷亡或財物毀損滅失之損害賠償。

二、船舶操作或救助工作所致權益侵害之損害賠償。但不包括因契約關係所生之損害賠償。

三、沈船或落海之打撈移除所生之債務。但不包括依契約之報酬或給付。

四、為避免或減輕前二款責任所員之債務。

前項所稱船舶所有人，包括船舶所有權人、船舶承租人、經理人及營運人。

第一項所稱本次航行，指船舶自一港至次一港之航程；所稱所稱運費，不包括依法或依約不能收取之運費及票價；所稱附屬費，指船舶因受損害應得之賠償。但不包括保險金。

第一項責任限制數額如低於下列標準者，船舶所有人應補足之：

一、對財物損害之賠償，以船舶登記總噸，每一總噸為國際貨幣基金，特別提款權五四計算單位，計算其數額。

二、對人身傷亡之賠償，以船舶登記總噸，每一總噸特別提款權一六二計算單位計算其數額。

三、前二款同時發生者，以船舶登記總噸，每一總噸特別提款權一六二計算單位計算其數額，但人身傷亡應優先以船舶登記總噸，每一總噸特別提款權一○八計算單位計算之數額內賠償，如此數額不足以全部清償時，其不足額再與財物之毀損滅失，共同在現存之責任限制數額內比例分配之。

四、船舶登記總噸不足三百噸者，以三百噸計算。

第 22 條　前條責任限制之規定，於下列情形不適用之：

一、本於船舶所有人本人之故意或過失所生之債務。

二、本於船長、海員及其他服務船舶之人員之僱用契約所生之債務。

三、救助報酬及共同海損分擔額。

四、船舶運送毒性化學物質或油污所生損害之賠償。

五、船舶運送核子物質或廢料發生核子事故所生損害之賠償。

六、核能動力船舶所生核子損害之賠償。

第 23 條　船舶所有人，如依第二十一條之規定限制其責任者，對於本次航行之船舶價值應證明之。

船舶價值之估計，以下列時期之船舶狀態為準：

一、因碰撞或其他事變所生共同海損之債權，及事變後以迄於第一到達港時所生之一切債權，其估價依船舶於到達第一港時之狀態。

二、關於船舶在停泊港內發生事變所生之債權，其估價依船舶在停泊港內事變發生後之狀態。

三、關於貨載之債權或本於載貨證券而生之債權，除前二款情形外，其估價依船舶於到達貨物之目的港時，或航行中斷地之狀態，如貨載應送達於數個不同之港埠，而損害係因同一原因而生者，其估價依船舶於到達該數港中之第一港時之狀態。

四、關於第二十一條所規定之其他債權，其估價依船舶航行完成時之狀態。

第二節　海事優先權

第 24 條　下列各款為海事優先權擔保之債權，有優先受償之權：

一、船長、海員及其他在船上服務之人員，本於僱傭契約所生之債權。

二、因船舶操作直接所致人身傷亡，對船舶所有人之賠償請求。

三、救助之報酬、清除沉船費用及船舶共同海損分擔額之賠償請求。

四、因船舶操作直接所致陸上或水上財物毀損滅失，對船舶所有人基於侵權行為之賠償請求。

五、港埠費、運河費、其他水道費及引水費。

前項海事優先權之位次，在船舶抵押權之前。

第 25 條　建造或修繕船舶所生債權，其債權人留置船舶之留置權位次，在海事優先權之後，船舶抵押權之前。

第 26 條　本法第二十二條第四款至第六款之賠償請求，不適用本法有關海事優先權之規定。

第 27 條　依第二十四條之規定，得優先受償之標的如下：

一、船舶、船舶設備及屬具或其殘餘物。

二、在發生優先債權之航行期內之運費。

三、船舶所有人因本次航行中船舶所受損害，或運費損失應得之賠償。

四、船舶所有人因共同海損應得之賠償。

五、船舶所有人在航行完成前，為施行救助所應得之報酬。

第 28 條　第二十四條第一項第一款之債權，得就同一僱傭契約期內所得之全部運費，優先受償，不受前條第二款之限制。

第 29 條　屬於同次航行之海事優先權，其位次依第二十四條各款之規定。

一款中有數債權者，不分先後，比例受償。

第二十四條第一項第三款所列債權，如有二個以上屬於同一種類，其發生在後者優先受償。救助報酬之發生應以施救行為完成時為準。

共同海損之分擔，應以共同海損行為發生之時為準。

因同一事變所發生第二十四條第一項各款之債權，視為同時發生之債權。

第 30 條　不屬於同次航行之海事優先權，其後次航行之海事優先權，先於前次航行之海事優先權。

第 31 條　海事優先權，不因船舶所有權之移轉而受影響。

第 32 條　第二十四條第一項海事優先權自其債權發生之日起，經一年而消滅。但第二十四條第一項第一款之賠償，自離職之日起算。

第三節　船舶抵押權

第 33 條　船舶抵押權之設定，應以書面為之。

第 34 條　船舶抵押權，得就建造中之船舶設定之。

第 35 條　船舶抵押權之設定，除法律別有規定外，僅船舶所有人或
　　　　　受其特別委任之人始得為之。

第 36 條　船舶抵押權之設定，非經登記，不得對抗第三人。

第 37 條　船舶共有人中一人或數人，就其應有部分所設定之抵押
　　　　　權，不因分割或出賣而受影響。

第三章　運送

第一節　貨物運送

第 38 條　貨物運送契約為下列二種：
　　　　　一、以件貨之運送為目的者。
　　　　　二、船舶之全部或一部供運送為目的者。

第 39 條　以船舶之全部或一部供運送為目的之運送契約，應以書面
　　　　　為之。

第 40 條　前條運送契約應載明下列事項：
　　　　　一、當事人姓名或名稱，及其住所、事務所或營業所。
　　　　　二、船名及對船舶之說明。
　　　　　三、貨物之種類及數量。
　　　　　四、契約期限或航程事項。
　　　　　五、運費。

第 41 條　以船舶之全部或一部供運送契約，不因船舶所有權之移轉

而受影響。

第 42 條　運送人所供給之船舶有瑕疵，不能達運送契約之目的時，託運人得解除契約。

第 43 條　以船舶之全部供運送時，託運人於發航前得解除契約。但應支付運費三分之一，其已裝載貨物之全部或一部者，並應負擔因裝卸所增加之費用。

前項如為往返航程之約定者，託運人於返程發航前要求終止契約時，應支付運費三分之二。

前二項之規定，對於當事人之間，關於延滯費之約定不受影響。

第 44 條　以船舶之一部供運送時，託運人於發航前，非支付其運費之全部，不得解除契約。如託運人已裝載貨物之全部或一部者，並應負擔因裝卸所增加之費用及賠償加於其他貨載之損害。

前項情形，託運人皆為契約之解除者。各託運人僅負前條所規定之責任。

第 45 條　前二條之規定，對船舶於一定時期內供運送或為數次繼續航行所訂立之契約，不適用之。

第 46 條　以船舶之全部於一定時期內供運送者，託運人僅得以約定或以船舶之性質而定之方法，使為運送。

第 47 條　前條託運人，僅就船舶可使用之期間，負擔運費。但因航行事變所生之停止，仍應繼續負擔運費。

前項船舶之停止，係因運送人或其代理人之行為或因船舶之狀態所致者，託運人不負擔運費，如有損害，並得請求賠償。

船舶行蹤不明時，託運人以得最後消息之日為止，負擔運費之全部，並自最後消息後，以迄於該次航行通常所需之期間應完成之日，負擔運費之半數。

第 48 條　以船舶之全部或一部供運送者，託運人所裝載貨物，不及約定之數量時，仍應負擔全部之運費，但應扣除船舶因此所減省費用之全部，及因另裝貨物所取得運費四分之三。

第 49 條　託運人因解除契約，應付全部運費時，得扣除運送人因此減省費用之全部，及另裝貨物所得運費四分之三。

第 50 條　貨物運達後，運送人或船長應即通知託運人指定之應受通知人或受貨人。

第 51 條　受貨人怠於受領貨物時，運送人或船長得以受貨人之費用，將貨物寄存於港埠管理機關或合法經營之倉庫，並通知受貨人。

受貨人不明或受貨人拒絕受領貨物時，運送人或船長得依前項之規定辦理，並通知託運人及受貨人。

運送人對於前二項貨物有下列情形之一者，得聲請法院裁定准予拍賣，於扣除運費或其他相關之必要費用後提存其價金之餘額：

一、不能寄存於倉庫。

二、有腐壞之虞。

三、顯見其價值不足抵償運費及其他相關之必要費用。

第 52 條　以船舶之全部或一部供運送者，運送人非於船舶完成裝貨或卸貨準備時，不得簽發裝貨或卸貨準備完成通知書。

裝卸期間自前項通知送達之翌日起算，期間內不工作休假日及裝卸不可能之日不算入。但超過合理裝卸期間者，船舶所有人得按超過之日期，請求合理之補償。

前項超過裝卸期間，休假日及裝卸不可能之日亦算入之。

第 53 條　運送人或船長於貨物裝載後，因託運人之請求，應發給載貨證券。

第 54 條　載貨證券，應載明下列各款事項，由運送人或船長簽名：

一、船舶名稱。

二、託運人之姓名或名稱。

三、依照託運人書面通知之貨物名稱、件數或重量，或其包裝之種類、個數及標誌。

四、裝載港及卸貨港。

五、運費交付。

六、載貨證券之份數。

七、填發之年月日。

前項第三款之通知事項，如與所收貨物之實際情況有顯著跡象，疑其不相符合，或無法核對時，運送人或船長得在載貨證券內載明其事由或不予載明。

載貨證券依第一項第三款為記載者，推定運送人依其記載為運送。

第 55 條　託運人對於交運貨物之名稱、數量，或其包裝之種類、個數及標誌之通知，應向運送人保證其正確無訛，其因通知不正確所發生或所致之一切毀損、滅失及費用，由託運人員賠償責任。

運送人不得以前項託運人應員賠償責任之事由，對抗託運人以外之載貨證券持有人。

第 56 條　貨物一經有受領權利人受領，推定運送人已依照載貨證券之記載，交清貨物。但有下列情事之一者，不在此限：

一、提貨前或當時，受領權利人已將毀損滅失情形，以書面通知運送人者。

二、提貨前或當時，毀損滅失經共同檢定，作成公證報告書者。

三、毀損滅失不顯著而於提貨後三日內，以書面通知運送人者。

四、在收貨證件上註明毀損或滅失者。

貨物之全部或一部毀損、滅失者，自貨物受領之日或自應受領之日起，一年內未起訴者，運送人或船舶所有人解除其責任。

第 57 條　運送人或船舶所有人所受之損害，非由於託運人或其代理人受僱人之過失所致者，託運人不員賠償責任。

第 58 條　載貨證券有數份者，在貨物目的港請求交付貨物之人，縱僅持有載貨證券一份，運送人或船長不得拒絕交付。不在貨物目的港時，運送人或船長接受載貨證券之全數，不得為貨物之交付。

二人以上之載貨證券持有人請求交付貨物時，運送人或船長應即將貨物按照第五十一條之規定寄存，並通知曾為請求之各持有人，運送人或船長，已依第一項之規定，交付貨物之一部後，他持有人請求交付貨物者，對於其賸餘之部分亦同。

載貨證券之持有人有二人以上者，其中一人先於他持有受貨物之交付時，他持有人之載貨證券對運送人失其效力。

第 59 條　載貨證券之持有人有二人以上，而運送人或船長尚未交付貨物者，其持有先受發送或交付之證券者，得先於他持有人行使其權利。

第 60 條　民法第六百二十七條至第六百三十條關於提單之規定，於載貨證券準用之。

以船舶之全部或一部供運送為目的之運送契約另行簽發載貨證券者，運送人與託運人以外載貨證券持有人間之關係，依載貨證券之記載。

第 61 條　以件貨運送為目的之運送契約或載貨證券記載條款、條件或約定，以減輕或免除運送人或船舶所有人，對於因過失或本章規定應履行之義務而不履行，致有貨物毀損、滅失或遲到之責任者，其條款、條件或約定不生效力。

第 62 條　運送人或船舶所有人於發航前及發航時，對於下列事項，應為必要之注意及措置：

一、使船舶有安全航行之能力。

二、配置船舶相當船員、設備及供應。

三、使貨艙、冷藏室及其他供載運貨物部分適合於受載、運送與保存。

船舶於發航後因突失航行能力所致之毀損或滅失，運送人不負賠償責任。

運送人或船舶所有人為免除前項前項責任之主張，應負舉證之責。

第 63 條　運送人對於承運貨物之裝載、卸載、搬移、堆存、保管、運送及看守，應為必要之注意及處置。

第 64 條　運送人知悉貨物為違禁物或不實申報物者，應拒絕載運。其貨物之性質足以毀損船舶或危害船舶上人員健康者亦同。但為航運或商業習慣所許者，不在此限。

運送人知悉貨物之性質具易燃性、易爆性或危險性並同意裝運後，若此貨物對於船舶或貨載有危險之虞時，運送人得隨時將其起岸、毀棄或使之無害，運送人除由於共同海損者外，不負賠償責任。

第 65 條　運送人或船長發見未經報明之貨物，得在裝載港將其起岸，或使支付同一航程同種貨物應付最高額之運費，如有損害並得請求賠償。

前項貨物在航行中發見時，如係違禁物或其性質足以發生損害者，船長得投棄之。

第 66 條　船舶發航後，因不可抗力不能到達目的港而將原裝貨物運回時，縱其船舶約定為去航及歸航之運送，託運人僅負擔去航運費。

第 67 條　船舶在航行中，因海上事故而須修繕時，如託運人於到達目地港前提取貨物者，應付全部運費。

第 68 條　船舶在航行中遭難或不能航行，而貨物仍由船長設法運到目地港時，如其運費較低於約定之運費者，託運人減支兩運費差額之半數。

如新運費等於約定之運費，託運人不負擔任何費用，如新運費較高於約定之運費，其增高額由託運人負擔之。

第 69 條　因下列事由所發生之毀損或滅失，運送人或船舶所有人不負賠償責任：

一、船長、海員、引水人或運送人之受僱人，於航行或管理船舶之行為而有過失。

二、海上或航路上之危險、災難或意外事故。

三、非由於運送本人之故意或過失所生之火災。

四、天災。

五、戰爭行為。

六、暴動。

七、公共敵人之行為。

八、有權力者之拘捕、限制或依司法程序之扣押。

九、檢疫限制。

十、罷工或其他勞動事故。

十一、救助或意圖救助海上人命或財產。

十二、包裝不固。

十三、標誌不足或不符。

十四、因貨物之固有瑕疵、品質或特性所致之耗損或其他毀損滅失。

十五、貨物所有人、託運人或其代理人、代表人之行為或不行為。

十六、船舶雖經注意仍不能發現之隱有瑕疵。

十七、其他非因運送人或船舶所有人本人之故意或過失及非因其代理人、受僱人之過失所致者。

第 70 條　託運人於託運時故意虛報貨物之性質或價值，運送人或船舶所有人對於其貨物之毀損或滅失，不負賠償責任。

除貨物之性質及價值於裝載前，已經託運人聲明並註明於載貨證券者外，運送人或船舶所有人對於貨物之毀損滅失，其賠償責任，以每件特別提款權六六六・六七單位或每公斤特別提款權二單位計算所得之金額，兩者較高者為限。

前項所稱件數，係指貨物託運之包裝單位。其以貨櫃、墊板或其他方式併裝運送者，應以載貨證券所載其內之包裝單位為件數。但載貨證券未經載明者，以併裝單位為件數。其使用之貨櫃係由託運人提供者，貨櫃本身得作為一件計算。

由於運送人或船舶所有人之故意或重大過失所發生之毀損或滅失，運送人或船舶所有人不得主張第二項單位限制責任之利益。

第 71 條　為救助或意圖救助海上人命、財產，或因其他正當理由偏航者，不得認為違反運送契約，其因而發生毀損或滅失時，船舶所有人或運送人不負賠償責任。

第 72 條　貨物未經船長或運送人之同意而裝載者，運送人或船舶所有人，對於其貨物之毀損或滅失，不負責任。

第 73 條　運送人或船長如將貨物裝載於甲板上，致生毀損或滅失時，應負賠償責任。但經託運人之同意並載明於運送契約或航運種類或商業習慣所許者，不在此限。

第 74 條　載貨證券之發給人，對於依載貨證券所記載應為之行為，均應負責。

前項發給人，對於貨物之各連續運送人之行為，應負保證之責。但各連續運送人，僅對於自己航程中所生之毀損滅失及遲到負其責任。

第 75 條　連續運送同時涉及海上運送及其他方法之運送者，其海上運送部分適用本法之規定。

貨物毀損滅失發生時間不明者，推定其發生於海上運送階段。

第 76 條　本節有關運送人因貨物滅失、毀損或遲到對託運人或其他第三人所得主張之抗辯及責任限制之規定，對運送人之代理人或受僱人亦得主張之。但經證明貨物之滅失、毀損或遲到，係因代理人或受僱人故意或重大過失所致者，不在此限。

前項之規定，對從事商港區域內之裝卸、搬運、保管、看守、儲存、理貨、穩固、墊艙者，亦適用之。

第 77 條　載貨證券所載之裝載港或卸貨港為中華民國港口者，其載貨證券所生之法律關係依涉外民事法律適用法所定應適用法律。但依本法中華民國受貨人或託運人保護較優者，應適用本法之規定。

第 78 條　裝貨港或卸貨港為中華民國港口者之載貨證券所生之爭
　　　　　議，得由我國裝貨港或卸貨港或其他依法有管轄權之法院
　　　　　管轄。

　　　　　前項載貨證券訂有仲裁條款者，經契約當事人同意後，得
　　　　　於我國進行仲裁，不受載貨證券內仲裁地或仲裁規則記載
　　　　　之拘束。

　　　　　前項規定視為當事人仲裁契約之一部。但當事人於爭議發
　　　　　生發另有書面合意者，不在此限。

第二節　旅客運送

第 79 條　旅客之運送，除本節規定外，準用本章第一節之規定。

第 80 條　對於旅客供膳者，其膳費應包括於票價之內。

第 81 條　旅客於實施意外保險之特定航線及地區，均應投保意外
　　　　　險，保險金額載入客票，視同契約，其保險費包括於票價
　　　　　內，並以保險金額為損害賠償之最高額。

　　　　　前項特定航線地區及保險金額，由交通部定之。

第 82 條　旅客除前條保險外，自行另加保意外險者，其損害賠償依
　　　　　其約定，但應以書面為之。

第 83 條　運送人或船長應依船票所載，運送旅客至目的港。

　　　　　運送人或船長違反前項規定時，旅客得解除契約，如有損
　　　　　害，並得請求賠償。

第 84 條　旅客於發航二十四小時，得給付票價十分之二，解除契
　　　　　約；其於發航前因死亡、疾病或其他基於本身不得已之事
　　　　　由，不能或拒絕乘船者，運送人得請求票價十分之一。

第 85 條　旅客在船舶發航或航程中不依時登船，或船長依職權實行
　　　　　緊急處分迫令其離船者，乃應給付全部票價。

第 86 條　船舶不於預定之日發航者，旅客得解除契約。

第 87 條　旅客在航程中自願上陸時，仍負擔全部票價，其因疾病上陸或死亡時，僅按其已運送之航程負擔票價。

第 88 條　船舶因不可抗力不能繼續航行時，運送人或船長應設法將旅客運送至目的港。

第 89 條　旅客之目的港如發生天災、戰亂、瘟疫，或其他特殊事故致船舶不能進卸客者，運送人或船長得依旅客之意願，將其送至最近之港口或送返乘船港。

第 90 條　運送人或船長在航行中為船舶修繕時，應以同等級船舶完成其航程，旅客在候船期間並應無償供給膳宿。

第 91 條　旅客於船舶抵達目的港後，應依船長之指示即行離船。

第三節　船舶拖帶

第 92 條　拖船與被拖船如不屬於同一所有人時，其損害賠償之責任，應由拖船所有人負擔。但契約另有訂定者，不在此限。

第 93 條　共同或連接之拖船，因航行所生之損害，對被害人負連帶責任。但他拖船對於加害之拖船有求償權。

第四章　船舶碰撞

第 94 條　船舶之碰撞，不論發生於何地，皆依本章之規定處理之。

第 95 條　碰撞係因不可抗力而發生者，被害人不得請求損害賠償。

第 96 條　碰撞係因於一船舶之過失所致者，由該船舶負損害賠償責任。

第 97 條　碰撞之各船舶有共同過失時，各依其過失程度之比例負其責任，不能判定其過失之輕重時，各方平均負其責任。

有過失之各船舶，對於因死亡或傷害所生之損害，應負連帶責任。

第 98 條　前二條責任，不因碰撞係由引水人之過失所致而免除。

第 99 條　因碰撞所生之請求權，自碰撞日起算，經過兩年不行使而消滅。

第 100 條　船舶在中華民國領海內水港口河道內碰撞者，法院對於加害之船舶，得扣押之。

前兩項被扣押船舶得提供擔保，請求放行。

前項擔保，得由適當之銀行或保險人出具書面保證代之。

碰撞不在中華民國領海內水港口河道內，而被害者為中華民國船舶或國民，法院於加害之船舶進入中華民國領海後，得扣押之。

前兩項被扣押船舶得提供擔保，請求放行。

前項擔保，得由適當之銀行或保險人出具書面保證代之。

第 101 條　關於碰撞之訴訟，得向下列法院起訴：

一、被告之住所或營業所所在地之法院。

二、碰撞發生地之法院。

三、被告船舶船籍港之法院。

四、船舶扣押地之法院。

五、當事人合意地之法院。

第五章　海難救助

第 102 條　船長於不甚危害其船舶、海員、旅客之範圍內，對於淹沒或其他危難之人應盡力救助。

第 103 條　對於船舶或船舶上財物施以救助而有效果者，得按其效果請求相當之報酬。

施救人所施救之船舶或船舶上貨物，有損環境之虞者，施救人得向船舶所有人請求與實際支出費用同額之報酬；其救助行為對於船舶或船舶上貨物所造成環境之損害已有效防止或減輕者，得向船舶所有人請求與實際支出費用同額或不超過其費用一倍之報酬。

施救人同時有前二項報酬請求權者，前項報酬應自第一項可得請求之報中扣除之。

施救人之報酬請求權，自救助完成日起二年間不行使而消滅。

第 104 條　屬於同一所有人之船舶救助，仍得請求報酬。

拖船對於被拖船施以救助者，得請求報酬。但以非為履行該施船契約者為限。

第 105 條　救助報酬由當事人協議定之，協議不成時，得提付仲裁或請求法院裁判之。

第 106 條　前條規定，於施救人與船舶間，及施救人間之分配報酬之比例，準用之。

第 107 條　於實行施救中救人者，對於船舶及財物之救助報酬金，有參加分配之權。

第 108 條　經以正當理由拒絕施救，而仍強為施救者，不得請求報酬。

第 109 條　船舶碰撞後，各碰撞船舶之船長於不甚危害其船舶、海員或旅客之範圍內，對於他船舶船長、海員及旅客、應盡力救助。

各該船長，除有不可抗力之情形外，在未確知繼續救助為無益前，應停留於發生災難之處所。

各該船長，應於可能範圍內，將其船舶名稱及船籍港並開來及開往之處所，通知於他船舶。

第六章 共同海損

第 110 條　稱共同海損者，謂在船舶航程期間，為求共同危險中全體財產之安全所為故意及合理處分，而直接造成之犧牲及發生之費用。

第 111 條　共同海損以各被保存財產價值與共同海損總額之比例，由各利害關係人分擔之。因共同海損行為所犧牲而獲共同海損補償之財產，亦應參與分擔。

第 112 條　前條各被保存財產之分擔價值，應以航程終止地或放棄共同航程時地財產之實際淨值為準，依下列規定計算之：

一、船舶以到達時地之價格為準。如船舶於航程中已修復者，應扣除在該航程中共同海損之犧牲額及其他非共同海損之損害額。但不得低於其實際所餘殘值。

二、貨物以送交最後受貨人之商業發票所載價格為準，如無商業發票者，以裝船時地之價值為準，並均包括應支付之運費及保險費在內。

三、運費以到付運費之應收額，扣除非共同海損費用為準。

前項各類之實際淨值，均應另加計共同海損之補償額。

第 113 條　共同海損犧牲之補償額，應以各財產於航程終止時地或放棄共同航程時地之實際淨值為準，依下列規定計算之：

一、船舶以實際必要之合理修繕或設備材料之更換費用為準。未經修繕或更換者，以該損失所造成之合理貶值，但不能超過估計之修繕或更換費用。

二、貨物以送交最後受貨人商業發票價格計算所受之損害為準，如無商業發票者，以裝船時地之價值為準，並均包括應支付之運費及保險費在內。受損貨物如被出售者，以出售淨值與前述所訂商業發票或裝船時地貨物淨值之差額為準。

三、運費以貨載之毀損或減失致減少或全無者為準。但運送人因此減省之費用，應扣除之。

第 114 條　下列費用為共同海損費用：

一、為保存共同危險中全體財產所生之港埠、貨物處理、船員工資及船舶維護所必需之燃、物料費用。

二、船舶發生共同海損後，為繼續共同航程所需之額外費用。

三、為共同海損所墊付現金百分之二之報酬。

四、自共同海損發生之日起至共同海損實際收付日止，應行收付金額所生之利息。

為替代前項第一款、第二款共同海損費用所生之其他費用，視為共同海損之費用。但替代費用不得超過原共同海損費用。

第 115 條　共同海損因利害關係人之過失所致者，各關係人仍應分擔之。但不影響其他關係人對過失之負責人之賠償請求權。

第 116 條　未依航運習慣裝載之貨物經投棄者，不認為共同海損犧牲。但經撈救者，仍應分擔共同海損。

第 117 條　無載貨證券亦無船長收據之貨物，或未記載於目錄之設備屬具，經犧牲者，不認為共同海損。但經撈救者，仍應分擔共同海損。

第 118 條　貨幣、有價證券或其他貴重物品，經犧牲者，除已報明船長者外，不認為共同海損犧牲。但經撈救者，仍應分擔共同海損。

第 119 條　貨物之性質，於託運時故意為不實之聲明，經犧牲者，不認為共同海損。但經保存者，應按其實在價值分擔之。

貨物之價值，於託運時為不實之聲明，使聲明價值與實在價值不同者，其共同海損犧牲之補償額以金額低者為準，分擔價值以金額高者為準。

第 120 條　船上所備糧食、武器、船員之衣物、薪津、郵件及無載貨證券之旅客行李、私人物品皆不分擔共同海損。

前項物品如被犧牲，其損失應由各關係人分擔之。

第 121 條　共同海損之計算，由全體關係人協議定之。協議不成時，得提付仲裁或請求法院裁判之。

第 122 條　運送人或船長對於未清償分擔額之貨物所有人，得留置其貨物。但提供擔保者，不在此限。

第 123 條　利害關係人於受分擔額後，復得其船舶或貨物之全部或一部者，應將其所受之分擔額返還於關係人。但得將其所受損害及復得之費用扣除之。

第 124 條　應負分擔義務之人，得委棄其存留物而免分擔海損之責。

第 125 條　因共同海損所生之債權，自計算確定之日起，經過一年不行使而消滅。

第七章　海上保險

第 126 條　關於海上保險，本章無規定者，適用保險法之規定。

第 127 條　凡與海上航行有關而可能發生危險之財產權益，皆得為海上保險之標的。

海上保險契約得約定延展加保至陸上、內河、湖泊或內陸水道之危險。

第 128 條　保險期間除契約另有訂定外，關於船舶及其設備屬具，自船舶起錨或解纜之時，以迄目的港投錨或繫纜之時，為其期間；關於貨物，自貨物離岸之時，以迄目的港起岸之時，為其期間。

第 129 條　保險人對於保險標的物，除契約另有規定外，因海上一切事變及災害所生之毀損滅失及費用，負賠償責任。

第 130 條　保險事故發生時，要保人或被保險人應採取必要行為，以避免或減輕保險標的之損失，保險人對於要保人或被保險人未履行此項義務而擴大之損失，不負賠償責任。

保險人對於要保人或被保險人，為履行前項義務所生之費用，負償還之責，其償還數額與賠償金額合計雖超過保險標的價值，仍應償還之。

保險人對於前項費用之償還，以保險金額為限。但保險金額不及保險標的物之價值時，則以保險金額對於保險標的之價值比例定之。

第 131 條　因要保人或被保險人或其代理人之故意或重大過失所致之損失，保險人不負賠償責任。

第 132 條　未確定裝運船舶之貨物保險，要保人或被保險人於知其已裝載於船舶時，應將該船舶之名稱、裝船日期、所裝貨物及其價值，立即通知於保險人。不為通知者，保險人對未為通知所生之損害，不負賠償責任。

第 133 條　要保人或被保險人於保險人破產時，得終止契約。

第 134 條　船舶之保險以保險人責任開始時之船舶價格及保險費，為保險價額。

第 135 條　貨物之保險以裝載時、地之貨物價格、裝載費、稅捐、應付之運費及保險費，為保險價額。

第 136 條　貨物到達時應有之佣金、費用或其他利得之保險以保險時之實際金額，為保險價額。

第 137 條　運費之保險，僅得以運送人如未經交付貨物即不得收取之運費為之，並以被保險人應收取之運費及保險費為保險價額。

前項保險，得包括船舶之租金及依運送契約可得之收益。

第 138 條　貨物損害之計算，依其在到達港於完好狀態下所應有之價值，與其受損狀態之價值比較定之。

第 139 條　船舶部分損害之計算，以其合理修復費用為準。但每次事故應以保險金額為限。

部分損害未修復之補償額，以船舶因受損所減少之市價為限。但不得超過所估計之合理修復費用。

保險期間內，船舶部分損害未修復前，即遭遇全損者，不得再行請求前項部分損害未修復之補償額。

第 140 條　運費部分損害之計算，以所損運費與總運費之比例就保險金額定之。

第 141 條　受損害貨物之變賣，除由於不可抗力或船長依法處理者外，應得保險人之同意。並以變賣淨額與保險價額之差額為損害額。但因變賣後所減省之一切費用，應扣除之。

第 142 條　海上保險之委付，指被保險人於發生第一百四十三條至第一百四十五條委付原因後，移轉保險標的物之一切權利於保險人，而請求支付該保險標的物全部保險金額之行為。

第 143 條　被保險船舶有下列各款情形之一時，得委付之：

一、船舶被捕獲時。

二、船舶不能為修繕或修繕費用超過保險價額時。

三、船舶行蹤不明已逾二個月時。

四、船舶被扣押已逾二個月仍未放行時。

前項第四款所稱扣押不包含債權人聲請法院所為之查封、假扣押及假處分。

第 144 條　被保險貨物有下列各款情形之一時，得委付之：

一、船舶因遭難，或其他事變不能航行已逾二個月而貨物尚未交付於受貨人、要保人或被保險人時。

二、裝運貨物之船舶，行蹤不明，已逾二個月時。

三、貨物因應由保險人員保險責任之損害，其回復原狀及繼續或轉運至目的地費用總額合併超過到達目的地價值時。

第 145 條　運費之委付，得於船舶或貨物之委付時為之。

第 146 條　委付應就保險標的物之全部為之。但保險單上僅有其中一種標的物發生委付原因時，得就該一種標的物為委付請求其保險金額。

委付不得附有條件。

第 147 條　委付經承諾或經判決為有效後，自發生委付原因之日起，保險標的物即視為保險人所有。

委付未經承諾前，被保險人對於保險標的物之一切權利不受影響。保險人或被保險人對於保險標的物採取救助、保護或回復之各項措施，不視為已承諾或拋棄委付。

第 148 條　委付之通知一經保險人明示承諾，當事人均不得撤銷。

第 149 條　要保人或被保險人，於知悉保險之危險發生後，應即通知保險人。

第 150 條　保險人應於收到要保人或被保險人證明文件後三十日內給付保險金額。

保險人對於前項證明文件如有疑義，而要保人或被保險人提供擔保時，仍應將保險金額全部給付。

前項情形，保險人之金額返還請求權，自給付後經過一年不行使而消滅。

第 151 條　要保人或被保險人，自接到貨物之日起，一個月內不將貨物所受損害通知保險人或其代理人時，視為無損害。

第 152 條　委付之權利，於知悉委付原因發生後，自得為委付之日起，經過二個月不行使而消滅。

第八章　附則

第 153 條　本法自公布日施行。本法中國民國九十八年六月十二日修正之條文，自九十八年十一月二十三日施行

參考文獻··········

一、期刊

曹有諒（2009），2009 年版英國協會貨物險條款共同條款修正釋義，**保險大道**，第五十八期。

曹有諒（2009），2009 年英國協會貨物險條款作對被保險人有利之修正釋義，**保險大道**，第五十九期。

曾文瑞（1999），英國海上保險法委付制度之研究─兼論海商法修正草案委付相關條文，**保險專刊**，第 55 輯。

曾文瑞（2000），英國海上保險法之損害防阻條款與我國新修訂海商法之比較探討（上）、（下），**航貿週刊**，第 200003 期、第 200004 期。

曾文瑞（2000），保險基本原則在海上保險之應用探討（上）、（下），**航貿週刊**，第 200040 期、第 200041 期。

曾文瑞（2000），從損害防阻觀點探討海上貨物被保險人之義務與保險理賠，**保險專刊**，第 59 輯。

曾文瑞（2001），我國海上保險之實務問題探討（上）、（中）、（下），**航貿週刊**，第 200118 期、第 200119 期、第 2000120 期。

曾文瑞（2002），論我國海上貨物保險之保險利益問題與解決建議，**運籌研究集刊**，第二期。

曾文瑞（2003），船舶運送業為旅客投保意外保險之問題及海上旅客運送責任保險制度之研究，**運輸學刊**。

曾文瑞（2005），2004 年約克安特衛普規則對共同海損制度與海上保險之影響，**核保學報**，第十三卷。

曾文瑞、李紀薇（2008），兩岸海上貨物保險代位權妨礙之效力研析，**保險經營與制度**，第七卷第一期，頁 79–104。

曾文瑞、林慧珊（2009），「海上貨物保險中有關適航性擔保之探討」，**2009 兩岸保險與危險管理學術研討會論文集**，頁 249–266。

曾文瑞、林慧珊（2011），自危險核保與理賠觀點論 ICC,2009 之保險期
　　間，**保險經營與制度**，第十卷第一期。

曾文瑞、曾國雄（2005，從損失分攤觀點論保險人對共同海損之賠償責
　　任，**保險專刊**，第二十一卷，第二期。（NSC93-2414-H-309-001）

曾文瑞、黃于瑄（2009），海上保險損害防阻費用之研究，**核保學報**，第
　　十七卷。

曾文瑞、廖芳伶（2010），從國際物流角度探討 ICC, 1982 保險期間之規
　　定與實務問題，**核保學報**，第十八卷。

黃正宗（1994），海上保險的基本性質與各當事人之基本定位，**船舶與海
　　運**，633 期。

鄭鎮樑（2000），英國勞氏保單中之附註條款與協會貨物條款之演化探
　　源，**核保學報**，第八卷。

鄭鎮樑、范姜肱、謝崇興（2010），英國 2009 協會貨物條款修正之探
　　討，**核保學報**，第十八卷。

二、書籍

2010 年版國貿條規編譯委員會（2010），**國貿條規 2010**。台北：外貿協
　　會。

王明芳（2016），**2015 英國保險法對海上保險之影響**。高雄：國立高雄
　　海洋科技大學航運管理研究所碩士論文。

王衛恥（1983），**海上保險法與共同海損**。台北：文笙書局。

王衛恥（1988），**海上保險的理論與實務**（第二版）。台北，文笙書局。

邱展發（2009），**海運提單實務**。台北：財團法人張榮發基金會。

姚玉麟（1985），**海上保險名詞釋義**。台北：航貿圖書。

徐當仁、曾文瑞（1999），**初學者海上保險基礎理論與實務**。台北：高皇
　　書局。

張慈民（2007），**船舶碰撞責任與保險理賠之研究**。高雄海洋科技大學航
　　運管理研究所碩士在職專班論文。

許曉民（1985），**海的危險事故**。台北：國立台灣海洋學院航海學會。

曹有諒（2010），**國際貨物運輸保險理論與實務**。台北：台市進出口商業
　　同業公會。

曾國雄、徐當仁（1993），**海商法（下）海上危險與海上保險（第二**

版）。作者出版。

曾國雄（1999），**海商法**。作者出版。

曾國雄（2008），**海運貨損理賠關鍵字釋義**。作者出版。

曾國雄、徐當仁（1993），**海商法（上）船舶與運送海商法（第二版）**。
作者出版。

黃正宗（2009），**我國海商法船舶碰撞法律規範研究**。

Arnould, Joseph (1981), *Arnould's Law of Marine Insurance and Average*,
London: Stevens & sons, 16th ed. Volume 2.

Cheng-Tsung Huang (1987), *A Programme of International Shipping and
Insurance Laws for our Future World*, Ph.D. in Law in the University
of Londan.

Donald O' May (1993), *Marine Insurance Law and Policy*, 1st Edition,
Sweet & Maxwell.

E. R. Hardy Ivamy (1984), *Marine Insurance*, 3rd Edition, Butterworth &
Co. (Publishers) Ltd.

E. R. Hardy Ivamy (1993), *Chalmers' Marine Insurance Act 1906*, 10th
Edtion, Butterworth & Co. (Publishers) Ltd.

J. Kenneth Goodacre (1996), *Marine Insurance Claims*, 3rd Edition, Witherby
& Co. Ltd.

N. Geoffrey Hudson, M. A. (19950, *The Institute Clauses*, 2nd Edition,
Lloyd's of London Press Ltd.

Robert H. Brown (1983), *Analysis of Marine Insurance Clauses–Book 1 The
Institute Cargo Clauses*, 2nd Edition, Witherby & Co. Ltd.

Robert H. Brown (1986), *Marine Insurance Volume 1–Principles and Basic
Practice*, 6th Edition, London Witherby & Co. Ltd.

Robert H. Brown (1989), *Dictionary of Marine Insurance Terms and
Clauses*, 5th Edition, Witherby & Co. Ltd.

Robert H. Brown (1998), *Marine Insurance Volume 2–Cargo Practice*, 5th
Edition, Witherby & Co. Ltd.

R. J. Lambeth (1990), *Templeman on Marine Insurance Its Principles and
Practice*, 6th Edition, Macdonald and Evans Ltd.

Susan Hodges (1997), *Law of Marine Insurance*, 1st Edition, Cavendish

Publishing Limited.

Susan Hodges (1999), *Cases and Materials on Marine Insurance Law*, 1st Edition, Cavendish Publishing Limited.

三、網路資源

1. Richards Hogg Lindley, http://www.rhlg.com/
2. Lloyd's Market Association, http://www.lmalloyds.com